Frontiers

Territory and State Formation in the Modern World

Malcolm Anderson

Polity Press

First published in 1996 by Polity Press
in association with Blackwell Publishers Ltd.

First published in paperback 1997.

Editorial office:
Polity Press
65 Bridge Street
Cambridge CB2 1UR, UK

Marketing and production:
Blackwell Publishers Ltd
108 Cowley Road
Oxford OX4 1JF, UK

Published in the USA by
Blackwell Publishers Inc.
350 Main Street
Malden MA 02148, USA

ISBN 0–7456–1652–6
ISBN 0–7456–2008–6 (pbk)

A CIP catalogue record for this book is available from the British Library and has been applied for from the Library of Congress.

Typeset in Times 10 on 12 pt by CentraCet Ltd, Cambridge
Printed in Great Britain by Hartnolls Ltd, Bodmin, Cornwall

This book is printed on acid-free paper.

Contents

List of Maps

Frontiers

Acknowledgements

I would like to thank Nigel Bowles, Eberhard Bort, François Crouzet, Desmond King and Jacqueline Larrieu who read the whole manuscript and offered many useful and stimulating comments. Richard Bellamy, Pierre Birnbaum, Mary Buckley and Anthony Cohen read parts of the text and saved me from egregious errors. The mistakes which remain are entirely my own responsibility.

Nicola Exley of the Reprographics Unit of the University of Edinburgh drew the maps, for which I am grateful.

Material support from the University of Edinburgh, especially of sabbatical leave, and the Economic and Social Research Council (a grant awarded for another project indirectly contributed to the writing of this book) have eased my task. I am grateful to the University of Edinburgh and the Fondation Nationale des Sciences Politiques in Paris for the use of their facilities. Personal support from colleagues in Edinburgh, Oxford and Paris kept at bay the lassitude which accompanies projects picked up and put down as a result of many interruptions, imposed and self-imposed.

To
Jacqueline

Introduction

All political authorities and jurisdictions have physical limits – a characteristic often regarded as so obvious that it does not warrant further comment. But where the limits are located, and the purposes they serve, influence the lives of all people separated by frontiers. Contemporary frontiers are not simply lines on maps, the unproblematic givens of political life, where one jurisdiction or political authority ends and another begins; they are central to understanding political life. Examining the justifications of frontiers raises crucial, often dramatic, questions concerning citizenship, identity, political loyalty, exclusion, inclusion and of the ends of the state. The general impact of frontiers[1] is rarely analysed by historians and social scientists.[2] This book attempts to fill a gap by specifying the nature of frontiers in the increasingly filled-up and fast-changing world of the late twentieth century.[3] A vast historical and philosophical background to this subject exists. The first step in the enquiry is to suggest a definition of frontiers.

Frontiers between states are institutions and processes. As institutions they are established by political decisions and regulated by legal texts. The frontier is the basic political institution: no rule-bound economic, social or political life in complex societies could be organized without them.[4] The questions, which have troubled philosophers since antiquity about all institutions may be asked about frontiers.[5] Are they needed? How can they be justified? The answers vary in different historical periods; different kinds of frontier existed before the modern state, and other kinds will emerge after its demise. The linear and exclusive state frontier, in the sense currently understood, scarcely existed before the French Revolution. Since then the frontier has defined, in a legal sense, a sovereign authority; the identity of individuals (claims to nationality and exercise of rights of citizenship) are delimited by it. But this particular form of frontier is not part of an immutable natural order and signs of a radical change in perceptions of frontiers are now apparent.

Frontiers as processes have four dimensions. First, frontiers are instruments of state policy because governments attempt to change, to their own advantage, the location and the functions of frontiers. Although there is no simple relationship between frontiers and inequalities of wealth and power, government policy on frontiers is intended to protect and to promote interests. Second, the policies and practices of governments are constrained by the degree of *de facto* control which they have over the state frontier. The claim of the modern state to be 'the sole, exclusive fount of all powers and prerogatives of rule'[6] could only be realized if its frontiers were made impermeable to unwanted external influences. The incapacity of governments in the contemporary world to control much of the traffic of persons, goods and information across their frontiers is changing the nature of states.

Third, frontiers are markers of identity, in the twentieth century usually national identity, although political identities may be larger or smaller than the 'nation' state. Frontiers, in this sense, are part of political beliefs and myths about the unity of the people, and sometimes myths about the 'natural' unity of a territory. These 'imagined communities', to use Benedict Anderson's phrase concerning nations,[7] are now a universal phenomenon and often have deep historical roots. They are linked to the most powerful form of ideological bonding in the modern world – nationalism. Other, usually weaker and less cohesive, imagined communities may transcend the confines of the state; myths of regional, continental and hemispheric unity have also marked boundaries between friend and foe.[8] But myths of unity can be created or transformed with remarkable rapidity during wars, revolutions and political upheavals.

Fourth, the 'frontier' is a term of discourse. Meanings are given both to frontiers in general and to particular frontiers, and these meanings change from time to time. 'Frontier' is a term used in law, diplomacy and politics, and its meaning varies according to the context. In the scholarly writings in anthropology, history, political science, public international law and sociology, it also has different meanings according to the theoretical approach adopted. Sometimes scholarship is the servant of political power and nationalist movements when frontiers are in dispute;[9] at other times it is part of the scarcely heard disquisition of the lecture hall. The term 'frontier' for people who live in frontier regions, or those whose daily life is directly affected by frontiers, is associated with the rules imposed by frontiers, and with popular images of the frontier as either 'barrier' or 'junction'.[10] What frontiers represent is constantly reconstituted by those human beings who are regulated, influenced and limited by them. The layers of discourse – political, scholarly, popular – always overlap; divergent mental images of frontiers are an integral part of frontiers as processes.[11]

Attitudes towards Frontiers

Emotions aroused by state frontiers became more widely shared and obsessive with the sacralization of homelands by nineteenth-century nationalism. Frontiers became associated with powerful images, symbols and (sometimes invented) traditions. The Italian sociologist Raimondo Strassoldo has reviewed the symbolic, psychological and sociological significance of frontiers.[12] They have a powerful hold on the imagination; many literary allusions are made to border crossing, to the passing of the frontier in terms of exile, danger and the discarding of rules, conventions and inhibitions.[13]

All frontiers have a psychological component[14] – indeed, some psychologists argue that each individual has a concept of bounded personal space.[15] Intrusion into this personal space, without invitation or consent, provokes emotional reactions of anxiety or hostility.[16] Governments show similar sensitivity to unregulated intrusions across frontiers, and to threats, real or imagined, to the territorial integrity of the state. In the nineteenth and first half of the twentieth centuries, during the great age of the nation-state in Europe, large populations and mass political movements came to share this sensitivity. Visual images of natural frontiers or approximate shapes – the boot of Italy, the islands of Britain and the face of France[17] – reinforced this view and were integrated into the sense of national identity. Feelings of violation were experienced at the threat of alienation of any part of this image of the motherland.

These feelings spread to states in the Third World, partly through the conduit of the educational systems established by the imperial powers and partly because indigenous nationalist movements required new mobilizing ideologies to unite disparate peoples. According to Lamb, writing about Asian frontiers after the end of the colonial period, the change in status from colony to fully independent state had profound consequences; the frontier was transformed into the 'cell wall of the basic unit of national identity', marking an emotional and psychological divide as well as a political–geographical line.[18] Any threat to the new frontier provoked a prickly nationalistic response. Thus, independent India reacted emotionally and with incomprehension to Chinese claims for territory on its northern frontier in the 1950s, in a manner quite different to the British imperial proconsuls (who had established the frontier), for whom frontier policy was part of a 'great game'.

The passions engendered by the nation-state are not necessarily a permanent feature of political life. Attitudes towards frontiers in the highly industrialized countries, and particularly in Europe, are once again changing. Instantaneous transfrontier communication of information and frontier crossings by individuals, annually numbering more than the total population of these countries, have transformed the psychological and practical importance of frontier controls. Frontiers are still regarded as useful for defending cultures, rights and interests, but more flexible attitudes than in the immediate aftermath of the Second World War now prevail about how frontiers should be policed. Nine of the fifteen member states of the European Union have already agreed to dismantle police controls at the frontiers between them.

Boundaries Defining Identities

In certain circumstances the frontier acquired a mythic significance in building nations and political identities, becoming the *mythomoteur* of a whole society. The pioneer frontier,[19] which was a zone rather than a line, was central to North American society as myth, symbol and practical influence on social life in the nineteenth century and remains a powerful idea in the United States to the present day. The Castilian nation was created on the Iberian frontier between Islam and Christianity. The nature of the Russian sense of identity and Russian imperialism can be understood only by reference to the steppe experience, in which the Russians successfully defended themselves against invaders from the east, and developed a tragic sense of history.[20]

Although all human communities have, to a degree, defined themselves according to their self-perceived boundaries, these boundaries have sometimes been self-consciously created to promote a sense of distinctiveness and separateness. This occurs even in relatively rich industrialized societies. Marianne Heiberg, writing about the 1960s and the first half of the 1970s, suggests that the Spanish Basques deliberately created an epistemic community in which people shared the same understanding of the political world: 'Political parties, artistic production, amnesty organisations, historical research, economic enterprises, schools, newspapers, public projects, popular festivals, publishing houses, etc. were forced into categories of *abertzale* (patriotic)/*españolista*, nationalist/non-nationalist, Basque/anti-Basque. Through the insistent pressure of this polarisation, the boundaries demarcating the Basque nationalist community and its exclusive institutions became explicit, consolidated and impermeable.'[21] But boundary-creating and maintaining mechanisms have usually come into being over much longer periods of time, the accumulated consequences of many individual actions and decisions, often directed towards other ends.[22]

State-building and a sense of territory have often gone hand in hand, but political identities have not always coincided with the frontiers of the modern sovereign state. Locality, social class, language, ethnicity, and religion have also been the basis of deeply rooted identities.[23] A non-state boundary may be an enduring basis of identity; the characteristics of peoples without a state, the Basques or the Scots, the Ladins or (until recently) the Slovenes, may change over time while their geographical boundaries remain in the same place; other groups, such as Gypsies and Jews, have no geographically defined frontiers yet retain strong boundary-maintaining mechanisms. Distinctive human groups without states have come to be known as 'minorities'. Pierre George suggests that there are three different types of minority: territorial minorities where a group has been associated for many generations with a particular area where it forms a majority of the population (Basques); minorities of the ghetto where enclaves are formed because of the reactions of the majority population (east European Jews prior to the Holocaust); and minorities without any specific geographical location which nonetheless retain strong communications networks (Gypsies).[24] The ways boundaries are maintained vary between these three types of minority. But the existence of minorities has conflicted with the objective of creating a homogeneous national identity bounded by the frontiers of states.

States and Transfrontier Relations

In recent history, the inter-state frontier has been regarded as fundamentally different to other kinds of boundaries because of the doctrine of sovereignty and the territorial principle. The territorial exclusivity of the 'nation'-state implied that there could be no intrusion by external jurisdictions and no political loyalties across the frontier. The people confined by a frontier were supposed to share a common fund of loyalties, values and characteristics. Exactly what these are may be vigorously and even violently disputed.

The more closed the frontier, the stronger has been its impact as a practical and symbolic threshold, the stronger rulers' belief that strict control of the frontier was essential to the maintenance of their power. The Iron Curtain with its surveillance systems and automatic killing machines, the militarized frontier of Franco's Spain, the imposed frontiers between Israel and its Arab neighbours, the 38th parallel separating the two Koreas, the unstable ceasefire line in Kashmir between India and Pakistan, the partition line separating Greek and Turkish Cyprus, the front line between Black Africa and the apartheid regime of South Africa and the frontier in the New Territories between Mao's People's Republic of China and the unfettered capitalism of Hong Kong are celebrated twentieth-century examples.

A pervasive, often almost superstitious, fear characterizes closed frontiers as lines of transition between two worlds – crossing them involves a passage to dangerous or forbidden lands; long residence on one side of the line requires a commitment to certain values and beliefs; those who pass regularly between the two worlds – such as Jews and Armenians between the Muslim and the Christian worlds for a millennium after the death of the Prophet, or private individuals who acted as intermediaries between east and west during the Cold War period – are admired, regarded as useful, but seen as deeply suspect. The completely closed frontier has always been an aspiration except for brief periods, during wars or other exceptional circumstances, it has scarcely existed. Transfrontier transactions and individual flight across the frontier occur despite the policies of authoritarian regimes.

Relations across twentieth-century international frontiers, between the populations which they separate, range along a continuum.[25] At one extreme, populations are alienated from one another, exchanges across the frontier are kept to a minimum and violence always threatens. Moving along the spectrum from this extreme, relations may be those of coexistence with strict control of exchanges, easily interrupted without causing serious economic and social breakdown. Further along the spectrum, economically integrated frontier regions are found where disruption of the pattern of exchanges would involve major social and population change. At the other extreme, frontier zones are fully integrated: people speak the same languages, or mutually comprehensible ones, economic and social life has melded together so that a *de facto* merger takes place.

Conditions for integrated frontier regions may sometimes appear to exist, but merging does not inevitably follow. Open and easily crossed frontiers remain barriers for important purposes, such as for legal systems, taxation, access to public services, flags, teaching of history and much else besides. The Canada–US frontier, which has scarcely any security function, has a separating effect and, as Beaujeu-Garnier and Chabod write about a particularly peaceful (although for a long time fortified) frontier, 'technical change has effaced physical barriers' but 'on the Franco-Swiss border the towns turn their backs on each other

... and face their respective countries'.[26] In the European Union, local and regional authorities now participate in transfrontier associations but some of these promote genuine joint activities while others do not.

In general, in the highly developed regions of the world, the frontiers of the nation-state have become more permeable and less clearly defined as the defensive lines of cultural and social identities.[27] New territorial questions have emerged in the late twentieth century. What purposes will frontiers serve between the member states of the European Union after the abolition of systematic frontier controls? Will the external frontier of the European Community become the equivalent of a state frontier encouraging the growth of a 'European nationalism'? What will be the resolution of shifting frontiers in the cataclysmic changes which in 1989 convulsed eastern Europe and subsequently the former Soviet Union; how long will frontiers in Africa and the Middle East survive in the midst of the economic, social, religious and political tensions in these regions? Will new continental groupings try to use frontiers in ways designed to improve their competitive position? In what ways will political frontiers adapt to new economic and demographic conditions? Will new technologies, bringing economic and social change in their wake, revolutionize attitudes towards territory and frontiers?

A speculative question underlying these others is whether other boundaries will become relatively more important than state frontiers in defining personal and group identity. The anthropologist Anthony Cohen has suggested: 'Where cultural difference was formerly underpinned also by structural boundaries, these have now given way to boundaries which inhere in the mind: symbolic boundaries. This transformation constitutes an important qualification to concepts of mass society, and has been manifest in the widespread assertion of sectional identities in the last twenty years.'[28] A process of delocalization of boundaries of identity may now be under way. More and more people are, like the 'wandering Jew', carrying their identity around with them.

Justification of Frontiers

What human purposes do frontiers serve? The question cannot be answered 'scientifically', in a neutral way. Frontiers are the limits of permissible behaviour but these limits are necessarily perceived in very different ways by different people. Evaluations of frontiers vary, ranging from regarding them as essential and precious protection, to accepting them as a fact of life, to considering them as tiresome and arbitrary constraints. Liberal pacifists have condemned them as the instruments for turning into enemies those who would prefer to live in harmony, and helping to maintain ancient hostilities when the causes for them have disappeared. Others in the liberal tradition have thought that clearly defined frontiers are essential for ordered, constitutional politics, the preservation of citizenship rights and the maintenance of community.

Liberals and Marxists may agree that boundaries are made and manipulated in order to ensure a certain distribution of power. But many Marxists, believing in the primacy of class struggle over any other form of conflict, contend that frontiers are transitory instruments for upholding particular forms of class domination. Without frontiers, conservatives and liberals concur, politics would be inconceivable; international relations in the current sense would disappear. The concept of the political, according to one famous argument by Carl Schmitt, is unintelligible without the notions of friend and foe, and therefore boundaries between them.[29] In addition to these familiar arguments, non-European traditions[30] have been incompatible with dominant European and American thinking: for Muslims historically, the external frontier of the Muslim world is a temporary truce line and the internal frontiers of Islam have no sound Koranic basis; in the Chinese classical tradition the only legitimate frontiers were those unilaterally imposed by the Chinese themselves.

But the western liberal view is the most influential in contemporary world politics, because the body of thought which can broadly be described as liberalism[31] has dominated constitutional thinking in nearly all of the highly industrialized countries, and has permeated international institutions and international law. Liberalism is a universal doctrine which attributes, in principle, equal rights and justice to all human beings. But universal notions of rights and justice are too abstract and too general for the purpose of deriving enforceable rules about who owes what to whom and in what circumstances. For this purpose a geographically bounded state is required. But liberalism offers a notoriously poor account of the territorial state because it proposes no argument about basic questions – why have a multiplicity of states, or why belong to one state rather than another?[32]

Vagueness and ambiguity characterize the liberal position on frontiers. Liberalism simply assumes, as a given, the existence of the territorial state, standing above civil society and regulating it. In the absence of a world state and universal liberalism, the territorially bounded state protects liberal values from internal and external enemies. But liberal universalism makes it potentially anti-pluralist, in that liberals tend to argue that all individuals should be integrated into a uniform liberal order – strong group identities and loyalties conflict with this position. Also, the practicalities of implementing liberal notions of equal liberties, equal opportunities and distributive justice make frontiers essential. For example, John Rawls argues[33] that policies should be pursued to promote equality, provided that these policies do not make the least favoured members of society worse off. Whether this is a tolerable principle without a strictly delimited state is doubtful because the sense of responsibility for the great majority of people does not extend to the whole of mankind and tends to diminish with social and geographical distance.

Attempts to popularize ideas of 'duties beyond borders'[34] extending outside groupings of like-minded states at comparable stages of economic development have not made much progress in large sections of opinion in any country. Some political theorists argue that the sphere of justice remains bounded by the frontier of a state.[35] In a morally pluralistic world, the argument runs, the state must be the final arbitrator of what is just and unjust. How frontiers are justified, and for what purposes, relate to these conceptions of spheres of justice.[36]

There is a preliminary matter of vocabulary: three words are in common use – 'frontier', 'boundary' and 'border' – and a fourth, now archaic, term – 'march' – which are applied to these outer limits. 'Frontier' is the word with the widest meaning, although its original meaning was military – the zone in which one faced the enemy. In contemporary usage, it can mean the precise line at which jurisdictions meet, usually demarcated and controlled by customs, police and military personnel. 'Frontier' can also refer to a region, as in the description of Alsace as the frontier region between France and Germany. In this sense it is the equivalent of the archaic 'march'. Even more broadly, 'frontier' is used in specific cases to refer to the moving zone of settlement in the interior of a continent and was used in this sense in Turner's famous classic, *The Frontier in American History* (Turner 1953). The term 'border' can be applied to a zone, usually a narrow one, or it can be the line of demarcation – the border between England and Scotland is both. It is the line running from the mouth of the Tweed to the Solway Firth, but in the plural it now refers to a Scottish region and, in the past, it was the 'debatable lands' where, in the fifteenth and sixteenth centuries, neither the law of Scotland nor the law of England was enforced. The word 'boundary' is always used to refer to the line of delimitation or demarcation and is thus the narrowest of the three terms. English is not unusual in having more than one term; French also has four – *frontière*, *front* (exclusively military), *limite*, *marche* (archaic as in English) – with only the first normally being applied to the international frontier. Spanish has three – *frontera*, *marca*, *limite* – and German, alone among major European languages, has only one term in common use – *Grenze*.

In this book the term 'frontier' is normally used to refer to the international boundary with variations in particular cases as, for example, the border between the Republic of Ireland and the United Kingdom Province of Northern Ireland; and 'boundary' is used to refer to the frontiers of political and administrative authorities below the state level. Prescott remarks that 'there is no excuse for geographers using the terms "frontier" and "boundary" as synonymous'[36] but this does not correspond to the ordinary language in the United Kingdom. By contrast, in the United States, 'border' is normally used to refer to the international frontier, because in American history 'frontier' referred to the zone mentioned above.

The Plan of this Book

This book treats a number of heterogeneous topics, united by the common theme that frontiers are inseparable from the entities which they enclose. The European origins and global spread of the sovereign state frontier are the subject of chapter 1. A specific conception of the frontier originated in the violent process of state formation in western Europe in the early modern period. Since then frontiers have marked the limit of an authority to rule, the sharp line at which sovereignty ran out. Wars were constantly fought to relocate frontiers and the nineteenth-century theorists sought to explain this competition; greater stability after 1950 stimulated a new set of theories.

The theme of chapter 2 is the changed basis of the legitimacy of frontiers. In traditional international law[37] there are broadly three bases of entitlement to territory – historical rights, agreements between states (treaties) and effective occupation. But the legitimacy, as opposed to the legality, of frontiers has been increasingly based on the liberal conception of the right of self-determination, sometimes regarded as the basic human right.[38] Aspects of the fragility of the territorial settlement in Africa and Asia are reviewed in chapter 3. Economic and social strains may not be contained by the existing frontiers, and European conceptions of frontiers may cease to be relevant in the quasi-sovereign states of the developing world.[39]

In western Europe there is a hierarchy of territorial units, ranging from regional groupings of states such as the European Community[40] to territorial units below the state level. Chapter 4 contains a review of aspects of territorial relationships below the state level, including the establishment of transfrontier associations of local and regional governments which suggested a fraying at the edges of the states. Chapter 5 is concerned with a core function of contemporary state frontiers – the control of the movements of people. The desire to retain cultural homogeneity, apprehension that large-scale immigration can undermine the cohesion of society and reluctance to extend the rights and privileges of citizenship to a large number of incomers all play a role in restrictions on immigration.

Chapter 6 discusses the contentious issues which have emerged in the last thirty years about boundary-making in uninhabited areas. The development of international regimes for these spaces has the potential to affect legal doctrines concerning, and political attitudes towards, inhabited territories. In conclusion, the slogan 'Europe without frontiers' is examined. European developments are of more than local interest because regional integration is occurring in other parts of the world and they may offer pointers to the future of frontiers.

1

The International Frontier in Historical and Theoretical Perspective

This chapter sets out elements of the intellectual context in which contemporary assumptions about frontiers have developed, with some references to the political processes through which the current international frontier has emerged. Frontier- or boundary-making has been a constantly repeated activity in the course of human history, but the characteristics of frontiers have varied considerably over time. Frontiers between states in post-Reformation Europe more and more resembled one another and became rooted, as institutions, in a common fund of ideas. Ideas of sovereignty, exclusive control over contiguous territory,[1] the nation-state and the juridical equality of states in an international society regulated by a voluntary acceptance of international law resulted in the spread of a common understanding of the frontiers of states.

Certain periods have, in retrospect,[2] made significant contributions to the ideas on which modern state frontiers are based – the Roman empire for notions of territoriality, the 'universalist' doctrines of the Middle Ages which offered an alternative project to the hardened frontiers of the states which emerged in Europe from the fifteenth century onwards, the development of the frontiers of France which prefigured those of the other European 'nation-states', the global spread of European notions of the frontier after the colonizing of lands in other continents, and the challenges to the frontier of the sovereign state in the post-Second World War international system. These landmarks in the history of frontiers mark an evolution in terms of stability of frontiers and the complexity of frontier functions.

The Legacy of Rome

Most ancient cultures and civilizations have left little mark on the territorial organization of the contemporary world. Their cosmologies, in which their sense of territory was rooted, are utterly alien to modern secular thought. But the modern international frontier and the related concept of sovereignty owe much to Roman ideas of territoriality, of *dominium* and *imperium,* transmitted through the Catholic Church, rediscovered by political theorists of the Renaissance and regarded as useful tools by jurists serving the interests of princes in the early modern period of European history. There are many problems associated with the reception of the Roman private law notion of property (*dominium*) and public law notion of undivided authority (*imperium*) in early modern Europe but only the main lines and understandings are relevant here.[3]

The influential features of Roman law and administration were developed from the first century BC. The relative density of population in Italy, from the period of the Roman Republic (509–27 BC), resulted in settlements being adjacent to one another, without the swamps, forests or uninhabited zones, which characteristically separated many pre-modern societies. As a consequence, clearly demarcated boundaries between settlements in ancient Italy were established (as they were in classical Greece, for the same reasons). When the Romans extended their empire into Gaul, they took this practice of demarcating boundaries with them. Often the old territorial divisions of indigenous peoples were confirmed by stone frontier-markers. The Romans also established a hierarchy of territorial divisions, commencing with the *pagus* at the base, then the *civitatis* and, at the apex, the *provincia* or *regio*.

The external frontiers of the Roman empire have seemed to the superficial observer, such as Rudyard Kipling,[4] to have been the archetype of the linear defensive frontier, dividing civilization from barbarism. The *fossatum* of North Africa, the *limes* of Syria, the Rhine and the Danube, the walls of Hadrian and Antonius (effectively occupied for only twenty years)[5] in Britain seem to have this purpose, if the archaeological evidence is viewed through the prism of the nineteenth-century experience of boundary-making. Even a sophisticated historian, Edward Luttwak, asserts that the Romans, like the British in India, sought fixed 'scientific frontiers' behind which the legions could defend the empire from external attack.[6] However, it seems more likely that they were means of policing the territory through which these great fortifications ran; Roman power and authority were felt by peoples far beyond them.[7] The relations between Imperial Rome and neighbouring peoples varied greatly during the centuries and between the different frontiers of the empire.[8] But Roman territorial organization – the outer limits of the march of the legions, as well as the internal Roman territorial divisions – continued to mark the social and political landscape long after the empire's disintegration.

The larger divisions of the empire, such as Hispania, Italia and Gallia, eventually became the territorial basis of the modern state system.[9] Some external Roman frontiers left an almost indelible impression. As Fernand Braudel writes: 'The frontier between the Rhine and the Danube was ... a cultural frontier *par excellence*: on the one side Christian Europe, on the other the Christian periphery, conquered at a later date. When the Reformation occurred, it was along virtually the same frontier that the split in Christianity became established: Protestants on one side and Catholics on the other. And it is, of course, visibly the ancient *limes* or outer limit of the Roman empire. Many examples would tell the same story.'[10] However, the great paradox in modern European political development, analysed by Stein Rokkan, is that the stable and strong states were established at the periphery of the territory of the Roman empire and the old core in Italy dissolved into loosely associated, competing and often warring, *civitates*.[11]

Within the territory they governed directly, the Romans were practical administrators who sought clear and comprehensive systems of rules – uncontrolled or unassigned territory was anathema to them. They also attempted to establish clear administrative hierarchies, and this included the hierarchical arrangement of territorial units. The final authority, the *imperium*, was at the apex of the hierarchy and the modern notion of sovereignty was derived from it. This association of final authority, of hierarchy and of territorial organization was taken over by the Catholic Church in the late Roman empire; the hierarchical system of archdioceses, dioceses and parishes with the bishop of Rome as the source of authority was well established by the fourth and fifth centuries.

The Middle Ages and Universalism

The uniformity of church territorial organization was disrupted by the collapse of the Roman Empire; from the sixth to the eleventh centuries there was a process described as the feudalization of the church.[12] However, clarity of territorial organization of the church remained an aspiration. As early as the ninth century all Christians were assigned to a specific parish and subsequently rules forbade them to listen to sermons in other parishes. The great councils of the Lateran, Lyon,

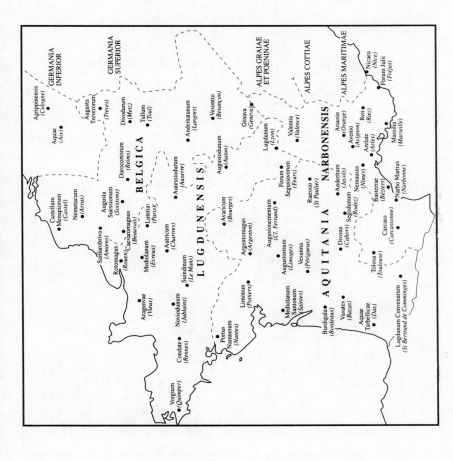

Map 1 Roman administrative areas in Gaul

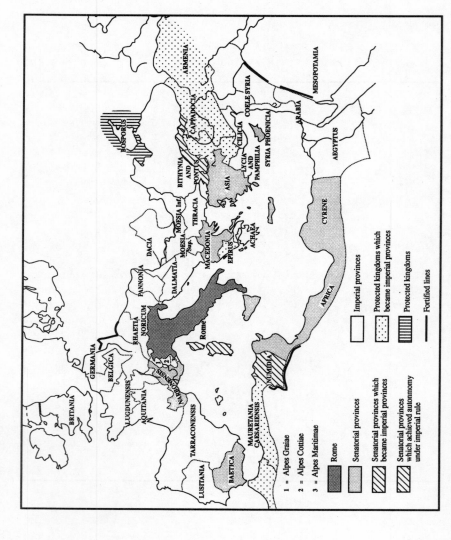

Map 2   The Roman empire at its greatest extent, showing main fortified lines

BRITANNIA

GERMANIA
BELGICA
LUGDUNENSIS
AQUITANIA
TARRACONENSIS
LUSITANIA
BAETICA

NARBONENSIS
RHAETIA
NORICUM
PANNONIA
DALMATIA
DACIA

Rome

MAURETANIA
CAESARIENSIS
MAURETANIA

NUMIDIA

AFRICA

MOESIA Inf.
MOESIA
Sup.
THRACIA
MACEDONIA
EPIRUS
ACHAEA

BOSPORUS

ARMENIA

BITHYNIA
AND
PONTUS
CAPPADOCIA

ASIA

LYCIA
AND
PAMPHILIA

CILICIA
COELE SYRIA
SYRIA PHOENICIA

MESOPOTAMIA

ARABIA

AEGYPTUS

CYRENE

1 = Alpes Graiae
2 = Alpes Cottiae
3 = Alpes Maritimae

Rome

Senatorial provinces

Senatorial provinces which became imperial provinces

Senatorial provinces which achieved autonomy under imperial rule

Imperial provinces

Protected kingdoms which became imperial provinces

Protected kingdoms

Fortified lines

Clermont and Dalmatia endorsed canons which made the church more bureaucratic and more hierarchical. They revived the Roman principles of territorial organization for the regular clergy. In this, the church was in advance, in principle if not always in practice, of the feudal secular order.[13]

By contrast with the church, land holding and allegiance in lay society were often highly fragmented. The land of the feudal nobility in the late Middle Ages was often not contiguous; a village could depend on more than one lord; lords could owe allegiance to more than one ruler; manorial courts, royal courts and ecclesiastical courts dispensed customary, statutory and church law to the same populations. Powerful rulers attempted to simplify the complexity of territorial organization in order to strengthen their authority. They initiated accurate record-keeping about land-holding, commencing with the Domesday Book in the late eleventh century in England, followed over a century later by a similar exercise in France.[14] This record-keeping was the basis of a new conception of territory in western Europe, which gradually spread to central and eastern Europe.

Several developments were associated with the new conception of territory, such as the institutionalization of secular administration and justice, rudimentary forms of representative assembly to approve taxes and legislation and conceptions of the political order based on more durable and impersonal loyalties than feudal relationships. Genealogy and genealogical myth remained as a basis of claims to authority, but they were first supplemented by others and then replaced – more quickly in western than in central and eastern Europe. Also, the myth of the universal empire, partly protecting and partly subordinate to a universal church, was slowly undermined. With hindsight, there is a sense of historical inevitability about the shift to state sovereignty; but absolute control of territory by rulers recognizing no superior authority was for a long time challenged by various forms of universalism. The core belief of universalism was that some high authority ought to hold sway over the whole of mankind or at least the civilized part of it. This belief came to be regarded as archaic or utopian in post-Reformation, post-Renaissance Europe. But it never entirely disappeared and eventually it took secular form.

Universalism was the philosophical and theological basis of the empire of Charlemagne (800–14) and remained that of the Holy Roman Empire, with diminishing plausibility, for a millennium. Even Charlemagne accepted that there were territorial limits to his empire; his authority neither extended to, nor clashed with, a competing universalism, that of Byzantium and the eastern church.[15] Systematic boundary-making within the empire commenced on Charlemagne's death when the patrimony was divided between his three grandsons at the treaty of Verdun in 843.[16] A third universalism emerged after the collapse of Byzantium, the tsar of all the Russias in conjunction with the Russian Orthodox Church. This partnership of throne and altar had more limited success and was eventually identified with an ethno-cultural exclusivity – pan-Slavism.[17]

These empires had an aspiration to suzerainty over the whole of Christendom but they never came near to achieving it and, despite this pretension, they always treated competing Christian rulers differently from non-Christian rulers. The practice of greater consideration, in diplomatic practices, by Christian rulers for each other survived as a polite gesture towards the belief in the unity and universality of Christendom during the growing secularization of politics of the eighteenth century into the age of European imperial domination of other continents in the nineteenth century. There were, of course, non-European, non-Christian empires, which also aspired to universal authority, emerging in the Muslim world and in China,[18] recurring during the successive dynasties which ruled the Chinese empire. These have not had the same influence as the Roman empire over the contemporary state system or over the attempts to overcome the defects of that system through international organization.

The Emergence of the Modern State System

In western Europe during the Middle Ages, the uneasy, sometimes conflicting, relationship between Pope and Holy Roman Emperor allowed the development of polities independent of both – the modern European states. The state system was anchored in the doctrine of the exclusive authority of the state within its own territory, subordinated only to the higher authority of God; states did not recognize the hegemony of any terrestrial ruler or universal church except, in the case of Catholic states, that of the Papacy in narrowly conceived spiritual matters. After the Reformation, according to the principle of *cuius regio, eius religio*, rulers imposed, where they could, the religion of their subjects.

Universalist thinking inspired by Christian doctrine survived in the new political order in various schemes for universal peace, such as those of the abbé Saint-Pierre and Immanuel Kant in the eighteenth century, and in ultramontane Catholicism which sought to revive the Papacy's influence over temporal matters by strengthening the Pope's spiritual authority. Even the late eighteenth-century Anglican conservative Edmund Burke was influenced by universalist thinking when he described Europe as 'virtually one great State having the same basis of general law' and that 'no citizen of Europe could be altogether an exile in any part of it'.[19] Universalism took a decidedly secular form during the French Revolution in the Declaration of the Rights of Man and the Citizen of 1789 and, more explicitly, in Marxism and in some other forms of nineteenth-century socialist thought. In political practice, those who upheld universalism were of marginal significance, except briefly after the French and the Russian revolutions, faced by the power and willingness of states to repress, and persecute, those who actively sought to put into effect universalist doctrines.

The contemporary international frontier developed as a result of a curious amalgam of universalism and particularist thinking. It is inextricably linked with the emergence of the concept of sovereignty in the theory and practice of European politics from the fifteenth to eighteenth centuries.[20] Sovereignty was not associated with a particular form of government – as Hobbes expressed it, the sovereign could be 'the one or the many' – but it was the basis of all properly established states.

The important implication of this doctrine for frontiers was that they were necessarily exclusive. The absolute nature of the authority exercised by the sovereign over territory and over individuals explicitly denied the possibility of the interpenetration of jurisdictions of the medieval polity in which kings, lords and clergy had autonomous judicial authority in the same territory. A single, supreme and independent sovereign was the hallmark of the state system of modern Europe, although competing authorities were common until the French Revolution of 1789. As far as crossing frontiers was concerned, the right of unimpeded exit for those individuals who had broken no law was admitted, but there was no equivalent right of entry. This right was in the gift of the sovereign, who could impose any conditions on foreigners who sought it; an important exception was made through the development of diplomatic immunity to the representatives of other sovereign powers.

The French Example

Establishing the identity of state-nation-territory, the underlying aspiration of the modern state, has been subject to many interpretations. But the linear frontier was the first requirement to establish this identity. This frontier was a rarity in the Middle Ages because of the virtual absence of continuous lines of fortification.[21] But in the late medieval and early modern periods, the kingdoms of western Christendom were virtually compelled to centralize in order to survive. Any weakness of central authority was ruthlessly exploited by internal and external enemies. An alternative model of political development, the city-state, which Braudel has called Europe's first fatherland,[22] showed remarkable vitality in northern Italy and in the Hanseatic towns of northern Europe, but it eventually could not resist the concentration of power in the kingdom-states. As Anthony Giddens has written, the nation-state replaced 'the city as the "power-container" shaping the development of capitalist societies'.[23] France was the great example of a kingdom compelled either to concentrate power or to fragment into a myriad local jurisdictions.

The historical problem, posed clearly by Lucien Febvre at the beginning of the twentieth century, concerns the aftermath of the Middle Ages: '. . . how and why these heterogeneous regions which no divine decree designated for unity . . . finally came together; this unity, first mentioned by Caesar in describing Gaul as having certain "natural limits", which was an approximate forerunner of France . . . How and why despite so many "offers" . . . despite so many failed initiatives to create Anglo-French, Franco-Iberian, Franco-Lombard or Franco-Rhenish nations, once seen as possibilities and sometimes established for limited periods, has Gallia succeeded in re-emerging after so many ordeals.'[24] An adequate explanation requires a detailed historical account of the interplay of chance and political choice over many generations but the main historical landmarks are clear. Fernand Braudel is the most recent of a line of distinguished French historians who have asked the question why the French state-nation-territory identity came into being. He concludes that it was the result of a combination of the European and Mediterranean context of France, of technology and economic organization, of imagination and of political action.[25]

The thoroughgoing expression of national sovereignty and the modern state frontier by the French Revolution had a long history. The great originality of French rulers was that they brought the various defining features of the modern frontier together – individually these features made their first appearance elsewhere. For example, the technical prerequisite of frontier delimitation, the accurate map, made a later appearance in France than in either Italy or England.[26] The first map of the French kingdom, attributed to Oronce Fine, was drawn in 1525, about a century after Ptolemy's *Geography* which stimulated the first generation of modern Italian cartographers, was rediscovered in Italy.[27] Strict demarcation of frontiers had, of course, long preceded modern maps. Frontier-markers were used in antiquity by the Greeks and the Romans[28] and some ancient polities in east Asia. In modern Europe, France was not the first in this field. The demarcated linear frontier made a precocious reappearance in fifteenth-century Muscovy;[29] frontier-markers were used at roughly the same time to mark the limits of Brabant.[30]

France was, however, the precursor of the centralized territorial state. The French kingdom grew unambiguously around one centre, the Île de France, in a series of piecemeal territorial acquisitions through conquest and dynastic marriages; the domains of the king of France eventually became (except for a few anomalies) a contiguous entity. France acquired a territorial clarity which contrasted with the fluctuations of imperial rule in Germany with its patchwork of fiefs, principalities, duchies, free towns and bishoprics; the religious division at the Reformation of the German-speaking peoples into Catholics and Protestants, as well as the non-German territorial interests of the Habsburgs, hindered the process of political unification and strengthened the contrast between German-speaking lands and France.

The beginnings of modern notions of a French territory were apparent in the thirteenth century. In 1244, the French king forbade his liegemen to hold land within the Holy Roman Empire and, in particular, banned the swearing of allegiance to both king and emperor (the notion of the king of France as 'emperor in his own domain' was developed). Marc Bloch considers that from this time there was what could legitimately be described as a frontier between France and the empire.[31] Towards the end of the thirteenth century royal power – military, fiscal, judicial – came to be felt in the marches of the realm. During this period, the customs policy of Philippe le Bel, who, sought to use the frontiers as a fiscal tool, required knowledge of the exact whereabouts of the frontiers.[32] The frontier became a focus of royal policy, with great practical as well as symbolic importance. Its symbolic importance was underlined by actions such as the two-year progress (1564–6) by Charles IX and his mother Catherine de Medici along all the frontiers of France.[33] But it was not until the middle of the sixteenth century that French monarchs could have a precise image of the extent of their territories because of the lack of accurate maps.[34]

In the second half of the sixteenth century, the idea of the natural frontiers of France, often wrongly attributed to Cardinal Richelieu, was revived by André Thevet to discredit the medieval divisions of French territory. The geographical image of France used by Thevet was derived from Caesar's *Gallic Wars* and from the classical geographer Strabo, who both described Gaul as bounded by the Pyrenees, the Rhine, the Alps and the seas. This idea of these natural frontiers was disseminated in French scholarly and educational literature from the sixteenth century onwards, and by the time of the French Revolu-

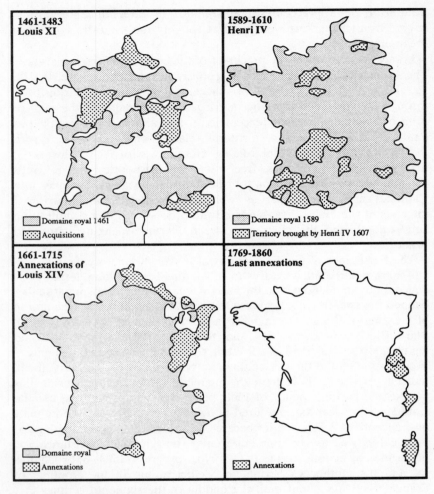

Map 3 The expansion of French territory

tion it had become generally accepted. The great orators of the
Revolution, Danton and Carnot, referred to natural frontiers,[35] like
their royal predecessors, to justify the expansion of French territory.
Thus Carnot, on 14 February 1794, stated to the Convention: 'The
ancient and natural limits of France are the Rhine, the Alps and the
Pyrenees. The parts detached have been usurped ... by diplomatic
pretensions, based on ancient possession, without any basis either in
judgement or in reason.' According to the revolutionaries, only peoples
were sovereign and had the right to decide the allocation of territory.

In this spirit, a crude public 'opinion poll' was held in 1795 on whether the Rhine should be the frontier of the French Republic and the results were published.[36]

The establishment of the modern French frontier was a process which took between three and five centuries – the demarcated frontier which was a boundary for legal, fiscal, administrative, political and ecclesiastical systems was not achieved until the French Revolution at the end of the eighteenth century. The assertion of uniform state power over the territory of France and the abolition of internal fiscal frontiers was not finally accomplished until the great abolition of privileges during the Revolution on 4 August 1789. This great act swept away the anomalies, particularisms, feudal jurisdictions and internal customs barriers of the *ancien régime* and created a united country. A radical reorganization of the internal boundaries of the country followed.[37]

After the Revolution it came to be widely, but erroneously, believed that, until 1789, it had been impossible to identify the exact location of the frontiers of France. Some of the most famous names in French academic geography at the beginning of the twentieth century – de Martonne, Gallois, Vidal de la Blache – propagated this belief in their contributions to a study group during the First World War.[38] Subsequent research has shown that they were wrong and that, under the *ancien régime*, although complicated, the frontiers were carefully and precisely negotiated. However, this notion of the uncertain frontiers of France served the cause of French expansionism by implying that claims opposing those of France had little legitimacy.

French expansion towards the Rhine had much success but was reversed by the defeat of Napoleon in 1814. Many, for example Victor Hugo in *Le Rhin*, continued to dream of France acquiring the whole of the left bank of the Rhine. The struggle over Alsace and part of Lorraine, which had been going on since the seventeenth century, continued. The conviction that the two predominantly German-speaking areas of Alsace and north-east Lorraine were indisputably French (because their populations wished to be French) became deeply entrenched in France in the nineteenth century. Franco-German rivalry assumed new bitterness when these territories, including some predominantly French-speaking areas, were annexed by the newly united German Reich after the 1870–1 Franco-Prussian War – only to be reacquired by France in 1919. After the two world wars of the twentieth century, French policy was to detach the Saar from Germany by creating an autonomous state, but this policy failed.

The modern frontier, in conventional thinking about the nation-state, separated two distinctive peoples or, to use a more pretentious term, 'civilizations'. A 'civilization' shared by all the inhabitants of French territory was completed only when the quasi-totality of the population became aware of their 'Frenchness'. This was achieved in the mid- and late nineteenth century when the state system of education, cheap newspaper press and the railways integrated the previously isolated and often non-French-speaking rural populations into the French nation.[39] The conviction that any intrusion across or any infringement of the frontier of the territory not expressly sanctioned by the French state should be firmly resisted came to be shared by the great majority of the population. Any attempt to detach territory, whether by separatist movements from within or by claims of another state from without, was regarded as a fundamental attack on the integrity of *la patrie*, on the one and indivisible French Republic, and on the French nation. There was virtual unanimity that Alsace-Lorraine was an integral part of France (except among a minority of the population concerned), after the annexation by the German Reich in 1871. This contrasts with the unsuccessful attempt to persuade the French population during the Algerian War of 1954–62 that the national territory stretched from Dunkirk to Tamanrasset, covering the whole of Algeria; de Gaulle and the great majority of the French electorate did not believe that the Algerian Muslims were or wished to be French.

The popular image of France as the 'hexagon', a term which, Eugen Weber has shown, has only recently become part of French political language,[40] now indicates that France has clear boundaries, disputed only by tiny numbers of Basque, Catalan and Breton autonomists. The Rhine frontier, the most problematic of France's frontiers in recent history, is no longer contested; the Alsatian 'malaise', synonym for autonomist sentiment in the inter-war period, has disappeared. The only part of French territory about which doubts remain is Corsica – Corsican cultural and social distinctiveness is recognized by the autonomy statute of 1982, the first time a special status for a segment of the national territory has been recognized by a French Republic. There is no longer controversy over any of the mainland frontiers of France.

Nation, Territory and International Relations

Although France is the exemplar of the development of the state-nation-territory identity and has had a considerable influence on the development of modern ideas about the international frontier, the French historical experience is different from that of other European nation-states. The geographical situation, the economic development, the enemies confronted and the political and administrative systems of the other strong states of the Atlantic seaboard which emerged from the fifteenth to seventeenth centuries – Spain, Portugal, England, the Netherlands and the Scandinavian monarchies – were extremely diverse. The concept of natural frontiers either made no sense, as in the Portuguese or the Dutch cases, or was self-evident, as in the English case; it could not play the same role in the statecraft of these countries as it did in France.

The idea of sovereignty *tout court* gained wide, almost universal, currency but 'national sovereignty' or 'sovereignty of the people' was either modified or not adopted at all in the constitutional principles of the other states. However, the state-nation-territory bonding exemplified by revolutionary France became the *mythomoteur* of nineteenth- and twentieth-century nationalism in Europe and in other continents as the European colonial empires declined in the mid-twentieth century. The nation-state introduced a precise sense of territorial identity and of territorial control. Rulers of these states, after societies reached a certain threshold of economic development, possessed the technical ability to police their territories and the military resources to offer credible resistance to armed intrusions across national boundaries.

The system in which the claim to absolute territorial sovereignty prevailed was as conflict-prone as the feudal system of personal loyalty which it replaced. In the absence of any universal authority, the only way to maintain peace and stability was to achieve a balance between the various independent entities. This resulted in an apparently endless process of territorial adjustments, or compensations as they were termed, to preserve the balance.[41] As in later imperial competition in Asia, the 'balance of power' resulted in various buffers, protectorates, clients, suzerainties, spheres of influence and neutral zones on the fringes of the great powers. The desire to make the balance more stable, and avoid the ruinous costs of war, resulted in two institutionalized practices which started to undermine the absolute nature of state sovereignty.

The first was the formulation of rules, 'the law of nations', to regulate the conduct of war and peace. At first, these did little more than codify existing practice and, in any case, were ignored with impunity by states. Eventually, these rules came to have the character of obligations in international law and constrained what most states did in most circumstances. The second practice was the meeting of heads of state, or their representatives, to legitimate a great settlement – a new balance of power. These took place after great wars – Westphalia in 1648, Utrecht in 1713, Vienna in 1815 and Versailles in 1919 (the first two were meetings of diplomats, the second two of heads of state) – but eventually the idea of a more permanent international assembly began to take shape, leading to the establishment of the League of Nations, then to

the United Nations and to regional European organizations after the
Second World War.

Under the old pre-1914 system, frontier disputes were of four main,
often overlapping, kinds. First, territorial disputes, supported where
possible by historic claims, ethno-nationalist arguments or assertions
about the equitable distribution of the spoils of war, were a means of
gaining advantage or domination over competing powers. Second, there
were 'positional' disputes over the precise location of the boundary
because of different understandings of the principles on which the
boundary was drawn. Some boundaries were demarcated only after a
considerable lapse of time and this could lead to different interpretations of what had been originally agreed.[42] Third, there were struggles
over sources of wealth and strategic areas, which led states to seize
territories, such as the annexation of Silesia by Frederick the Great.
Fourth, the whole system of territorial adjustment was called into
question by revolutionary states, notably by the French revolutionary
state (followed in the twentieth century by Russia, Germany, China,
Libya and Iraq) which set out to change fundamentally the political
map.[43]

Explanations of Frontier Disputes and of the Decline
of these Disputes

The great crisis of legitimacy which followed the French Revolution of
1789 necessitated new bases for political authority. This stimulated
secular explanations of territorial and frontier disputes. Sometimes
explanations of territorial conflict were ideological justifications of
expansionism. Geopolitical scenarios, such as Sir Harold Mackinder's
heartland and rimland to explain the nineteenth- and early twentieth-
century imperial struggle in the Eurasian land mass were clearly, in
retrospect, a justification of the pursuit of British imperial interests.[44]
But all explanations of conflict in the nineteenth and early twentieth
centuries were useful to some interests and inimical to others; their
claim to objectivity has little basis.

The four most influential nineteenth-century explanations of territorial disputes can be drastically summarized under the headings of
economic determinist, liberal nationalist, social Darwinist and *Realpolitik*. The best-known representative of the first school was Karl
Marx, although there were non-socialist, even liberal, versions of this
position. Marx was the first to suggest that there are systematic connections between economic organization, technological development and
the political map. In the Marxian theory of scientific socialism the role

of rulers and governments under capitalism was relegated to that of agents of the bourgeoisie, itself the product of the underlying economic organization of society. The factory system resulted in the accumulation of capital in fewer and fewer hands and a drive for access to larger markets. Marx regarded the large nation-state as the political form best suited to capitalism because such states supplied homogeneous markets which could be dominated by bourgeois rulers; but the bourgeois class would, in his view, become increasingly competitive as successive crises of over-production caused a more and more intense struggle for markets.[45] Extending state territory was one aspect of the life-and-death struggle to capture markets – a theory used by Lenin to explain the imperialism of the European powers in the late nineteenth century to colonize what remained of the less developed regions of the world.

When the last remaining markets had been cornered, according to Lenin, the stage would be set for the struggle which would bring about the collapse of capitalism. Lenin's prophetic vision turned out to be incorrect, although latter-day Marxists have argued that the United States, in association with other core capitalist states in Europe and Japan, has assumed the mantle of the nineteenth-century European colonial powers, with the less developed countries in a dependent relationship with them. This view derives directly from Lenin's famous tract on imperialism: '... finance capitalism and its foreign policy ... give rise to a number of *transitional* forms of state dependence. Not only ... the two main groups of countries, those owning colonies or the colonies themselves, but also the diverse forms of dependent countries which, politically, are formally independent, but in fact, are enmeshed in the net of financial and diplomatic dependence ...'.[46] The stage is therefore still set, according to 'dependency' theorists,[47] for the final crisis of capitalism.

The liberal nationalist position is often regarded as the polar opposite of Marxism.[48] It is associated with the contractarian political thought of the seventeenth and eighteenth centuries and, more loosely, with *laissez-faire* economic liberalism. The liberal nationalist position was based on a conception of the natural rights of man and on the idea of government by consent.[49] Liberal nationalists assumed the inevitability of conflict between rulers, and between them and the people whom they ruled, as long as they claimed to derive their authority from God, genealogy and historic rights. In the liberal nationalist world view there could be no lasting peace and stable territorial settlement until 'peoples' were emancipated and the boundaries of nations coincided with the boundaries of states.

Most liberals assumed that free peoples would have no reason to make territorial claims against one another. In 1834 the great liberal campaigner for Italian unity Mazzini founded, in an action which seems paradoxical in the light of subsequent history, the Young Europe movement as an 'international of nationalists'. In his view nationalists of all nations could cooperate harmoniously. Some thinkers in this tradition considered that harmonious relations between free peoples required international organization; Victor Hugo, the French republican poet, proposed a European Federation in 1849, and Carlo Cattaneo, the Italian liberal, suggested a European Senate a year earlier. The idea of free peoples cooperating in an international institution to resolve disputes is the core of the liberalism of Woodrow Wilson and the inspiration for the League of Nations.

There was an element of utopian thinking in the liberal nationalist position. The existence of nations or peoples was simply assumed and the fact that some were deliberately created by violence, intimidation and manipulation was ignored. To the objection that nationalism has been the most fertile source of violent conflict in the nineteenth century, the liberal response is that the nationalism in question was not based on liberal principles. The liberal theory of the nation was held by those who took the view that nations are not free associations of people but natural entities bound together by language, history and ties of blood. In the later nineteenth century this way of thinking became associated with new biological theories, and could loosely be described as social Darwinism. Theorists such as William Houston Chamberlain and Gobineau gave a racialist bias to it. The central proposition was that natural competition between nations or human species resulted in the survival of the fittest or best adapted and the extinction or subjection of the weaker.

The most ambitious project to apply organic views of state and nation to territory and frontiers was a book entitled *Politische Geographie* published in 1897 by the German geographer Frederik Ratzel. Ratzel argued that states could be considered as living organisms and frontiers as equivalent to a skin. States were in constant competition with each other in order to increase their relative power and in the course of this struggle sought to maintain or acquire the most effective frontiers – the shortest, enclosing the largest practical geographical space, the least complicated and the easiest to defend. Ratzel also developed the idea of *Lebensraum*, which he conceived as the space necessary for a people to support itself and to develop the various cultural and social forms associated with it.

Ratzel intended his work to be a contribution to the science of geography, and thus morally neutral, but his view of the struggle of states to achieve the best configuration of territory removed all moral or normative considerations from acts of inter-state violence, in effect giving general sanction to them. Ratzel was attacked by French human geographers such as Lucien Febvre, who rejected his view that territory 'determines the fate of peoples with a blind brutality' in favour of a more voluntarist conception – 'there are no necessities but everywhere there are possibilities' – in which human intelligence and imagination were crucial in deciding the purposes to which territory was put.[50] In the recent revival of geopolitics, writers have attempted, with mixed success, to integrate this more voluntarist approach.[51]

The concept of *Lebensraum* was given an explicit prescriptive content by Ratzel's pupil Karl Haushofer. The latter argued that the dynamic state must acquire the frontiers necessary to secure optimal internal development; if the dynamic state had the need and the power to develop the territory of a neighbouring or competing state, it had the right to lay claim to seize it. *Lebensraum* and the other social Darwinist concepts of the German geopolitical school were taken over and used by the Nazis to support their racialist and expansionist policies.[52] Theories of a biological basis to human territoriality have been revived in popular works such as those of Robert Ardrey and Richard Dawkins,[53] and this belief has formed the unsatisfactory background of some sociological accounts of territory.[54] Whether the compulsive boundary-making of human beings is determined by instinctual human 'nature' or a 'rational' response to specific situations, or some combination of the two, continues to be a matter of speculation. Despite attempts to reconstruct a science of sociobiology,[55] it has proved impossible to formulate questions which can be rigorously answered according to currently acceptable scientific criteria.

Realpolitik was a practice rather than a theory, as is exemplified by Otto von Bismarck, who ruthlessly pursued the interests of the state, Prussia, of which he became Chancellor in 1862. He brought about the unity of Germany under the Hohenzollern emperor by the unscrupulous use, in the famous phrase, of 'blood and iron'. Placing the interests of their state above all other considerations and prudently pursuing its interests was what most nineteenth-century statesmen considered they were doing. General explanations of politics belonged, in their view, to philosophy which had no part in the practical business of statecraft. Nonetheless, they were basing their actions on certain philosophical assumptions which derived from Machiavelli (1469–1527), who argued that rulers were not bound by morality but should use guile and force, from Bodin (1530–96) who suggested that sovereignty meant that rulers had no superior[56] and from Hobbes (1588–1679), who argued that in an original contract individuals handed over to the sovereign all power (except that of life and death) to conduct affairs of state.[57]

Hobbes formulated a position which has been widely accepted down

to the twentieth century – sovereigns are in a state of nature in
relationship with one another because there is no authority superior to
them. They are therefore at liberty to make war on one another when
their interests are served by doing so; they lose their entitlement to rule
only if they can no longer defend the lives of their subjects. The view of
international society as composed of states relentlessly pursuing their
interests is the basis of the twentieth-century realist school of international relations.

Marxist, liberal and neo-Darwinist theories and *Realpolitik* had
considerable plausibility in a world in which conflict, war and transfer
of territory were accepted as repeated and banal occurrences. Where
they lacked plausibility was in their common failure to explain the
complexity of disputes whose participants were often ensnared in 'a
maze of the greatest complexity', and this 'maze had not been built in a
day and the way out was long'.[58] Another common feature was that,
with the exception of *Realpolitik*, the classic nineteenth-century theories
envisaged the possibility that the struggle over territory would come to
an end, although only Marxism explicitly envisaged an 'end of history'
and the emergence of a harmonious society. Except for short periods of
time, and in special circumstances, none of these theories seemed to fit
accurately the actual conduct of relations between states.

Explanations of Territorial Stability

Between 1950 and 1990, important changes in the global political map
took place but, compared with previous historical periods, frontiers
were relatively stable. Despite the persistence of territorial claims,
changing the location of frontiers no longer seemed to have the same
priority for governments. How is this to be explained?

The realist and neo-realist schools of international relations remained
convinced that states formed an essentially anarchic society. The reason
for the greater stability of the global political map was, according to
realists, the increased expected cost of using military force to acquire
territory and the diminishing value, in the general struggle between
states for power and influence, of direct control of territory. The
competition between the superpowers of the United States and the
Soviet Union, from the closing stages of the Second World War to the
mid-1980s, was not so much to gain sovereign control of territory but a
struggle for territorial spheres of influence. From this starting-point,
Kenneth Boulding proposed a general theory[59] and used the tools of
economics to analyse competition between states; with assumptions
derived from a realist framework, he argued that states always seek to

maximize their territorial influence. He suggested that the costs of competing for territory (influence over territory rather than sovereign control) increase with distance just as costs for firms in a particular market increase with that market's distance from the point of production. Territories far distant from the metropolitan heartland might be given up to a competing power without a contest, but each state has a critical frontier across which a competing power cannot cross without a fight.

The concept of the critical frontier differs from the boundary of a sphere of influence, because the latter implies a tacit or explicit agreement between states about where the boundaries are, whereas the critical frontier is unilaterally defined by the state concerned. The Cuban missile crisis of October 1962 provided a timely illustration of Boulding's idea of a critical frontier because the USSR placed missiles with nuclear capability in what had been considered, since the early nineteenth century, as 'America's backyard'. The contention of Boulding and other writers in the realist school was that the incidence of armed conflict over territory diminished if the costs became too high. The Mutually Assured Destruction (MAD) strategic doctrine of the superpowers, their quasi-monopoly over nuclear weapons, their economic, military and political domination of their client states and the weakness of the states outside the two blocs created a situation in which any major and deliberate revision of the political map became very costly indeed. With the relative decline of the United States *vis-à-vis* the other highly industrialized countries and the collapse of the USSR as a hegemonic power in the late 1980s, the Boulding theory would predict increasing prevalence of territorial disputes. This, indeed, seemed to happen.

Others argue that the ground rules of the international system have been changing since the end of the Second World War, reducing the importance of territorial competition between states. Examples are 'interdependence' and 'integration' theorists who suggest that states, particularly the highly industrialized states, have become so locked into one another that territorial competition between them has become impractical and irrelevant. There is no clear distinction between the two schools of thought, but interdependence arguments tend to stress systemic factors such as new communications technologies, market forces and changing forms of economic organization while integration arguments stress the importance of political action and institutional factors.

An example of the interdependence theory is the work of the neo-Marxist historian, Immanuel Wallerstein, who traces the origins of the world capitalist economy to the sixteenth century.[60] At that time a trade

financed by a nascent capitalist economy began to bring goods from
distant sources such as India, China and the Americas on to the
European market. The relative power of European societies was quickly
and profoundly influenced by the ways in which they related to the new
trading system and in which their economies were inserted into this
global economy. Economic and associated political power moved from
Florentine and Venetian hands, with the loss of Italian control of the
oriental trade, first to Iberia, as a result of the Portuguese discovery of
the maritime route to India and Spanish conquests in Central and South
America, then to the Low Countries, with Dutch dominance of maritime
trade and, finally, by the beginning of the nineteenth century, to the
United Kingdom, whose dominance was based on sea power and cheap
manufactured goods. These changes in the European political economy
had their roots in the structure of the world economy. Greater integration of world markets and increasing concentrations of capital in the
core capitalist societies was, according to Wallerstein, part of an
inexorable historical process. Global integration (or globalization as it
is currently called) abolishes the significance of geographical distance
and makes all frontiers permeable; this eventually has the indirect effect
of diminishing the interest of rich and powerful countries in changing
the location of frontiers.

The basic factors leading to a global economy are common ground
between this Marxist view and many liberal interpretations of economic
development – division of labour, expansion of trade and new technologies lead to the interdependence of economies. But Marxists, while
giving some importance to political action, interpret the changes in
political structures and in territorial relationships as emerging from the
necessities of class domination and the contradictions arising from the
basic characteristics of capitalism. Liberals, for the most part, regard
these changes as partly arising from political will, and partly from
market forces.

Writers in both schools are agreed that sovereign independence has
been rapidly eroded and, in the economic domain, that no state has
genuine autonomy. As Charles Kindelberger, representing a liberal
view, wrote in 1969 in colloquial language, 'the nation State is just about
through as an economic unit'. Developing this proposition Keohane and
Nye write: 'the problem is not loss of legal sovereignty but the loss of
autonomy. States still have the policy instruments to implement their
policies but they are less and less able to use them in order to arrive at
objectives which they have chosen.'[61] For those in the Marxist tradition
the loss of economic autonomy emerged from the necessities of 'late
capitalism' and the increasing concentrations of capital in the United
States, Japan and western Europe. The diverse group of writers in the

dependency school argued that the rest of the non-socialist world was dependent on, and exploited by, this core with the proletarianization of the great majority of the world's population in the Third World or the so-called 'South'.

The two main strands of interdependence theory have both been subject to searching criticisms. Marxist theory is no longer influential, partly as a result of the collapse of Communist regimes in the 1980s and partly because of an intellectual assault which has tended to discredit the evidence used to support dependency theory. Conventional liberal positions have also been sharply criticized for failing to take account of the role of concentrations of economic and political power. Although there are considerable differences within as well as between the two schools of thought, both share a common starting-point, namely that economic change is the motor of political change. The frontiers between political units are subject to the inexorable forces of economic change; pressures almost inevitably build up to revise the location and functions of frontiers.[62]

Integrationist theorists have been mainly concerned to explain the development, and predict the future course, of European integration. They may be crudely classified under two headings, federalist and neo-functionalist. The best known of the former school is Altieri Spinelli, the Italian Communist member of the European Parliament until his death in 1986, who considered that Europe would be integrated by a series of deliberate political decisions which would eventually establish a true federation. Political will and constitutional inventiveness of leading groups and individuals are essential to federate Europe. The neo-functionalists argue that certain functional requirements ensure that steps towards integration should take place, but that the form and consequences of integration are nevertheless the outcome of political bargaining and decisions.

Jean Monnet, the inspirer of the French system of economic planning after the Second World War and the first president of the European Coal and Steel Community, was the most influential exponent of the neo-functionalist view. Monnet urged 'sectoral' integration, in other words, introducing close cooperation, with elements of supra-national authority, in a given important area of activity.[63] This, in his view, would almost inevitably necessitate cooperation in other spheres. Economic integration requires a high level of political cooperation both internally and externally for trading relations with the rest of the world. Thus the Treaty of Rome led inevitably to European Political Cooperation, to the Single European Act and finally will require political union in which the frontiers between states will be of no more significance than the boundaries between administrative units.

The great nineteenth-century theories – Marxism, neo-Darwinism, and *laissez-faire* liberalism – contributed to a secular, 'social scientific' way of considering frontier and territorial disputes. Although intended to be of universal validity, they are rooted in a specific historical period; they provide unconvincing explanations of the frontier disputes at the end of the twentieth century. The more recent theories attempting to explain the temporary stability of territorial relations are also embedded in a particular historical context. They do not take account of the explosive potential of territorial ideologies.

Territorial Ideologies and the Permanence of Frontier Disputes

Both the theorists of territorial conflict and those who have sought to explain a lessening of these conflicts have tended to underestimate the importance of territorial ideologies. Within western Europe there was an attempt, following the Second World War, to banish territorial ideologies from public debate, even when there was a territorial issue at stake, as in the Saarland. The European frontier invested with ideological significance was the frontier between the eastern and western blocs running through central Europe. The Iron Curtain symbolized a Manichaean world view, a struggle between good and evil.

Disputes about state frontiers were regarded by progressive politicians and technocratic administrators as a relic from a past, the pursuit of archaic quarrels engaged in by immature states which had not completed the 'modernization' process. However, some kind of territorial ideology – namely, a set of beliefs about the relationship of the population to the area which it inhabits – is a necessary part of the basis for any political order. Although it is submerged in western Europe, except for small and allegedly unrepresentative minorities such as Irish and Basque nationalists, there is no inevitability that this will remain the case.

In particular circumstances, territorial ideologies can resurface and fuel bitter conflicts. Under Slobodan Milosevic in the late 1980s a greater Serbian territorial ideology was revived, after it had long been submerged during the Tito period. Serbs claimed the indisputable right to control lands in which they were a majority; even Kosovo, with its overwhelming Albanian majority, is regarded as the cradle of the Serbian nation. This ideology has served as a justification for the removal of non-Serbs from 'Serbian' lands by the notorious policy of 'ethnic cleansing'. A similar territorial ideology was influential in Israel with the designation of the West Bank of the Jordan as Samaria and Judea and therefore part of the biblical Kingdom of Israel. The Greek territorial ideology in which the lands and symbols of classical Greece are the basis of the legitimacy of the contemporary Greek state generates conflicts with Turkey and Macedonia.[64] Belief in the 'natural' unity of the island of Ireland supports a continuing nationalist struggle for a united Ireland.

Sometimes these territorial ideologies, although appealing to history for their justification, are based on flimsy historical evidence. An example is the Iraqi claim that Kuwait is the nineteenth province of Iraq, based on dubious assertions about the internal administrative divisions of the Ottoman empire.[65] Stateless nations or ethnic groups claiming political independence often construct a historical identity and a territorial ideology. These territorial ideologies emerge and become powerful instruments of political mobilization in local situations. When they will emerge and how influential they will be in capturing the imagination of significant numbers of people is unpredictable. But general trends towards global interdependence and regional integration are unlikely to prevent them from being highly divisive. Disadvantaged populations adversely affected by processes of economic and political change seize on them as an instrument for altering balances in their favour. Territorial ideologies, in this sense, are more likely to be espoused by populations in a weak and vulnerable position.

Other ideologies about frontiers, focusing on their function of social protection, have resurfaced in Europe. In western Europe, with the disappearance of the external threat from the USSR, this function of frontiers has particularly been linked with controlling movements of population, vulgarized into fears of being 'flooded' by immigrants; this is discussed below in chapter 4. A permeable frontier has, in this view, the potential to create intolerable conditions, with large numbers of the world's poor crossing frontiers to improve their lot. Fear of immigration can be coupled with the aspiration to construct the widest territorial entity which can be effectively integrated into an area of political stability and economic prosperity in a dangerous world. 'Fortress Europe' is a slogan that expresses this way of thinking. But these fears may result in temptations to withdraw or hold up larger groupings: an illustration is the determination of the UK to preserve frontier controls within the European Union.

Territorial ideologies may be interpreted as rhetorical justifications for claims made for other reasons, to convince a sceptical international community of their legitimacy. Ideology, it may be argued, is merely a cynical cover for the promotion of material interests. But no claim, in contemporary circumstances, is acceptable to the international community or can mobilize a population to the point of making it a life-and-death matter, without a convincing form of legitimation. What suffices as legitimation will depend on the circumstances of the period and the characteristics of the population involved. The content of territorial ideologies varies according to time and place but their content is a crucial factor in initiating and sustaining a struggle for territory. Whether they are influential depends on the instabilities present in particular societies. If frontiers divide relatively stable societies, the longer the frontiers last, the harder they are to change. As Braudel remarks: 'Frontiers tends to entrench frontiers and make them seem natural phenomena.'[66]

2

Self-Determination, Secession and Autonomy: European Cases of Boundary-Drawing

The principle of self-determination has been one of the most influential ideas in the nineteenth and twentieth centuries; it has been a call to rebellion against states as well as becoming a basis for state legitimacy, embedded in international law.[1] While the great majority of the world's frontiers were established by force and intimidation, they are, in the long term, considered sustainable because *ex post facto,* they rest on self-determination or consent. But there are formidable objections to self-determination as a universal principle. It seldom points, clearly and unambiguously, to a solution to territorial conflicts when two groups lay claim to the same land.

The English term 'self-determination' probably originated from a translation of the German *Selbstbestimmungsrecht* in the nineteenth century, but the idea of self-determination derives from the Reformation, which established the primacy of the individual conscience, and from the contractarian political philosophers of the seventeenth and eighteenth centuries. Hobbes, Locke and the Scottish jurist Stair based their political philosophies on the axiom that societies and polities were established by an original contract, informed by natural law. Individuals agreed to this contract in order to improve on the unsatisfactory conditions which they endured when no polity existed. The ideal of self-determination was, therefore, supposed to produce a morally superior form of government because it rested on consent.

In certain circumstances, such a contract could be broken and the parties to the contract revert to a 'state of nature' where force was the only arbitrator, until a new contract was agreed. In the eighteenth century Rousseau produced what has been regarded as a radical democratic version of contract theory; he argued that the self-government achieved by people coming together in a social contract produced a superior form of freedom to that of the natural state. In a properly constituted society, Rousseau argued, each individual remained part of the sovereign and only the sovereign could legislate on matters which affected all citizens. If a ruler usurped sovereignty, citizens were then free of the obligations imposed by the original contract. For Rousseau, as for Hobbes and Locke, the frontiers of polities were unproblematic – they were defined by the territories occupied by the people who participated in the original contract.[2] This contract, for Locke and Rousseau, was the basis of all free societies. The core of the notion of self-determination was that people could withdraw from a polity, if their rights were abused, and set up another one.

The contractarian political philosophers influenced political practice, even though their ideas were modified in the light of political circumstances and sometimes by the misunderstandings of those who sought to apply them. The makers of the American Revolution of 1776 and the framers of the Constitution of the United States in 1787 drew on the ideas of Locke (as well as of Montesquieu). The leaders of the French Revolution and the French Constitution-makers of 1789 to 1793 absorbed the ideas of Rousseau and of the thinkers of the French Enlightenment. Conservatives reacted sharply against the ideas of both revolutions, rejecting as a pernicious doctrine the notion that political authority rested on the will and consent of the people, as opposed to the will of God and tradition. They considered that those who put their faith in human reason to discover the bases of political authority were dangerously undermining all authority.

In the politics of nineteenth-century Europe the principle of self-determination, because it was explicitly democratic, challenged existing political authorities as well as the territorial status quo. A turning-point came in the early twentieth century, when the principle was espoused by US President Woodrow Wilson in his declaration of US war aims during the First World War. For Wilson, national self-determination was a liberal ideal which provided a moral basis for the war against Germany, Austro-Hungary and Turkey. He agreed with the proposition of John Stuart Mill that 'free institutions are next to impossible in a country made up of different nationalities'.[3] America's European allies (Britain, France and Italy) adopted the principle as a useful propaganda weapon to subvert the domination by the Turks and the Austrians of south-east and central Europe; but they showed little inclination to accept it for their own subject peoples. Even US Federal officials saw the drawbacks of putting the principle into practice; Wilson's Secretary of State, Robert Lansing, roundly denounced it as a utopian idea which stimulated false hopes and would inevitably lead to new conflicts.[4] In the treaties which followed the war, the principle was applied to the vanquished and was ignored when it ran counter to the interests of the victorious powers. In the peace negotiations the great powers, as Tudjman observes, 'were primarily concerned with what they conceived to be their own interests'.[5]

The Russian Revolution of October 1917 also gave political impetus to self-determination. Although Lenin's espousal of the idea appears cynical in the light of subsequent history, he accepted Engels' view of the historical necessity of breaking Russian reactionary domination of subject peoples. In Marxist-Leninist theory, national aspirations and national movements were assessed in class terms. The independence or autonomy of peoples was a valid objective if it coincided with the 'objective' interests of the working class. Irish nationalism was, therefore, regarded as a positive phenomenon by Engels because it weakened the hegemony of the British bourgeoisie and undermined the privileged position of the British working class, based, so he argued, on the imperial wealth of Britain.

Marxist positions on nationalism changed according to circumstances, but the basic Marxist doctrine held nations to be the expressions of the class structure of society. However, Marxists took account, to a greater or lesser extent, of the practical importance of national sentiment. The founding myth of the Soviet Union is expressed by the Soviet jurist, Gregori Tunkin: 'The Communist Party fought for the unification of all the nations ... because this was necessary in the interests of the proletarian revolution: the struggle for unification was free and each nation expressed its right to self-determination by the free choice to unite with all the other socialist Republics.'[6] The military victories of the Red Army contributed much more than the free choice of peoples to the establishment of the USSR; the violent repression of some nationalities demonstrates that the interests of the leadership of the Communist Party were of overriding importance for Stalin and his colleagues.[7] Although the right to self-determination, in the guise of the right of the republics to secede from the Union, was included in Stalin's new Constitution of 1936 and reaffirmed by the Brezhnev Constitution of 1977, it was, for most of the time, regarded as purely theoretical; it was contradicted by the Leninist principle of party organization, democratic centralism.

Despite the experience of Stalinist repression of national minorities, the association of Marxism-Leninism with nationalism during the decolonization process after the Second World War proved influential in the Third World. From Cuba to Mozambique, from Nicaragua to Vietnam, it was the mobilizing myth of national revolutions. Linking the theme of social revolution to national emancipation in a simple but persuasive intellectual framework was attractive to successive generations of nationalists in less developed countries. To create new nations from highly fragmented populations, a social revolution was necessary, and to explain economic backwardness to peoples whose expectations had been raised by decolonization, a theory of exploitation by the rich countries was helpful. For analogous reasons, it was adopted by leaders of nationalist minority movements in western Europe such as the Basque Homeland and Liberty (ETA) and the Irish Republican Army (IRA). It remains the ideology of some separatist movements such as the Kurdish Workers Party (PKK).

In the post-Second World War period the right to self-determination was regarded as mainly applicable to the colonial possessions of the European imperial powers. After the collapse of the Soviet Union, it has been invoked by the nations and ethnic groups involved in the political disintegration of the USSR, Yugoslavia and Czechoslovakia. Political forces appealing to it now pose serious threats to the integrity of multinational successor states such as the Russian Federation, Serbia and Bosnia-Herzegovina as well as other multi-ethnic federal states (even those with stable democratic practices and institutions, such as Canada and India). In western Europe, where state boundaries have secure legal foundations as well as broad consent, the right of self-determination has been used by minorities to attack the territorial status quo. Consideration of the principle is, therefore, necessary to any general enquiry into the durability and legitimacy of contemporary frontiers.

The Boundaries of the Nation

A fundamental problem arose when the notion of self-determination (which was, at its simplest, an aspiration to self-government) was combined with the nation in the concept of national self-determination. In this combination, as Ivor Jennings observed, for a people to determine its own form of government, the prior decision was to decide who the people were (and who had the authority to take this prior decision): 'On the surface (self-determination) seemed reasonable: let the people decide. It was in fact ridiculous because the people cannot decide until someone decides who are the people.'[8] The practical implications of the principle, taken to extremes, were pointed out by

Rupert Emerson: 'In its most extreme version, the right of self-determination could mean the right of any group of disaffected people to break away at pleasure from the State to which they presently belong and establish a new State closer to their heart's desire.'[9] The risk was that any group, no matter how small, could decide they were a people and secede from the polity of which they disapproved, creating instability and insecurity.[10]

The American and French revolutionaries did not see this as a problem and issued stirring declarations in the name of the peoples they claimed to represent. The people were those (males) who resided in the territories called France and America, the boundaries of which were, in part, determined by nature and, in part, decided by the free consent of the people.[11] There were problems in America, both with black slaves imported from Africa and with the native Indians, and in France with the awkward fact that the majority of the rural population in France spoke local dialects and languages rather than French, and were sometimes resistant to the new revolutionary ideas put to them. For the first time it seemed necessary 'to force people to be free' and recognize their highest allegiance was to the republican nation; the alternative presented to them was exile or death. In both France and America it was decided that the possession of certain qualities or attributes was necessary in order to be a member of a people and a fully qualified citizen – an 'active citizen' to use the term of the French Constitution of 1791.

Self-determination and nationalism have coexisted uneasily since the French Revolution.[12] Four analytically distinct concepts of the nation with broad appeal to nationalist politicians and activists emerged in the nineteenth and twentieth centuries, and all have had variants.[13] The first is the idea of the nation as a contractual or quasi-voluntary association; a nation existed because a large number of people identified themselves with it. Nations could disappear when this sense of identity faded and new identities could emerge. 'The Nation', as Ernest Renan expressed it in a famous aphorism, 'is an everyday plebiscite.'[14] An opposing view was expressed by Fichte, reacting against the ideas of the French Revolution. He wrote, in a much quoted sentence from his *Address to the German Nation* (1808): 'The distinction between the other nations of Europe and the German nation was created by nature. The Germans are united in a nation, distinct from any other nation, because of a common language and common natural characteristics ... they were bound together by nature herself long before human will intervened.' According to this view, individuals do not choose their nationality by identifying with a nation, they are born into a nation and cannot escape or deny their national identity.

The third theory influential in the nineteenth century was the nation as a metaphysical ideal or as an impersonal will; this became vulgarized as the nation as a set of images, aspirations and highly selective historical references. The most celebrated twentieth-century example of this ideal can be found in the first pages of the war memoirs of General de Gaulle in which he invokes symbols, historical figures, battles, ideas and family experiences in order to explain what 'France' means; it is a France curiously devoid of the people.[15] A fourth theory of the nation emerged later in the nineteenth century and was called 'east European nationalism' by John Plamenatz, although it is now more familiar as Third World nationalism.[16] The nation, in this view, is the political project of an elite minority which regards itself as the embodiment of the values of the nation. The elite has a self-assigned mission to integrate different ethnic and social groups into a nation with the purpose of modernizing a society to render it less vulnerable to external domination.

All four types of theory have two common threads. First, the nation is the basis of political legitimacy. Second, all assume that the nation is bounded, that it has frontiers: 'The nation is imagined as *limited* because even the largest of them, encompassing perhaps a billion human beings, has finite, if elastic, boundaries beyond which lie other nations.'[17] The central problem is that, unless a state authoritatively declares who is a member of a nation, there is no agreement about the limits of the nation. To rest the legitimacy of a state on a nation is therefore problematic.

Universal Acceptance of Self-determination

The principle of self-determination received world-wide assent by its inclusion in the Charter of the United Nations (Articles 2.4 and 55). Although not mentioned in the 1948 UN Declaration of Human Rights, it was reiterated in the 1960 Declaration on the Granting of Independence to the Colonial Countries and Peoples and eventually integrated into international law through two 1976 UN agreements, the Covenant on Social and Economic Rights and the Covenant on Civic and Political Rights. An authoritative commentary on these agreements by F. Capotorti, published by the UN in 1979,[18] presented self-determination as the basic human right because all other rights derive from it. The right of every nation to self-determination was also included in the Final Act of the Helsinki Conference on European Security and Cooperation in 1975. Even the Papacy, a firm opponent of liberalism and nationalist ideology in the nineteenth century, became a wholehearted supporter of the principle. John Paul II, on a visit to his native Poland in 1979, said that every people has the right to its homeland, culture, freedom and self-determination.

Martin Wight argues that, during the decolonization process after the Second World War, self-determination came to mean a combination of things – majority rule, the exclusion of racial minority governments and domination by people of European descent in non-western regions.[19] Sceptical voices, repeating old conservative arguments, criticized the implications of the right and the difficulties of applying it in practice, *inter alia* the risks of establishing non-viable states, and of creating insoluble disputes over territory with 'trapped minorities' and 'stranded majorities'. When a new frontier is proposed giving self-determination to an oppressed minority, a new minority (of members of the former majority such as the Hungarians of Slovakia, Transylvania and Vojvodina) is often created, trapped on the wrong side of the new frontier; a majority of the existing state may lose a vital strategic advantage such as access to the sea, which was the case for Austria and Hungary after the First World War, or a resource essential for maintaining collective life such as, in the African secessionist crises of the 1960s, the oil of Biafra or the copper of Katanga. The morality of a rich province leaving a poor country is often contested on the grounds that minorities have obligations to the majority in a state, just as majorities have obligations towards minorities. It is not generally regarded as justifiable for a majority to expel a minority it does not like. In other words, a majority vote in Great Britain to expel a troublesome and costly province like Northern Ireland, or in Italy to expel Calabria and Sicily, because they are economic and social liabilities, would, quite apart from the legal difficulties of doing so, be regarded as an abandonment of responsibility. The responsibility of the minority to the majority, while not as strong as that of the majority to the minority, nonetheless exists.

The practical questions associated with implementation of self-determination were exhaustively discussed in the literature of the inter-war period.[20] The most difficult question centred on the drawing up of the electoral roll (who was to do this, and the principles of inclusion and exclusion); whether a simple majority of voters or a majority of those entitled to vote or some previously agreed qualified majority should be decisive; who determined the choices put to the electorate (including the wording of the questions); whether a territory was divisible if a locality strongly dissented from the majority opinion; and whether the parties to the conflict must agree on the voting procedures. The additional problem of who controlled an area was clearly apparent in the plebiscites at the end of the First World War. Examples include the disagreement between Poland and Lithuania in 1920–1 over the Vilna plebiscite,[21] the Silesian plebiscite when German *Freicorps* operating in the region clearly influenced the outcome, and the plebiscite in the German-speaking area of Eupen-Malmédy when voters, if they wanted a return to Germany, were required to sign a register in the presence of Belgian officials who cancelled food ration cards and the right to travel of those who had the temerity to do so.[22] Plebiscites can only be fair, it is often argued, if they are held under neutral auspices. This is always difficult and sometimes impossible, even when an international authority assumes control.[23]

During decolonization, such problems were relatively unimportant, and where there were disputes, as in the case of the partition of India, rough-and-ready solutions were imposed. When demands were seriously pressed by minorities in both western and eastern Europe, or by secessionist movements in the Third World, the difficulties in the application of the principle pointed out by Jennings and Emerson, as well as the practical questions raised by the post-First World War plebiscites, became central. Clear answers have not been provided, either by the United Nations or by the various autonomist and secessionary crises, to the questions: Who are the 'people' with the right to self-determination? In what circumstances? With what limitations? With what relationship to other principles of international law such as respect for the territorial integrity of states[24] or non-intervention in the domestic affairs of states?

The 1976 UN Covenant on Civic and Political Rights states that self-determination implies 'the free association or the integration within an existing State or the introduction of another political status freely chosen by the people'. The way in which the people should freely decide is not stated, but a regime of free elections is implicit. The Covenant recognizes that the exercise of the right does not necessarily involve the redrawing of international boundaries but may, instead, be satisfied by some form of devolution of power or of political autonomy, provided that such an option is freely chosen by the people – a prudent position because only about 10% of the members of the UN are ethnically homogeneous, leaving about 90% with two or more ethnic groups on their territory. If every nation or ethnic group were to assert the right to statehood, the international system would be destabilized. In practice, the international community of states has been hostile to secession. Governments can count on at least the passive support of other states until secession is a *fait accompli.* The widespread acceptance of the principle has, however, had a crucial negative effect: it is very difficult for states to acquire territory – an act which was common until the middle of the twentieth century – without reference to the wishes of their population.[25]

Self-determination of Minorities in Western Europe

In western Europe a range of possibilities for territorial minorities exists between, on the one hand, complete independence and, on the other, total integration with the larger entity. But, even given this consensus, it is still difficult to arrive at satisfactory understandings about which people have the right to decide, the process by which the decision should be taken, and the territories in which a democratic consultation should take place. Three cases of west European minorities – South Tyrol, the Swiss Jura and Northern Ireland – illustrate these difficulties.[26] In South Tyrol and the Swiss Jura, the demand for autonomy was based, like many demands for independent statehood elsewhere, on the necessity to defend a particular culture; the division between Ulster Protestants and the Catholic Republicans has also been described as a 'cultural divide'.[27] The cultural argument can be as exclusionary as arguments based on blood relationships, particularly when language and religious allegiance are used as cultural markers. Solutions in these three cases have been sought, with varying degrees of success, through constitutional concessions.

South Tyrol

The South Tyrol conflict is a case of a minority trapped on the 'wrong' side of the frontier as a result of the outcome of wars and of the perceived national interest of Italian governments.[28] The origins of the dispute are in the vision of the 'natural' frontiers of Italy in the nineteenth century; the contention that the watershed of the Alps was the natural frontier became part of Italian nationalist thinking. Italy's opportunity to gain the Alpine watershed came in the First World War. To attract Italy away from her alliance with Austro-Hungary and Germany, Britain and France, as allied powers, offered Italy the territory up to the Brenner in the secret Treaty of London in 1915. This included the province of South Tyrol (the Alto Adige) which, according to the Austro-Hungarian census of 1910 had a population of 86% German speakers, 8% Italian, 4% Ladin (Rhaeto-Romansch) and 2% others (mainly soldiers). The Austrian loyalties of the majority of the population were not in doubt; honouring the Treaty of London by the Treaty of Saint Germain, between the victorious coalition and Austria, was a flagrant breach of the principle of self-determination. Although the Liberal government of Italy, then in power, undertook to maintain the linguistic and cultural rights of the German speakers, Mussolini's

Fascist regime went back on this undertaking by introducing a radical programme of Italianization. When Hitler determined to make an alliance with Mussolini, the South Tyrolese German speakers were invited to choose either integration in the Italian state and Italian nation or emigration to the Third Reich. In a plebiscite held in the summer of 1939, two-thirds of this population chose emigration. The war intervened and only 70,000, predominantly town-dwellers, had left before other Axis objectives became of more pressing importance.

After the Second World War another agreement (the 1946 De Gaspari–Gruber Agreement) guaranteed the linguistic and cultural rights of the population. But the South Tyrolese suspected the Rome government of deception and of secretly aiming to absorb the German speakers into Italian society. Legislation in 1948 integrated the province of South Tyrol in a broader region of the Trentino–Alto Adige; the Alto Adige (South Tyrol) was accorded the status of a province, but most of the more important powers were granted to the region. Within the region, the Italians had a 70% majority in the regional assembly. The impressive political solidarity of the South Tyrolese, with over 90% voting for the Südtiroler Volkspartei (SVP), kept alive the issue of the status of province.

A small minority of the South Tyrolese adopted violent tactics: in 1956, the first bomb was exploded by German-speaking militants. There were subsequent attacks on a wide range of targets, producing a long crisis in the relations between the South Tyrolese and the Rome government. Austria tried, with partial success, to internationalize the issue by placing it before the UN General Assembly, a move resented by the Italian government; the Italians agreed, nonetheless, to negotiate directly with the SVP and recognized that the Austrian government had a legitimate interest in the dispute. The negotiations followed a tortuous path until the signing in 1969 of a package agreement – a very detailed document containing 137 articles. The principal features were that the province of Alto Adige was given increased powers, particularly in the crucial areas of agriculture and tourism, which had previously belonged either to the region or to the central government; the principle of 'proportionality' of different ethnic groups in public employment (except the police) was to be standard practice; the province was to receive a specified proportion of total Italian public expenditure (a higher proportion of central government revenues was accorded to the Alto Adige than was the case for *Land* Tirol in Austria); German was permitted in all public business and all officials had to be competent in both German and Italian; the place of German in the school system was guaranteed.

Partly due to the prosperity of the province, German speakers could

Map 4   South Tyrol

not be recruited in sufficient numbers into public sector employment. The SVP opposed Italians filling jobs reserved for Germans, except on a temporary basis; Italians were therefore denied jobs in a part of Italy at a time of relatively high national unemployment. Italians increasingly felt themselves to be a beleaguered minority in South Tyrol. The system of proportionality introduced a form of ethnic/linguistic apartheid. Individuals had to make a declaration of their language at each ten-year census and important privileges were reserved to the German speakers. The policy ran counter to the accepted basis of individual rights in the rest of western Europe and was at odds with developments in South Tyrolese society itself – among other things, the spread of bilingualism,[29] mixed marriages, integration of the younger generation of German speakers into Italian society, the participation by the political elite in national Italian politics, increased prosperity (checked by the provincial government to prevent immigration of Italian labour), the heightened sense of European identity and the ending of provincial isolation through the Brenner motorway. The linguistic frontier has, however, remained remarkably stable; despite radical changes of political regime and many social changes, it has been in virtually the same place since the end of the Middle Ages. The position of South Tyrol is not entirely resolved because issues concerning the package agreement recur from time to time, such as the delay in the implementation of bilingual courts envisaged for May 1993. However, the conflict officially ceased to be an international issue when in 1992 the Austrian and Italian governments asked the Secretary General of the United Nations to remove the South Tyrol question from the UN agenda.

The Swiss Jura

German speakers of South Tyrol and the Francophone population of the Swiss Jura both won constitutional concessions at about the same time. In the Swiss case the victory was the establishment, in 1979, of the canton of Jura (the first new canton in Switzerland since 1815) by secession from the canton of Berne. This was a significant move in a confederation where citizenship rights derived from the locality of origin rather than the confederation.[30]

The demand for the autonomy of the Jura was longstanding – the first autonomist movement began in 1826, fading in 1831 when the government of Berne made concessions, but autonomist demands were revived at regular intervals. Two characteristics – the French language and the Catholic religion – distinguished the autonomist population from the majority of the canton of Berne. Memories of the religious wars of the sixteenth century lingered in the popular imagination; several politico-religious crises in the nineteenth century helped to maintain the religious division.[31] The southern Jura, while French-speaking, is overwhelmingly Protestant, and has never identified with the autonomist cause.

The process leading to the setting up of the canton of Jura commenced in 1947 with the Moekli affair. The legislature of the canton of Berne rejected the nomination of Georges Moekli as director of public works on the grounds that the post was too important to be held by a French speaker. Since Moekli in the course of his career had been a member, and then president, of the executive of the canton, this refusal

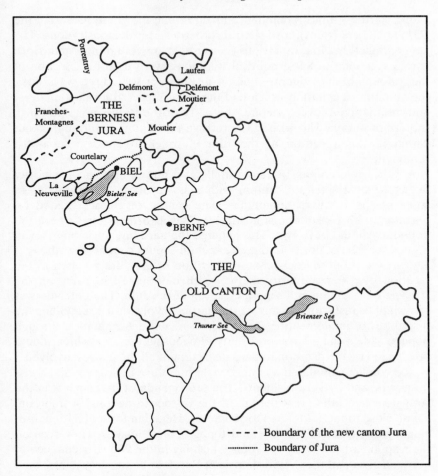

Map 5 Jura and the canton of Berne

was regarded as highly provocative. The French speakers were divided in their responses but in 1948 a separatist movement was established which, in 1952, was named the Rassemblement Jurassien (RJ). In the south of the Jura, Force Démocratique, began campaigning for the unity of the canton of Berne.

The first referendum on separation of the Jura from Berne took place in the communes of the Jura in 1959, and resulted in a narrow defeat of the proposal. But some communes in the north recorded very strong majorities in favour of separation, which encouraged the autonomist movement. A militant wing of the movement, the Jura Liberation

Front, started a minor bombing campaign while the youth section of the RJ, the Béliers (rams), instigated disorderly street demonstrations. The Jura conflict became notorious because arson, bombings and riots, considered alien to Swiss political traditions, were used by a section of the autonomist movement. Opinion in the Jura split three ways: first, the autonomist coalition which had the most impact at local, confederal and international levels; second, the party of the status quo; and third, the compromisers who wished to preserve the canton of Jura but create within it a half canton of the Jura in order to appease separatist sentiment.

Another referendum was held in 1974, resulting in a small minority in favour of a separate canton, with massive majorities in favour in some of the northern communes. The canton of Berne decided on partition, with consultations at the local level to determine where the boundary should be drawn. This angered the hard-line autonomists who argued that the majority in the referendum should commit the whole of Jura to the proposed new canton. Partition of the Jura resulted in the creation of a new minority in the south determined to carry on the struggle for a united and separate canton of the Jura. The outcome was not wholly satisfactory to any of the parties involved. It exemplifies the difficulties of implementing the principle of self-determination through popular vote – the near-impossibility of choosing the area which should be affected by the decision to the satisfaction of all the parties involved.

The conflict stimulated a considerable literature by foreign and Swiss observers, and by Jura residents. The propaganda of participants in the struggle reflects the great themes of the European nationalist tradition. Those close to the RJ tended to promote a Hegelian form of nationalism comprising historical, cultural and topographical images. They accused their opponents of losing the roots which lay in the 900-year connection between Jura and the Archbishopric of Basel, of being lackeys of Berne and of ignoring the perils of Germanization.[32] The case presented for the south of Jura remaining with Berne canton were analogous to Northern Ireland unionism – the north and south of Jura had little in common. (Even their linguistic unity was misleading because the north was formerly *langue d'oil*, the northern French dialect which became standard French, and the south *langue d'oc*, which remained a southern French dialect; the two halves of Jura were culturally different with the result that inhabitants manifested different characteristics and behaviour; there was no linguistic conflict with the German speakers and no risk of Germanization.[33]) The argument for maintaining the unity of the canton was that this unity was longstanding and that partition was contrary to the interests of the population.

The three main types of explanation of the conflict by outsiders were based on notions of cultural difference, relative deprivation and centre–periphery conflict. The cultural argument was that the conflict was the result of the clash of two value systems (based loosely on two religious traditions), which produced different attitudes towards social and political issues. The relative deprivation argument suggested that the economic decline of the north of Jura, and loss of economic autonomy with the disappearance of traditional watch manufacture, provoked a demand for a compensatory political autonomy. The centre–periphery argument was based on empircal observation of physical and human geographical indices – distance from Berne, altitude, proportion of French speakers in the population, rates of outmigration; all the communes in which autonomist sentiment was strong had high scores when placed on a centre–periphery scale. This location needed only a trigger to provoke a typical peripheral revolt against the centre. No criteria for settling the rival claims of these theories exist and all rest on unreliable data.

Ireland

The long crisis in Northern Ireland began in 1969, when the British army was called in to aid the civil power to contain serious civil disorder. The intervention was followed by a prolonged terrorist campaign by the Provisional Irish Republican Army. The crisis is the direct result of the partition of the island by the Government of Ireland Act (1920) and the Anglo-Irish Treaty (1921). The roots of the problem lie deep in the history of Anglo-Irish relations; some Irish nationalists date its origins from the 1169 Anglo-Norman invasion of Ireland. Historians of all persuasions agree that the majority of the Irish population was imperfectly integrated into the rest of Britain. The failure of assimilation became a strategic weakness when, after the Reformation, continental Catholic powers calculated that they could strike at the Protestant holders of the English crown through disaffected Catholic Ireland. The result was that the later Tudors and the first Stuart king, James I, attempted to change the composition of the population by organized migration of Protestants to Ireland. This policy of 'plantations' eventually established a Protestant, mainly Scottish Presbyterian, majority in the north-east of Ireland and a minority Protestant 'ascendancy' in the rest of the island.

Although the rebellion of 1798, widely regarded as the starting-point of modern Irish nationalism, was led by Protestants, the great majority of the Protestant population in the nineteenth and twentieth centuries has unequivocally supported maintaining the Union with the United

Kingdom. In the first great Home Rule crisis of 1885, the cause of unionism adopted the sectarian slogan 'Home Rule means Rome Rule' – in other words, the devolution of power to Ireland would inevitably mean the political domination of the Roman Catholic Church. A combination of influential support for the Ulster cause in the Conservative Party as well as more generally in the civil and military establishment in Britain, the heroic battlefield record of the Ulster regiments during the First World War and the weapons in the hands of the Ulster Protestants prevented the imposition of Home Rule on the whole of Ireland. Six of the nine counties of Ulster were allowed to opt out and acquired, initially against their wishes, their own devolved government and parliament at Stormont.[34]

When the Republic of Ireland was declared in 1949, all constitutional links between the United Kingdom and Ireland were broken, but without breaking all ties between southern Ireland and the UK. Irish citizens continued to have unrestricted right of entry to Britain and automatically acquired citizenship rights in the UK through residence. Social, cultural, sporting and professional ties between south and north and between both and the rest of Britain were retained. In sport, for example, rugby union is organized on an all-Ireland basis, Association football on a divided north-south basis, swimming is all-Ireland, cycling partitioned; in trade unions, sixty-eight out of eighty-nine are exclusive to the Irish Republic but five are all-Ireland and sixteen (including some of the most politically sensitive such as the National Union of Journalists) are all-British Isles.[35]

Despite the tissue of relationships between Britain and both parts of Ireland, two separate communities were deeply entrenched in Northern Ireland. The two communities were divided by symbols, traditions, religion, education, political allegiances and historical memories. Most of the historical memories relate to violent confrontation between the two communities since the sixteenth century and beliefs about the threat represented by the other community. As in the case of the Jura, a wide variety of explanations has been offered for the persistence and intractability of the divisions in the Province. These have been neatly categorized into Marxist and non-Marxist, traditional unionist and traditional nationalist, endogenous and exogenous explanations.[36] Most of these explanations regard the conflict in Northern Ireland as only incidentally a territorial dispute. The partition has merely helped to sustain a conflict which predated 1921 and will doubtless continue despite repeated attempts to construct a settlement.

The nub of the problem facing British and Irish policy-makers is that those wanting political change, the majority of the Catholic population, are a minority of the population of the Province and the Protestant

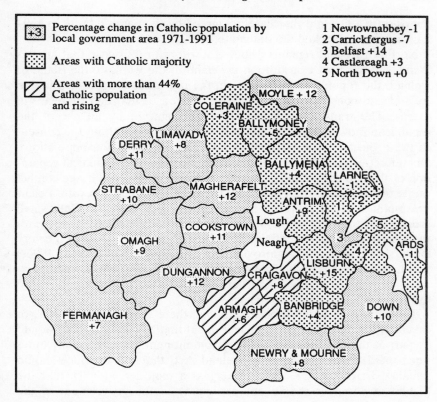

Percentage change in Catholic population by local government area 1971-1991

Areas with Catholic majority

Areas with more than 44% Catholic population and rising

1 Newtownabbey -1
2 Carrickfergus -7
3 Belfast +14
4 Castlereagh +3
5 North Down +0

MOYLE + 12
COLERAINE +3
BALLYMONEY +5
LIMAVADY
DERRY +11
BALLYMENA +4
LARNE -1
MAGHERAFELT +12
STRABANE +10
ANTRIM +9
Lough
COOKSTOWN +11
Neagh
OMAGH +9
LISBURN +15
ARDS -1
DUNGANNON +12
CRAIGAVON +8
BANBRIDGE +4
DOWN +10
FERMANAGH +7
ARMAGH +6
NEWRY & MOURNE +8

Map 6   Population changes in Northern Ireland

majority are implacably opposed to change. Demographic trends are moving against the Protestant population. The western half of the Province is becoming increasingly Catholic, and the long-feared Catholic majority in the whole Province may emerge in the first quarter of the twenty-first century. The presence of intransigents on both sides of the communal divide – the Provisional Irish Republican Army (PIRA) and Sinn Fein on the Catholic–nationalist side and the Protestant para-militaries and the Democratic Unionist Party of Ian Paisley on the Protestant–unionist side – has made it impossible for moderates to reach agreement from fear of losing support to the intransigents. Determined efforts to bring the two sides together by the British government in 1973 at the Sunningdale Conference, the Prior initiative on 'rolling devolution' at the beginning of the 1980s, then joint efforts by the British and Irish governments with the Anglo-Irish Agreement at Hillsborough in 1985, the Joint Declaration on the future of the

Province in 1993, and the ceasefire agreed by the paramilitaries in 1994 have not yet unblocked the stalemate.

Northern Ireland remains disputed territory in the sense that articles 2 and 3 of the Irish Constitution lay claim to the whole of the island of Ireland; the republican movement in the north has fought for a united Ireland and constitutional nationalists aspired to that end by peaceful means. The transfer of sovereignty is recognized by all except the republican movement in the north to be impossible without the consent of the Protestant unionist community (about 57% of the population). One effect of the troubles has been the increasing geographical separation of the two communities, but no large group involved in the conflict wants to repartition the Province, leaving only those areas with a clear Protestant unionist majority in the Union with the UK. Only small groups of Protestant paramilitaries and some others have toyed with the idea of an independent Northern Ireland, partly because of the very large transfer payments (approximately £3 billion annually in the 1990s) that London makes to the Province to pay for social services, unemployment benefits and policing. There is, therefore, no straightforward territorial solution to the problem.

The Protestant unionist position is that there should be an unequivocal commitment by the British government that Northern Ireland should be part of the UK (not the qualified commitment, repeated many times since the 1949 Government of Ireland Act, that the Province should remain part of the UK only as long as a majority wish it); that the Dublin government should not participate in the government of the Province; that the Catholic–nationalist population should become reconciled to the constitutional status quo when there was no possibility of a united Ireland. This solution commands very little support in the main British political parties or indeed anywhere outside the Protestant community of Northern Ireland.

The joint Anglo-Irish approach to the problem is based on the position that both communities should be able to express freely their national aspirations; strict non-discrimination should be enforced in education, employment and housing; there should be power-sharing between them in managing the internal affairs of the Province; the Irish dimension and the Dublin government's legitimate interest in the affairs of Northern Ireland should be recognized; cooperative arrangements between Northern Ireland and the Republic of Ireland should be put in place; the wishes of the majority in Northern Ireland on the constitutional question should be respected. This approach is deeply suspect in the Protestant unionist community as a strategy to unite Ireland by stealth; the paramilitary and evangelical wings of Protestant unionism are unlikely ever to be reconciled to it.[37] The practice of self-determination through a popular vote is only a small part of a solution to the problems of Northern Ireland. The referendum of 1973 (popularly called the 'border poll') was a failure because it was boycotted by the Catholic–nationalist population; it is unlikely that the referenda envisaged by the Anglo-Irish Declaration of 1993 will make more than a marginal contribution to a settlement.

The Northern Ireland problem is unusual but has parallels elsewhere in western Europe. Regions with distinctive social and cultural characteristics and distant from metropolitan centres are often pulled in several directions in a process of adaptation to complex changes. Corsica is an example of the phenomenon with an idiosyncratic political structure, a 'unionist' majority, and a violent and troublesome autonomist movement, the banned Front de Libération National Corse (FLNC). A special regime was introduced for the island in 1982, with a regional assembly and executive; the arrangements have, however, functioned badly because Corsica's political fragmentation results in the absence of a stable majority. Subsequent initiatives, such as the 1988 'plan Joxe' and the 1991 Special Statute, aimed at providing a framework in which traditional clientelism would be replaced by a system allowing strong political leadership, have met with no success.[38] Complicating factors include the 'dérive mafieuse' – the spread of criminal conspiracies linking Corsican nationalists and criminal networks, and the dependence of the Corsican population on grants from the French government and the EU.

There are also certain analogies between Northern Ireland and the Basque problem. The extreme nationalists in both regions have demanded a revision of the international frontier. In the Basque case it is the suppression of the Franco-Spanish frontier in the western Pyrenees and the creation of a united Basque political entity uniting the four Spanish Basque provinces with the three French Basque provinces. In both cases only a minority (in the case of the French Basques, a tiny minority) of the population support this aim and an even smaller proportion identify with the violent campaign associated with it. Both extreme nationalist ideologies espouse a view of history in which national identities have been established over many centuries and have been ruthlessly suppressed by foreign invaders. The Basques have attracted much interest because of the mystery surrounding their origins and their language.[39]

Even if a demand for self-determination can, in principle, be satisfied within the framework of an existing state frontier, the question of how small a minority should exercise the right is still relevant. An example of the difficulty posed by very small populations is the group of villages in Belgium, Les Fourons, a French-speaking enclave in Flanders. The

56 *Boundary-Drawing in Europe*

wish of the inhabitants to be attached to the French region of Belgium
has caused the fall of governments and a constitutional crisis. Interference with the linguistic frontier imperilled the process of federalizing
the country which began after the Second World War and culminated
in 1988 and 1993 when a series of competences were accorded to
the regions and the language communities.[40] Specific interests were
involved in Les Fourons, but the issue of principle is whether,
how and why a population as small as 4,000 should be allowed to
override the wishes of large numbers of people who want to preserve
the territorial status quo. There is no clear basis for an answer to this
question except a *Realpolitik* assessment of the balance of forces and
interests, which often supplies no answer except that of crisis
management.

Self-determination in Central and Eastern Europe

The frontiers in central and eastern Europe are of more recent origin
than in western Europe. In the mid-nineteenth century the present
states of east and central Europe did not exist but were the provinces
of the multinational empires of the Habsburgs, the Hohenzollerns, the
Romanovs and the Ottomans. The retreat of Ottoman power allowed
first an independent Greece and then the restoration of ancient Balkan
kingdoms, submerged by four centuries of Ottoman rule. After the First
World War, Poland, Czechoslovakia and Yugoslavia (as the kingdom of
the Serbs, Croats and Slovenes) were established. The frontiers of
Russia were pushed to the east with the setting up of the small Baltic
states of Latvia, Lithuania and Estonia, and the acquisition by Poland
of Russian and Ukrainian territory.

In the early twentieth century there was, in eastern Europe, a great
fluidity of frontiers, almost all of which were contested. In the new
states, there were important ethnic, religious and linguistic minorities.
The most dangerous for the stability of the region were those minorities
who belonged to the dominant nationality of a neighbouring state, such
as the Sudeten Germans (during the first Czechoslovak Republic), or
who had close affinities with it. This situation was unavoidable because
the nations of eastern Europe did not inhabit clearly defined territories,
and parts of the region were an ethnic mosaic which could not be
accommodated by the drawing of frontiers of the new states. In Walter
Kolarz's terms, the new states were territorial states rather than nation-
states.[41] The absence of homogeneous populations led to hazardous
nation-building processes, including the forcible integration of minorities, the transfer of populations and the invention of national myths.

Attempts at enforced assimilation were frequently defended by their perpetrators as either raising the cultural and material standards of backward peoples or as righting historic wrongs. The Frederick the Great, king of Prussia at the time of the first partition of Poland in 1772, had a deep contempt both for the Polish nobility and the Polish peasantry and thought that Germanization was the only way of turning them into useful members of society.[42] This German attitude persisted until the end of the Second World War. Magyarization policies were partly a response to the laying waste of the country by the Turks and the decimation of the Hungarian population, and based on a belief that the illiterate 'history-less' peasant peoples were civilized by such policies. The contemporary Slovak, Romanian and Serbian attitude towards their Hungarian minorities (which number at least 3.5 million) is, in part, a reaction to historic wrongs of enforced Magyarization.[43]

The problems of frontiers in central and eastern Europe were not limited to ethnic complexity. The appeal to an actual or to a mythic past led to claims on territory not held by the 'nation' in question. The most striking example is Kosovo, over 90% of whose people are Albanian, but claimed by Serbs to be the heartland of Serbia and the cradle of the Serbian nation.[44] This belief is kept alive by the inclusion of epic songs and legends in the Serbian school curriculum of the famous 1389 defeat of the Serbs by the Ottoman Turks at Kosovo. The Albanians are regarded as recent interlopers very much as Irish nationalists have regarded the Ulster Protestants as colonists and the Greek Cypriots have regarded the Turks as intruders, although in all three cases the population settlements occurred before the establishment of the modern state system. Some historic claims, such as those of Lithuania for the restoration of the extensive lands of medieval Lithuania, have virtually disappeared, but others may be revived.

The transfer of populations and the new frontiers imposed by the Soviet Union at the end of the Second World War simplified the ethnic composition of states. Poland, through the expulsion of the Germans and the shift westwards of the frontier with Germany and with the Soviet Union, experienced a drop in the non-Polish population from about a third (according to the 1921 census) to less than a twentieth of the total after 1945. Czechoslovakia, with the expulsion of the Sudeten Germans in the west, the destruction of the Jews in the Holocaust and the loss of Ruthenia to the Soviet Union in the east, became a two-nation (Czechs and Slovaks) rather than a four- or five-nation state. Hungary's minorities were reduced in numbers but Slovakia (with a small but significant Hungarian minority), Serbia (with a Hungarian minority in Vojvodina and an Albanian majority in Kosovo), Romania (with a large Hungarian minority), Bulgaria (with a Muslim/Turkish minority and a small Hungarian minority), Albania (with a Greek minority) and Greece (with a Turkish minority) remained. Under Communist regimes, the minority questions were kept under control by harsh repressive measures, sometimes to the extent of denying that a minority actually existed, such as the Greeks of Albania, or by attempted assimilation, as in the case of the Germans, Turks and Magyars of Romania.[45]

East-central Europe and the former territories of the USSR comprise a complex cultural and political area; generalizations about recent developments across this huge territory are hazardous.[46] Some new states came into being amid bloodshed and hatred while others aspired, with at least temporary success, to democracy and good neighbourliness. Despite ethnic diversity some states for a time appeared stable, whereas others, such as Armenia, Moldova and Georgia, have been the scenes of bloody confrontation. Some states have relatively uncontentious boundaries while others are threatened by serious secessionist movements and sometimes by territorial claims by neighbouring states. Examples include Russian designs on Ukrainian territory (Sebastopol, the home port of the Black Sea fleet, was a sensitive issue – the Khrushchev 'gift' to the Ukraine of Crimea was called into question by a pro-Russian electoral victory in 1994) and on areas of eastern Ukraine (where Russian immigrants predominate), and Armenian claims to the Azeri territory of Nagorno Karabakh. New political entities may emerge on the basis of regional groupings such as the Commonwealth of Independent States which included eleven[47] of the fifteen republics of the former USSR (with Georgia, on the verge of disintegration, asking for membership in 1993); in central Europe, the Visegrád three was established in 1991 (this became four in 1992 with the break-up of Czechoslovakia); and the Council of Baltic states which has provided a framework for cooperation between Latvia, Lithuania and Estonia and their western neighbours. The stability of these, and present territorial arrangements in general, is uncertain although coalitions in favour of the status quo may ensure at least temporary stability for the major states.

The slow disintegration of Soviet Communism during the second half of the 1980s and the rapid collapse of Soviet hegemony over central and eastern Europe in 1989 was followed by a revision of frontiers which had previously happened only after major wars. The initial euphoria of 'freeing the nations from the yoke of Communism' encouraged minority nationalist claims in western Europe, from Scotland to South Tyrol.[48] The encouragement to west European regionalist and minority movements waned as the violent and anti-democratic aspects of east European nationalism became apparent. In eastern Europe itself, the three

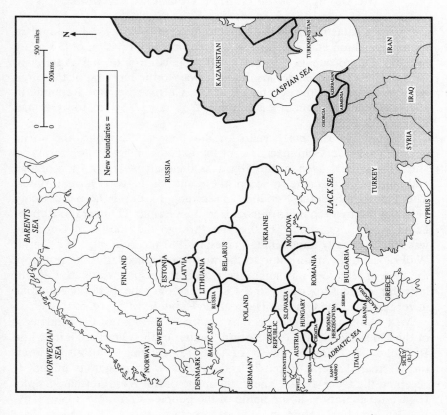

Map 7 New frontiers in central and eastern Europe after 1989

most important outcomes of the events of 1989 were unification of Germany, intractable conflict in Yugoslavia and encouragement of disintegration of the USSR. Other consequences for territorial organization, some of which will take many years to resolve, are most evident in Czechoslovakia, the Russian Federation and the southern borderlands of the former USSR.

The Collapse of the German Democratic Republic

Germany's catastrophic defeat in the Second World War resulted in both its partition and a major loss of territory. The division of Germany in 1945 into occupation zones under the control of the American, British, French and Soviet armies gave way to the merging of the three western zones and the setting up of the German Federal Republic in 1949 and the subsequent establishment by the USSR of the German Democratic Republic.

Although, in the early years of the Federal Republic, the social democratic leader Schumacher kept the issue of unification on the West German political agenda, the Germans themselves, at both the official and popular level, came to accept the reality of the two German states. The German Federal Republic (according to the 1972 basic treaty between the two republics) recognized the German Democratic Republic as a sovereign state. The frontier through the middle of Germany was made virtually impossible to cross; in 1961 the building of the Berlin Wall blocked the main route to the west and reduced, but did not stop, the flow of East German migrants. However, in some respects, particularly for citizenship rights and trade relations, the Federal Republic never regarded the German Democratic Republic as a foreign state.[49]

West Germany came reluctantly to accept the loss of the lands east of the Oder–Neisse line, the eastern frontier of the German Democratic Republic. The Warsaw Treaty of 1970, regularizing relations between the German Federal Republic and Poland, was ambiguous in that it accepted the Oder–Neisse line in the name of the West German people. It gave no guarantee in the name of the people of a reunited Germany. In October 1989, after months of procrastination, Chancellor Kohl repeated the undertaking of the Warsaw Treaty in the name of the whole German people.

The location of Poland's eastern borders were also at stake. The Polish government felt obliged to issue a forceful statement in April 1990 that it would not advance any claims on the territories to the east which included the former Polish cultural centres and university towns of Lvov and Vilna (Vilnius). These statements accepted that, after the

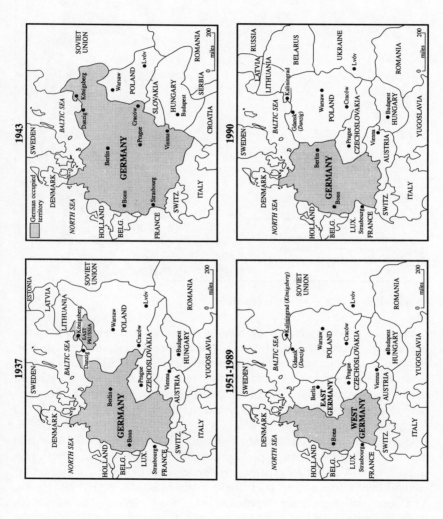

Map 8 Germany in 1937, 1943, 1951–89 and 1990

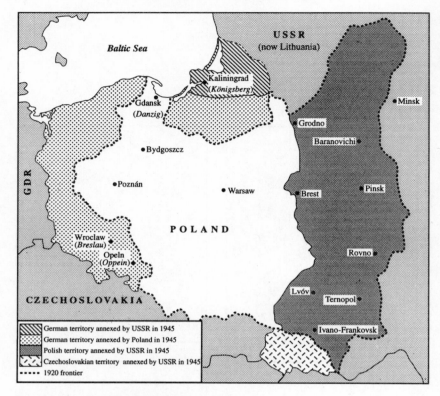

Map 9   Poland's 1920 and 1945 frontiers

passage of a certain length of time, a territorial arrangement imposed
by military force had legitimacy, if there were strong reasons for this.
After the collapse of the inner German frontier in 1989, any German
aspiration to recover former German territories was subordinated to
the political requirement that the united Germany should reassure both
its eastern neighbours and its western allies that it harboured no
territorial ambitions in the east.[50]

Germany's unification was the outcome of a changed global situation
and had little to do with implementing the principle of self-determination. The will and the capacity of the Soviet Union to maintain its
control over east and central Europe evaporated during the late 1980s.
The ideas of democracy, openness and economic reform advanced,
from the mid-1980s, by Mikhail Gorbachev eventually affected all the
People's Democracies of eastern Europe and led to the overthrow of
all the Communist regimes. In the German Democratic Republic, open
protest against the regime could not be repressed with the same

ruthlessness (Honecker ordered repression but local Communist leaders defied his order) which had been used in East Germany in 1953, Hungary in 1956 and Czechoslovakia in 1968 because Soviet backing was absent.[51]

The immediate trigger for the collapse of the regime was the loss of control of its frontiers. Fortification of the inner German frontier had been reduced in 1984, when 50,000 automatic 'death machines' (guns triggered by sensing devices) were dismantled, but the order to shoot-to-kill those who attempted to escape the GDR remained in force until 1989. The major problem for the GDR came in the summer of 1989 when thousands of East Germans on holiday in Hungary and Czechoslovakia refused to return home. First Hungary, then Czechoslovakia opened their frontiers, allowing them to go to the Federal Republic where constitutionally they had citizenship rights. The GDR could not resist mass exodus because it could not close its eastern as well as its western frontier for more than a few days without serious economic and political consequences.[52]

Germany was the only member state of the European Community whose territory changed because of the collapse of Soviet Communism. With a strong economy and a stable political system, regime change and frontier revision in Germany were quite unlike those of eastern Europe. The espousal (partial in the case of Romania and Bulgaria) by the former Communist states of pluralist political systems and the market economy, the evident desire of the new governments either to become members of, or to be associated with, the European Community seemed to herald the healing of the great schism between Communist and non-Communist Europe. But social and economic conditions as well as the new territorial politics of central and eastern Europe maintained a continuing divide between east and west.

The Failure of Yugoslavia

With six republics arguably based on six peoples (and, in addition, a million Albanians in the province of Kosovo), three major religions (Catholic, Orthodox and Muslim), Yugoslavia was a country with strong centrifugal tendencies. It resembled the USSR, with a mosaic of different nationalities (with one dominant nationality), religious divisions and marked differences in regional economic development.[53] The intermingling of peoples is sometimes more complex in Yugoslavia than in the ex-USSR: in one formerly autonomous region, Vojvodina, there were six officially recognized languages and twenty officially recognized ethnic minorities.[54] But Russia has a long history of statehood and has

Map 10   Ethnic composition of the states of former Yugoslavia

been regarded as a major power since the beginning of the eighteenth century, whereas Yugoslavia achieved unity and a precarious independence only in 1918.

The north-west Balkans had been a zone of confrontation between the Habsburgs and the Ottoman Turks, between Christian and Muslim for over 400 years.[55] The militarized and violent frontier zone left a difficult legacy for the newly independent state. It has also given the Serbs a tragic sense of history, exemplified in the novels of Dobritsa Tchossitch[56] in which the Serbian people are misunderstood, sacrificed, caught in a situation from which there is no escape and betrayed by allies to whom the Serbs have been faithful.

Percival Dodge, the American representative to the Serbian government, wrote in 1917: 'all those who know the three nations express doubts that they could unite happily in one state.'[57] Tensions were soon apparent. Assassination (which began in 1928 with the killing of Croatian deputies in parliament) gave way to slaughter in the Second World War when the Nazis set up an independent Fascist state in Croatia and its militias massacred Serbs. Only the iron hand and the prestige of Tito, who had a Croat father and a Slovene mother, managed to preserve the peace between the peoples in the quarter of a century after the Second World War; nevertheless cracks were appearing before his death.

The internal frontiers of Yugoslavia were redrawn immediately after the Second World War to create state territories of roughly equal size which fragmented the dominant nationality, the Serbs, an outcome which Serbian nationalists subsequently interpreted as a deliberate manoeuvre to hold them in check. The federalization of the country, begun in the 1960s, did not stem the slide towards confrontation and disintegration. In the south-east of the country, the clash of Serbs and Albanians which continued throughout the 1980s was contained, but the growing disenchantment of the richer western republics with Serbian dominance unleashed a process which inevitably led to a major territorial reorganization.

The difficult relationship between Croats, Serbs and Bosnians (or Muslims) is not based on ethnicity, since they are ethnically indistinguishable, but on history, religion and political allegiance. The Serbs regard themselves as an ancient people who, during the centuries of subjection to the multinational empires, kept their distinctive identity. The Croats, long the loyal subjects of the Habsburgs, Roman Catholic in religion, using a Latin script, also regard themselves as a distinctive people and accepted as such by all but a small minority of Serbs. The Muslims did not enjoy equal status, and during the current conflict many attempts have been made to de-legitimize their claims to such status. The argument has parallels with some Israeli attempts to undermine the claims of the Palestinians to recognition as a nation – the Muslims are not a people but a religious community wrongly elevated by Tito and the Yugoslav Communists to a political entity. The 1971 census was the first at which Slavs could declare themselves as ethnically Muslim, and the 1974 Constitution was the first to give to Serbo-Croat Slavs identifying with the Muslim tradition the status of one of the peoples constituting Yugoslavia.

The break-up of Yugoslavia occurred with dramatic speed.[58] In 1989, the first plans for seccession were made by Slovenia. In August of that year, a new constitution was introduced to prepare for separation from the Yugoslav federation. In December 1990 a referendum in Slovenia resulted in a 90% majority in favour of independence. These moves coincided with a renaissance of greater Serbian nationalism led by the president of the Serbian Republic, Slobodan Milosevic. His belligerent declarations exacerbated relations between Serbs and others in the neighbouring republics of Bosnia-Herzegovina and Croatia. The Slovenes, undeterred by threats from Belgrade, moved ahead with legislation setting up an independent currency and taxation and banking systems, and declared sovereign independence in February 1991. The response of the Serbs was a clumsy military intervention which met with international disapproval and determined opposition from the Slovenes. The Serb-led federal army withdrew in July 1991, paving the way for a much more serious confrontation in Croatia and Bosnia-Herzegovina. The declaration of Croatian independence was countered by a move by Serbian militias backed by the federal army to defend what they considered to be the Serbian parts of Croatia.

In the initial stages of the crisis some western governments, particularly the British and French, and the Soviet Union were opposed to the break-up of Yugoslavia. But the reactions of the international community were insufficient to hold in check the mutual antagonisms of it's peoples. Once violence had broken out, it was impossible, even by the intervention of the European Community and the United Nations, to stop the spiral downwards into military aggression, 'ethnic cleansing' and atrocity. Initially, the leaders of the regional governments of Yugoslavia, other than Serbia, and the foreign governments which backed the independence of Slovenia, Croatia and then Macedonia and Bosnia-Herzegovina believed that a stable settlement could be reached by respecting the frontiers of the federal states drawn by Tito. This seriously underestimated the fears of those who would be dominated by other ethnic groups, in the absence of an authoritarian government to repress dissent. A new political map which makes concessions to Serb aspirations to unity is the only possible outcome of the conflict.

The Disintegration of the USSR

A near-consensus in the rich countries (Japan being a marginal dissenter) supported the maintenance of the territorial integrity of the USSR. But the Soviet empire could be kept in being only by repression and the denial of self-determination. The thesis of 'imperial overreach' popularized by Paul Kennedy provides a convincing explanation for the collapse of the Soviet Union; the productivity of the economy of the USSR was inadequate to finance the means required to maintain the Soviet empire.[59] The Second World War increased the ethnic diversity of the Soviet Union in ways which, from the late 1980s, created continuing political problems. The forcible annexation of the Baltic states (Latvia, Lithuania and Estonia) after the 1939 Molotov–Ribbentrop pact, the absorption of Polish and Uniate Christian populations in Byelorussia (Belarus) and the Ukraine in 1944 and the reacquisition of Moldova from Romania were all sources of difficulty. The whole of the western marches of the USSR, like its southern Caucasian region, was potentially unstable, since force was the only basis of political authority.

The internal organization of the USSR seemed definitively established by the Stalin Constitution of 1936 and by the iron grip of the Communist Party. Some flexibility appeared when Gorbachev showed a willingness to right historic wrongs, and Volga Germans and Crimean Tartars, exiled by Stalin, were given new hope.[60] However, the Russian population of the former German Volga autonomous region opposed the re-establishment of the German autonomous region on the grounds that there were too few Germans left. Nonetheless, on 28 November 1989 the Supreme Soviet voted for the principle of re-establishing an autonomous geographical entity for the Volga Germans.[61] The Crimean Tartars, deported by Stalin to Siberia during the Second World War, were allowed to return under Gorbachev, but their numbers were small and in 1993 made up only 10% of the Crimean population.

These minor concessions were overwhelmed by the disintegration of the Soviet Union which officially took place in 1991, after the passing of a law allowing secession and the Minsk Agreement which recognized that the USSR no longer existed.[62] These acts symbolically marked the reversal of a process, which had begun in the thirteenth century, of Russian imperial expansion. The series of secessionist crises was initiated by the Baltic republics. Although these republics have small populations, their people showed a capacity for political organization based on memories of independent statehood, between the Treaty of Brest–Litovsk in 1917 and the Molotov–Ribbentrop pact of 1939. The

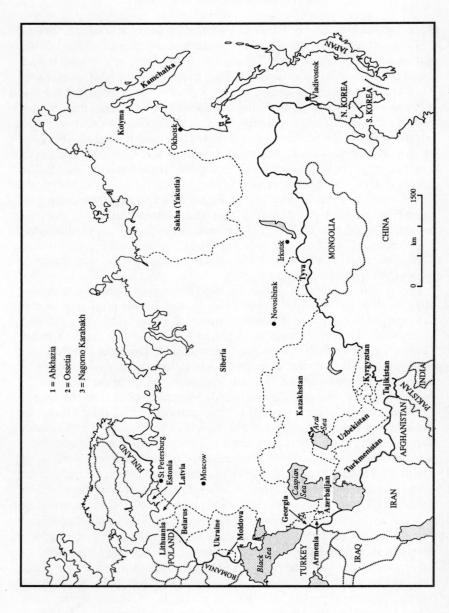

Map 11 Russia and neighbouring states after the break-up of the USSR

1990 declaration by Lithuania of independence from the Soviet Union was resisted by President Gorbachev. His intimidation (with limited use of force) of the Lithuanians was unsuccessful. Declarations similar to the Lithuanian one were made by Latvia, Estonia and the Russian Federation under the leadership of Boris Yeltsin. Eventually all the republics of the Union claimed their 'sovereignty'. The Soviet leadership offered a new union treaty, to be approved by referendum on 17 March 1991.

The Baltic governments would not co-operate with the March 1991 referendum on the grounds that they would be drawn into the Soviet constitutional system. They argued that their forcible annexation by the Soviet Union in 1940 meant that they were not legally part of the USSR. They feared intimidation by Soviet armed forces stationed in the region and also argued that 'there's no use conducting a poll to ask if a prisoner wants to be free – it's clear enough.'[63] However, they were prepared to hold referenda approving complete independence; the results were recognized by Boris Yeltsin in August 1991.

Latvia and Estonia contained large Russian minorities, although when referenda were held on independence many Russians supported independence.[64] In Estonia in 1992, 77.8% voted in favour of independence on an 82% turnout, despite Russian speakers comprising 40% of the population. In Latvia the vote was 72% for independence on an 86% turnout despite the presence of almost 60% Russian speakers in the population. The number of Russian speakers almost certainly exaggerated the number of those who identified themselves as ethnic Russians – but these may have been over a third of the population in Latvia and around 30% in Estonia. The high level of popular support for independence led the international community – first Scandinavian countries, Canada and Argentina, then the European Community[65] and finally the USA to recognize the Baltic States.[66]

Russian minorities caused continuing tension and dispute. Defence of these minorities by Russia was a potential source of instability. The Estonian citizenship law passed in July 1993 made knowledge of the Finno-Ugric language of the country a necessary, but not a sufficient, condition of citizenship. In a referendum the Russian-dominated city of Narva in the north-east of the country promptly voted by a large majority in favour of autonomy.[67] The Latvian parliament approved a bill in November 1993 stipulating that only those who had lived in the country for ten years, who could pass a language test, and who were not former Soviet army or KGB officers, would be eligible for citizenship; even then there would be unspecified citizenship quotas for those of Russian origin. Latvians are outnumbered by Russians by two to one in

Riga, the capital, and explicit discrimination has potentially explosive consequences.

The lack of national or ethnic homogeneity is common to all the republics of the former USSR. The Russian minorities posed immediate difficulties: those with more than an estimated 10% Russians are Ukraine with 22% (11.4 million), Kazakhstan with 38% (6.4 million), Belarus with 13% (1.4 million), Kyrgystan with 22% (1 million) and Turkmenistan with 10% (0.4 million). All the estimates are subject to serious dispute[68] but, nonetheless, there are large numbers of Russians who feel themselves unwanted, and even threatened, in the newly independent states. Russia retains overwhelming military force and calls to defend the interests of Russian minorities may result, after the nationalist gains in the December 1993 elections in the Russian Federation, in an increased willingness to use that force. Some situations are more complicated than those found in the Baltic states because, as well as minority tensions, national groups straddle existing international frontiers.

In the Moldovan Republic, for example, the majority of the population is Romanian-speaking. There are also two important minorities – one Russian, around the industrial towns of Bendery and Tiraspol on the lower Dniestr, the other Gagauz, Christians of Turkish ethnic origin numbering about 150,000. The Gagauz declared their independence in August 1990 and proceeded to elect their own parliament. This provoked the Moldovan authorities into declaring a state of emergency and depriving ten of the thirteen Gagauz members of the Moldovan parliament of their seats. After the failed coup in Moscow, Moldova proclaimed its independence with a view to eventual re-unification with Romania[69] and the leaders of the Gagauz and the Russians of the trans-Dniestr were arrested for having supported the coup.[70] This display of force did not work and the trans-Dniestr Russians, supported by a large Russian garrison, remain effectively outside the authority of the Moldovan Republic.[71]

Russian minorities in the Ukraine are also potentially a destabilizing element. In a December 1991 referendum Crimea, with a population of about 90% Russian speakers, voted with a 54.2% majority in favour of independence from the Ukraine. This was confirmed by the election of a Crimean parliament with a majority firmly in favour of union with Russia. The Kharkov mining basin, 'given' by Russia to the Ukraine in the early 1920s to counteract Ukrainian nationalist tendencies, also has an overwhelming majority in favour of close relations with Russia. In both cases, the policy of Moscow has been cautious, doubtless with a view to drawing the whole of the Ukraine back into the Russian orbit. In the light of increasing economic difficulties in the Ukraine and popular disillusionment with the Ukrainian nationalist government, this policy is not unrealistic. The elections of March–April 1994 in the Ukraine showed a large pro-Russian minority in the east of the country. In 1995, however, the Ukrainian government disarmed the Crimean presidential guard and closed the Crimean parliament.

After the break-up of the USSR, forces of disintegration threatened the unity of the Russian Federation itself[72] to the extent that an aide of Boris Yeltsin in the corridors of the 1993 Constitutional Conference of the Russian Federation described the autonomist fever as 'political AIDS'.[73] The demands for autonomy were mainly initiated by ethnic and national movements, but some regions were also motivated by economic considerations. These considerations are especially important in the Pacific regions of the Russian Federation – Sverdlovsk and Vladivostok populated overwhelmingly by ethnic Russians – and in oil-rich Tartarstan, because they subsidized the rest of the Federation through the tax system. Distance from Moscow plays a role and, even in the nineteenth century, encouraged a Siberian independence movement. The reassertion of presidential power in the bloody confrontation between president and parliament in October 1993, and the nationalist success in the December 1993 elections mark a less tolerant policy towards autonomist demands (exemplified by repression in Chechnya in 1994–5) and a step towards a partial reconstitution of the former USSR.[74]

The Southern Borderlands of the Former Soviet Union

The Caucasian and trans-Caucasian region of the USSR is a shatter zone where armies have clashed since ancient times. From the fourteenth to the twentieth centuries the Russians confronted the Ottoman Turks in the region. The Persians managed to keep a precarious independence during the great period of European imperialism because of Anglo-Russian rivalry. The smaller peoples of the region – the Armenians, Georgians and Azeris – were, however, dominated by the larger ones. The drive of the Russians towards the south, which started in earnest in the eighteenth century, eventually had disastrous consequences for the Armenians. The Turks, as Russian pressure increased, considered the Armenians to be a strategic threat, and repressed them in the notorious massacres of 1915. A brief moment of independence, after the Bolshevik revolution, for Armenia, Georgia and Azerbaijan, ended with the invasion by the Red Army in 1920 and the signing of the Soviet–Turkish Treaty of March 1921. All three peoples retained distinctive cultural identities and separate languages; in the early 1990s they all proclaimed their sovereignty.

Two of the three have important minority problems within their borders. Georgia declared itself independent in 1991 and elected a government fiercely hostile to autonomy for its minorities, the Muslim Ossetans and the Abkhazis. The territory of the Ossetans has been divided since 1922 into the autonomous region of North Ossetan in the Russian Federation and the autonomous region of South Ossetan in the Republic of Georgia. In 1989, the South Ossetans revived an old claim to be reunited with the North Ossetans in the Russian Federation. After his election as president of Georgia in 1990, Zviad Gamsakhourdia declared that South Ossetan no longer existed, renaming it Central Kartlia, whereupon the Ossetans declared secession from Georgia. President Gorbachev annulled both the Georgian and the Ossetan declarations and, faced by an invasion of Ossetan by Georgia, sent in Ministry of Interior troops to separate the two sides. The capture of the capital of Abkhazia, Sukhumi, by Abkhazi rebels in September 1993, which the new president, Eduard Shevardnadze, asserted could not have been done without Russian help, threatened to plunge the whole of Georgia into anarchy. The rebels asserted their right to restore the 1925 constitution for an independent Abkhazia, associated with Russia, thereby raising two spectres: first, a fragmentation of the former USSR into tiny warring statelets (the ethnic Abkhazis probably number less than 100,000); second, exploitation by Russia of ethnic minorities to reassert their power over the territory of the former USSR. A situation was created in which Georgia could not survive without Russian goodwill and, as Shevardnadze's authority weakened, he asked to join the CIS and requested Russian assistance.

Like the Moldovans–Romanians, the Azeris also straddle the international boundary. The Russian empire had annexed part of Azerbaijan in 1828; there are, therefore, two Azerbaijan provinces: the ex-Soviet Union province has an Azeri population of about 7 million, and the Iranian province one of about 10 million. Azeris on both sides of the frontier are Shi'ite but the Soviet Azeris were not strongly influenced by Iranian 'fundamentalism'.[75] In January 1991 the Soviet Azeris made an attempt at reunification with the Azeris in Iran by breaking down the frontier fence between the two countries.[76] Important material pressures prevent the reunification of Azerbaijan. The major Soviet oil city of Baku is situated in Azerbaijan and Russia regards the oilfield of Azerbaijan as of major strategic interest. Although Iranians stirred separatist feelings in the Muslim republics by broadcasting in several languages such as Turkic, Tajik and Turkmen, the Iranian leadership had overriding interests in good relations with Russia. President Rafsanjani was the first Iranian leader to visit (on 22 June 1989) Soviet Azerbaijan and to seek closer ties with the USSR and, subsequently, Russia.

All the non-Russian republics on the southern border, stretching from the Caucasus to Mongolia, have moved to establish their independence, thus creating the potential for considerable instability of frontiers. For example, the frontiers which delimit Uzbekistan and Tadjikstan do not follow the ethnic division of the population; the largest Tadjik towns are Samarkand and Bukhara, which are in Uzbekistan, and a fifth of the Tadjiks speak Uzbek. There is a similar problem with Kyrgystan because the important Kyrgyz town of Osh is in Uzbekistan. Despite rapid population growth, different ethnic groups living in the same territory and disparity in resources, territorial conflict did not occur immediately, partly because of continuity of political leadership. The Communist Party remained in power, but its system of rule was based on clientelist networks and had little to do with ideology. An alliance formed between the Communist rulers and the Islamic clergy aimed to contain the spread of Muslim fundamentalism. Since the Muslim republics of central Asia are not economically viable, independence may in future provoke a struggle for resources, with consequent territorial disputes.[77]

The Division of Czechoslovakia

After the breakdown of Soviet control of eastern Europe, central and eastern European countries increasingly felt the economic attraction of Germany and the European Community. This attraction encouraged the disintegration of Czechoslovakia.

The Czechs had a proud history, constituting the heart of the old kingdom of Bohemia and, in more recent history, participating fully in the industrial revolution of nineteenth-century Europe. The Slovaks had no history of independent statehood (with the partial exception of a Nazi puppet state during the Second World War). They remained a predominantly agrarian people; the industries which had been developed during the Communist period were poorly adapted to market conditions. Although both countries were within the Habsburg domains, the Czechs were linked closely to Vienna, while the Slovaks were subject to intense efforts of Magyarization by the Hungarians who called Slovakia 'Upper Hungary'. The Communist regime, from 1947 to 1989, did not remove the sense of Slovak subordination and relative deprivation.[78] Although the Slovaks probably gained from union with the Czechs, the latter were perceived as the dominant partner because the Czech territories had twice the population (approximately 10 million as opposed to 5 million), produced, in 1991, 74% of the GNP and accounted for just over 70% of industrial production.

The Slovaks demanded, and obtained, a federal constitution in 1990, but the 1991 parliamentary elections produced diametrically opposed results in the two countries, with a government in Bratislava determined to press for complete independence. This was agreed by the Czechs, and, in July 1992, the separation ('the velvet divorce') of the two countries was proclaimed. The Czech prime minister, Vaclav Klaus, saw the advantages of a rapid and decisive split: a separate Czech republic would escape the conflictual relations with Hungary, shed some intractable industrial reconversion and economic problems and allow speedier membership of the European Community.

Although the separation was amicable, the practicalities were complicated. The two states had to renegotiate the 2,800 documents which regulated the relationships between Czechoslovakia and the outside world, as well as divide assets and debts and reorganize postal, transport, telecommunications and all other public services.[79] The negotiations proceeded smoothly; significantly, binationality (Czech and Slovak) became a simple formality, thus avoiding the difficult choice of Slovaks resident in the Czech Republic and vice versa.

The immediate consequence of the divorce was to create an important psychological divide, limiting the Czech Republic's exposure to the east and making Slovakia seem closer to the economically distressed Ukraine and linked via the Danube to the unstable Balkans. This impression of identification with the east was increased by the tension between Slovaks and the Hungarian minority in the country. Other factors also played a role. The Czech Republic attracts western tourists to its baroque and Renaissance cities; inward investment has continued to flow into the Czech Republic, but is virtually non-existent in Slovakia.[80]

Specific political developments were also driving the fledgling states apart. After the tightening of Germany's asylum law in 1993, the Czechs (like the Poles) were willing to filter out, at their own frontiers, would-be economic migrants from the former Soviet Union and eastern Europe before they arrived at Germany's frontiers, so turning the frontier between Slovakia and the Czech Republic into a new east–west border. Although freedom of movement across the frontier is guaranteed for inhabitants of the frontier region, the border has come to have the characteristics of a tightly controlled international frontier.

Conclusion

The history of the claims of nations and peoples to avoid oppressive and alien rule is richer and more diversified than the nationalist effervescence in eastern and western Europe in the late twentieth century suggests. It also transcends the philosophies of the contractarian theorists of the seventeenth and eighteenth centuries from which the contemporary doctrine of self-determination derives. There have always been human groups who have been fiercely attached to particular territories, prepared to die on the spot rather than be removed from their homelands and equally prepared to die rather than be ruled by alien people. Ideas of captive and free peoples have frequently involved religious beliefs and historical myths which conferred on them a unique destiny.

Certain peoples have acquired an exemplary status of universal and tragic significance. In the case of the Jews, their plight as a captive people in Egypt and their later expulsion from their homeland after the defeat at Masada in AD 73 and definitively after the failure of Bar Kochba's revolt in AD 132–5, has been given cosmological and theological significance couched in concepts which could scarcely be more foreign to the language of liberalism. The Armenians, the allegedly innocent Christian victims, suffered intermittent persecution by the Turks over five centuries. Gladstone espoused their cause in the celebrated 1876 Midlothian campaign, and they became the first victims of a modern genocide. But their understanding of their own plight had more to do with the teachings of the Armenian Church than anything within the liberal tradition based on Locke and the Enlightenment, at least until President Wilson aroused new and false hopes during the First World War.

In nineteenth- and twentieth-century Europe, certain nations acquired the heroic status of tragic martyrs. Amongst the most celebrated are the Poles in the nineteenth century who, after three partitions in the eighteenth century, lost all independent control of territory while maintaining a high degree of national consciousness; the Irish, after an avoidable famine, forced emigration and the repression of nascent nationalism, were placed in a situation which seemed alien to the values of Victorian England.[81] In the twentieth century, the black populations of South Africa, who had previously demonstrated military prowess against the British empire, became subject to a small white minority. The Kurds, an ancient people spanning Turkey, Syria, Iraq, Iran and the ex-USSR, who were promised an independent Kurdistan by the Treaty of Sèvres in 1920 and saw this undertaking annulled by the Treaty of Lausanne in 1923, remain persecuted and divided down to the present day. The Palestinian people were dislodged by the Israelis in 1948 and harassed by Israeli military action when the Palestine Liberation Organization tried to undermine the Israeli state.

These peoples, with greater and lesser intensity, have been seen as victims in the grip of a fate from which there is no escape without a revolutionary change. In these, often genuinely tragic, situations, ideas of social contract, limited government, the rule of law and of citizenship rights do not arouse the passions necessary to endure a condition of oppression and, if possible, to escape from it. Appeals to blood ties which are elemental and exclusive, and revolutionary ideologies which demonize their opponents, seem necessary to their struggle. They need a Sorelian myth to keep fighting against the odds.

The concept of self-determination has therefore been useful but, at the same time, marginal to those people engaged in the fiercest struggles for a piece of territory, no matter how small, in which they think they can be free. But self-determination, in its pure social contract form, remains a concept central to the project of constructing a 'united nations' world order; in this project there has to be some principle which legitimizes control of territory and the boundaries of that territory. No alternative to the principle of self-determination is available. But difficult theoretical problems are linked with practical issues of central importance. Tension between the rights of nations or majorities and the rights of individuals or minorities is inescapable. In practice, this tension is often seen at its most intense in language policies which often result in practices and policies oppressive to minority and individual rights.

Although the 'language of rights' has become dominant in arguments about disputed frontiers, a movement away from rights towards concepts concerning social practices and the competences of public authorities is more helpful in cases where national or ethnic groups have to live together in the same territory. Ensuring access to education and employment, sharing power through specially designed constitutional mechanisms, providing economic opportunities for previously excluded groups, fragmenting the notion of citizenship so that it can become shared or dual, constructing joint authorities across international frontiers to administer matters of common interest are more constructive in solving practical problems in disputed territories such as Northern Ireland. Solutions may be achieved by processes of negotiating and bargaining in which the doctrine of national self-determination is set aside.

3
Themes in African and Asian Frontier Disputes

African and Asian frontiers differ from European frontiers because of radically different economic, political and demographic environments. Acute tensions over frontiers occur in Africa and Asia of a kind which have disappeared from the European Union and North America. The presence of Islam and its radical variants, the legacy of traditional ideas of territory and frontiers, the experience of European imperialism and the disruption caused by superpower rivalry remain among the many complicating factors in the territorial politics of Africa and Asia.

The distribution between states of valuable resources, particularly of oil and water in the Middle East, is determined by the location of frontiers. The inequitable results of frontier delimitation lead to attempts to delegitimize frontiers. World views, such as those proposed by Muslim 'fundamentalists' who hold that territory belongs to no particular human group but to God, support these attempts. In a belief based on the Koran, strict Muslims hold that the only true frontiers are those of faith, and not those drawn by men on maps or on the ground. Also, according to strict Muslim doctrine, citizenship does not depend on place of birth but on religion.[1] Although Muslim governments became accustomed to a plurality of territorial entities,[2] a radical current, since the founding in the early twentieth century of the Muslim brotherhoods in Egypt, has rejected the division of the Muslim world. After the acceptance by the Sublime Porte in the nineteenth century of European rules of diplomacy, the relationship of the teachings of the Prophet to the practice of Muslim rulers has been tenuous. The regime of Ayatollah Khomeini in Iran, though ostensibly restoring the purity of Muslim doctrine, was impregnated with western ideology of nationalism, even racism; the regime was eventually compelled to come to terms with the existing state system and the international frontier.

The conditions which have prevailed in western Europe, allowing territorial questions to fade from the political agenda, have been absent in Africa and Asia. Except on the Asian Pacific rim, the *sine qua non* of political stability – economic well-being – has not been present. Population pressures, scarce resources and, in extreme cases, famine conditions are associated with instability and strife. Despite this environment, frontiers have changed relatively little. In Africa, a deliberate attempt to maintain the stability of frontiers was made by the newly independent regimes. By contrast, in Asia, where most frontiers were negotiated by the imperialist powers with well-established and ancient peoples, almost every frontier has been the locus of some kind of dispute over the last three decades. The great schism between Communism in its various forms and the west had a more direct effect on Asian than African territorial organization and led to the partition of three countries, Korea, Vietnam and Yemen.[3] However, Asian frontiers have been much more stable than a perceptive observer, such as Alastair Lamb in the 1960s, thought likely.[4]

The themes of this chapter are common to both Africa and Asia but they have a different significance within, as well as between, these continents. These themes are territorial disputes based on a struggle for resources, disputes left over from the colonial period, the uncertain legitimacy of some states (making their territory vulnerable), the inability of weak states to control territory and police frontiers and the broad consensus among states against secession but in favour, in principle, of the application of self-determination to populations within existing frontiers. Africa and Asia are vast land masses containing many variations and contrasts in cultures, social development, wealth, demography, climate and topography. Despite nineteenth-century stereotyping concerning the dark continent and the mysterious orient,[5] they cannot be considered as entities for purposes other than the geographical and cartographical.

African Difficulties

Sub-Saharan African frontiers are almost entirely the result of European intrusion into the continent. As A. I. Asiwaju writes, 'while Africa was not the first or the last part of the world to experience European or Euro-centric political partition, the scale of the operations made the African case the most dramatic.'[6] Only parts of the Moroccan–Algerian and the Algerian–Tunisian frontiers were in existence in 1800, while the remainder were created in the late nineteenth and early twentieth centuries.

The political and social organization of pre-colonial Africa had little effect on the politics of colonial boundary-making. Although sophisticated pre-colonial societies existed, there were no analogies of states in the political entities of pre-colonial sub-Saharan Africa. Boundaries of tribes were rarely demarcated and the power of pre-colonial African empires and kingdoms simply faded the greater the distance from the centre.[7] The view that colonial boundaries took no account of indigenous populations has been revised in recent years. J. Gallais has convincingly argued that the state boundaries have 'a certain validity ... the partition [of Africa] was arbitrary to the extent that the colonial power could choose between different possibilities, but the choice made was never made on a purely arbitrary basis, and high on the list of principles of territorial organisation was the taking into consideration of the ethno-demographic distribution of population some of which was long-standing.'[8] Nonetheless, colonial boundaries often cut through tribal territories.[9] But imperialism so disrupted African societies that pre-colonial legacies have had relatively little effect on post-colonial boundary disputes, except as a legitimating argument for some separatist claims.

Boundary-making by Europeans in Africa has a number of special characteristics. African topography (rivers and relief features) sometimes led European colonial powers to draw political boundaries cutting across ethnic boundaries. Rivers form the current boundaries between Zambia and Zimbabwe, and Zaire and the Congo;[10] and relief features make up over a quarter of boundary features in tropical Africa.[11] In many places, ill-defined African watersheds serve as centres of population rather than, as in Europe, clearly dividing populations.[12] African rivers have attracted settlement, with the same ethnic group settling on both banks, particularly in semi-arid areas where flood-plains are suitable for agricultural use. Using rivers as political boundaries has met similar difficulties in Europe but, at least in western Europe (for example, on the upper Rhine), these have largely been overcome by the successful integration into the nation-state of the riverine populations.

A completely different kind of boundary, the geometric boundary, is more common than river boundaries in Africa; the former either follow lines of longitude or latitude, as with Egypt's western and southern boundaries, or are lines joining two specified points as, for example, the boundary between Nigeria and south-western Cameroon. Boundaries are often a composite of topographical features, geometrical lines and

African and Asian Disputes

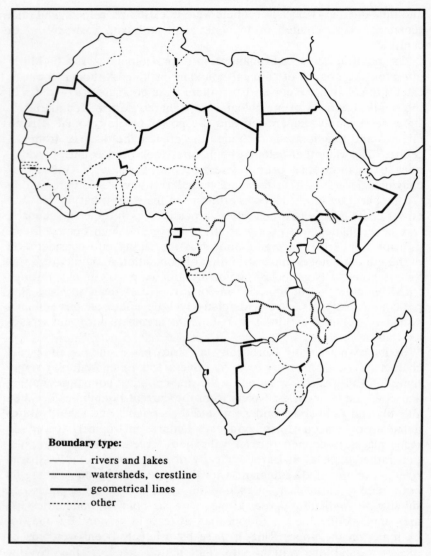

Map 12 Africa: topographical, geometric and 'human' boundaries

concessions to the patterns of human settlement.[13] African boundaries were therefore delimited by the colonial powers according to a variety of principles. Most have been relatively uncontroversial, although reasons for discord are easy to find.[14]

African frontier disputes, since the great period of decolonization in the late 1950s and early 1960s, which are more significant than the numerous technical demarcation disputes, are few enough to be listed.[15]

Morocco and its neighbours (Spain, Algeria and Mauritania)[16]
Egypt and Sudan
Libya and its neighbours (Algeria, Niger and Chad)
Nigeria and Chad and Cameroon
Togo and Ghana
Somalia and Ethiopia and Kenya
Malawi and Tanzania
Mozambique and Zambia
Zambia and Zaire
Guinea-Bissau and Senegal
Lesotho and South Africa

Secessionist crises have been more serious because the territories involved are large compared with those in inter-state disputes: in some cases, for example, in the Horn of Africa and in the Casamance and Senegal–Guinea-Bissau dispute, a separatist crisis and an inter-state dispute are intertwined. In the cases of Biafra and Katanga and of Tigre and Eritrea (the only secession yet to succeed, after the referendum of April 1993), there have been ambitions to establish new states. In addition there are transboundary resource disputes mainly concerning water, potentially the most important of which is between Egypt, Sudan and Ethiopia over the Nile.[17] A peculiar kind of resource competition took place in Southern Africa before the de Klerk government decided in 1989–90 to dismantle apartheid and reach an accommodation with the African National Congress, in that the Republic of South Africa tried to weaken the front-line states coalition against it by a policy of beggar my neighbour.[18]

The relative stability of African boundaries was supported by a broad international consensus on preserving the territorial status quo, shared by the newly independent African states and by the former imperial powers. South Africa, an outcast power because of its apartheid policies but the most powerful country, militarily and economically, on the continent, was more concerned to manipulate and control neighbouring countries than to redraw boundaries. African nationalist movements and elites sought to create territorial nations in attempts to govern and to change the societies which emerged from colonial domination.[19] The nationalist movements were determined to exclude ethnic criteria as the basis of state territory for the very practical reason that instead of fifty-one states (fifty-two after the independence of Eritrea) Africa would contain at least ten times as many, depending on the criteria used to define a people.[20]

The UN General Assembly in 1960 and 1961 (sessions 15 and 16) resolved in favour of maintaining the colonial boundaries; even more important, the Organization of African Unity at its inaugural meeting in 1963 and in a more specific 1964 resolution on border disputes[21] accepted the principle of *uti possidetis ita possideatis* (that which you possess, you continue to possess), with the dissenting voice of Somalia and the reservations of Morocco.[22] This principle originates in Roman law, but the most influential precedent was the agreement of Latin American states to accept existing boundaries when they threw off Spanish and Portuguese control at the beginning of the nineteenth century.[23]

Most of the inter-state disputes over territory in Africa resulted from the legacy of colonialism. The demarcation of frontiers (many of which still remain undemarcated) has sometimes been the cause of conflict because the principles of delimitation agreed could not be uncontroversially implemented on the ground,[24] or because unilateral demarcation by one state was declared unsatisfactory by the neighbouring state or even because boundary markers were surreptitiously moved.[25] An example of a dispute left over from the colonial period is that between Libya and Chad. This dispute arose from the unwillingness of Chad, and of the former colonial power France, to recognize the unratified cession of the Aozou strip by Laval to Mussolini in 1935.[26]

The Aozou strip, an area of desert of 114,000 square kilometres, possibly containing exploitable uranium deposits, was occupied by Libya in 1973. The border dispute was then complicated by political instability, coup and counter-coup in Chad, and French military intervention. Libya retained the upper hand until 1987, when Chad forces unexpectedly drove the Libyans out of the strip. A truce was agreed in Algiers in 1989 which included recourse to the International Court of Justice;[27] in February 1994, the International Court of Justice decided that the strip formed part of the sovereign territory of Chad. The court did so on the grounds that in 1955 France (the colonial power at the time) and Libya had signed a treaty of friendship and good neighbourliness in which both parties assumed a definitive frontier along the existing line of delimitation. In March 1994 Libya accepted this judgement, announcing that the dispute was definitively terminated.

The dispute between Egypt and the Sudan is similar to the conflict over the Aozou strip because it arises from different views of an agreement reached by colonial powers and continues because of the presence of natural resources. The boundary between the two was drawn by an 1899 agreement between the puppet government of Egypt, effectively controlled by the British Resident in Cairo, Lord Cromer, and the Sudan, then an Anglo-Egyptian condominium. The traditional boundary was at Wadi Haifa, at the second cataract on the middle reaches of the Nile.[28] This is situated on the 22nd parallel and the frontier was simply extended along that parallel both west and east. A problem arose because this delimitation ignored the territories of tribal homelands between Wadi Haifa and the Red Sea. As a consequence, there was an administrative adjustment in 1902 to take account of the homeland of the Bacharia (or Bishareen) tribe, and the new frontier followed a zigzag line from a point about 100 miles east of Wadi Haifa to terminate on the Red Sea well to the north of the 22nd parallel.

Nasser's nationalist regime reasserted a claim to the 22nd parallel in 1956, but the Sudanese held firmly to the view that the 1902 adjustment was the valid international frontier. In December 1991 the Egyptians called for tenders for offshore oil exploration on the 22nd parallel, with the consequence that the dispute flared up.[29] As with most frontier disputes this clash is complicated by other issues, particularly the Sudanese belief that Egypt is an overbearing neighbour which takes scant account of Sudanese interests and sensibilities. The Egyptian government, on its side, has shown alarm over support for Islamic fundamentalist subversion from Sudan.

However, not all frontier disputes are the result of the legacy of the colonial powers. Other factors included the specific administrative/ political history of the area involved, inter-ethnic violence, political rivalries, economic resources (notably oil in the case of Biafra, copper in Katanga), and occasionally the peculiar geography and topography of the country.[30] The argument could sometimes be made, especially for Katanga,[31] and to a lesser extent Biafra, that secession would have left 'stranded majorities' of people deprived of the means of subsistence because valuable resources had been removed from the state.

Where pre-colonial tribal territories crossed the frontiers of the post-colonial states they have often been the cause of friction because people in the frontier regions tended to ignore the international boundaries in day-to-day behaviour. Some cause security and public order problems. For example, the nomadic Tuaregs pose security problems for Algeria, Mali and Niger. Although the Tuaregs are a particularly warlike people, they illustrate the general problem of policing African boundaries. African states lack the trained personnel, the technology and the financial resources to prevent the unauthorized movement of persons and goods across their frontiers. Movements from one state to another of starving people, ethnic groups threatened with massacre, migrant workers, guerrilla fighters, diamond smugglers, drugs and weapons dealers can threaten the interests of a neighbouring state. International

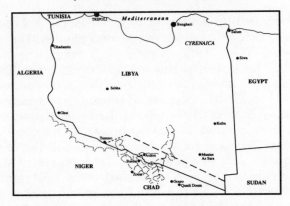

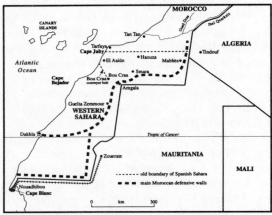

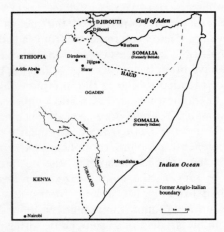

Map 13 (*a*) The Aozou Strip; (*b*) the western Sahara; (*c*) the Horn of Africa

tension results if the conviction grows that more could be done by the 'exporting' state to control the problem, and that this neglect is wilful.

Ethnic groups straddling international boundaries have rarely provoked serious irredentist movements or claims, except in the cases of Eritrea, Somalia and the western Sahara. These instances are remarkable because they involved states having some characteristics similar to those of west European nation-states. The longstanding irredentist claims of the Moroccans and the Somalis were held in check until the departure of the colonial powers. In 1975, Spain accepted the UN proposition that self-determination should be accorded to Spanish Morocco.[32] But the Spaniards, under pressure from a peaceful invasion of the Spanish Sahara by 350,000 Moroccans, negotiated a settlement with the king of Morocco, ceding the north and the centre of the territory to Morocco and the south to Mauritania. The agreement was not accepted by the UN and was opposed by Algeria, Libya and a national liberation movement, the Polisario, founded in 1973 in anticipation of decolonization. The grounds for opposing a Moroccan takeover were that a distinctive people, the Saharawis, inhabited the territory. In 1979, Mauritania renounced the southern part of the western Sahara and signed a peace accord with the Polisario but the Moroccan army pre-empted the move by occupying part of the territory and building a wall 2,000 kilometres long to enclose the economically useful part of the western Sahara (containing phosphates).

Morocco's long history as a political entity, only partially interrupted by a colonial protectorate (1905–54), provides part of the explanation of this conflict. Its territory had been more extensive in the pre-colonial period. The Moroccan position, explained in detail before the 4th Committee of the UN General Assembly in 1979, was that reintegration of the western Sahara was a return of territory to the mother country; this return did not infringe the principle of respect for frontiers because the principle applied only to independent states with internationally recognized frontiers.[33] In 1988, the UN Secretary General produced a plan for a ceasefire and a referendum in the western Sahara under UN supervision.

The UN peace plan was accepted in principle by all parties; in September 1991, a representative of the Secretary General, assisted by 3,000 police, soldiers and administrators, started to organize a referendum. Points of contention in this agreement were the composition of the electorate (whether close relatives of 1974 residents were allowed to vote, whether all ethnic Saharawis, many of whom traditionally lived in southern Morocco, should vote), the question to be asked in the referendum, the role of the Moroccan administration and the army after the ceasefire and the nature of the relationship between the former belligerents.[34] The determination of the Algerians, the backers of the Polisario, to bring the conflict to an end, as well as the conviction of Hassan II that a settlement would be to Morocco's advantage, were decisive.[35] The referendum was, however, delayed because finally no agreement could be reached between Morocco and the Polisario on who should vote in the referendum.[36]

Somalis claimed to have formed a more or less united entity from the sixteenth century until the arrival of the Europeans, but the historical facts are obscure.[37] They have a strong ethnic–cultural and kinship definition of the Somali nation, which seems as strongly held by Somalis living in Kenya, Ethiopia and Djibouti as by those living in the Somali Republic.[38] The strongest colonial power in the region, Britain, recognized the problem but failed to resolve it partly because the various clans which made up the Somali people showed unity only when threatened by the neighbouring Amharic Christians.[39] The irreconcilable positions of the states involved led to a bitter war in the Ogaden between Ethiopia and Somalia, with superpower involvement (the USSR backing first one side then the other) because of the strategic importance of the Horn of Africa.[40] Radical proposals were made for a socialist federation of the states with the arrival in power of socialist regimes in both Ethiopia and Somalia, in the 1970s, but the conflict did not cease. Only the collapse of both regimes in 1990–1, in Ethiopia through regional revolts in Eritrea and the Tigre, and in Somalia through inter-clan civil war and famine, temporarily removed the issue from the international agenda.

Disintegration of states in Africa, since independence, seemed a more likely cause of frontier revision than seizure by one state of a neighbour's territory. The only successful secession, Eritrea, was the outcome both of colonial history and of the instability of central government in Ethiopia. The Italian imperial administration (1890–1941) defined Eritrea as a political entity separate from Ethiopia because the latter was conquered by Italy much later (1925); both were liberated by British military action during the Second World War. The Ethiopian argument was that Eritrean separatism was the outcome of a typical imperialist strategy of divide and rule: the inhabitants of Eritrea had no obvious characteristics in common.

With nine ethnic groups and mixed Muslim–Christian religious allegiance in the population, the sense of common Eritrean identity was created by thirty years of armed combat against the troops first of the Emperor Haile Selassie and then of the Marxist regime led by Menguistu Haile Maryam. The taking of the capital of Asmara in May 1991 by the Patriotic Front for the Liberation of Eritrea (PFLE) was made possible by the disintegration of the Marxist regime in Addis Ababa. After this military victory, the proclamation of independence became inevitable and followed a referendum on 23–5 April 1993, when 99.8% of the population voted for independence. For the first time the principles of the intangibility of African frontiers and opposition to secession were breached, but in a way which conformed to the basis of the other African frontiers – the colonial frontier was restored.

The weakness, sometimes virtual absence, of policing on African frontiers has resulted in large population flows from poorer to richer countries (such as Ghanaians to Nigeria in times of Nigerian prosperity), movements of refugees escaping political or ethnic persecution and the flight of starving people from famine conditions. Occasionally African countries, such as Nigeria, will round up illegal immigrants in the urban areas and deport them, but there is little the Nigerian authorities, or other governments faced by illegal immigration, can do to stop them entering the country. Frontiers are often in remote and sparsely populated regions, and many frontiers remain undemarcated except on roads. The lack of ability to control frontiers and large tracts of territory enclosed by these frontiers means that African countries have not acquired sovereign statehood, defined as effective control of territory.

Asian Contrasts

A major contrast between the African and Asian experience of European imperialism is that, in Africa, no territory escaped European rule (even the ancient kingdom of Ethiopia was briefly subjected to Italian domination until the Emperor Haile Selassie was restored by the British in 1941), whereas in Asia, Turkey, Persia, Afghanistan, Siam, Nepal, Tibet, China and Japan remained formally independent, although often submitting to demands by imperial powers which would have been intolerable to a European sovereign state.[41] Moreover, their frontiers (except in the case of Japan) were redefined by the intervention of the European powers. In one instance this led to a country, Afghanistan, being granted territory (by the British) in the east, which it had no desire to possess. In other cases, there were strong feelings of dispossession, particularly in the case of China with the seizure of trading posts, the so-called treaty ports, and the forcible opening of the interior to western trading interests, most notoriously to opium traders. In the post-1949 period (after the Communist takeover in Beijing), the most potentially dangerous frontiers in Asia have been those of the People's Republic of China. The Chinese frontier is the longest of all land frontiers (22,000 kilometres); there are large national minorities in frontier regions, a series of complex transfrontier relations with thirteen neighbours, and continuing frontier disputes.

Chinese adjustment to the intrusion of European powers and European ideas about international relations was tortuous and difficult. The development of Chinese civilization over a period of three millennia, with a claim to a continuous history of statehood during most of that period, and the absence of other neighbouring peoples of similar size, resources and level of culture, encouraged the growth of specifically Chinese attitudes about relations with other polities. The imperial Chinese view about frontiers was very different from those prevailing in Europe, although they bore a distant resemblance to those found in the 'universalisms' referred to in chapter 1. According to Confucian teachings, the Chinese emperor, as son of heaven, had the authority to rule the 'Middle Kingdom' which encompassed the whole world, both the 'civilized' (Chinese in culture) and the not yet 'civilized', or barbarian.[42] Imperial China, therefore, did not recognize equal states or powers, and nor did her occasional barbarian conquerors from the central Asian Khanates when they became Chinese emperors; her neighbours were treated as clients, vassals or uncivilized peoples.

The frontiers of Imperial China were self-defined; a treaty about delimitation of frontiers was, according to the Chinese view, unequal. Any treaty which resulted from a negotiation with another power was regarded as imposed. Imperial China also held the view that the empire had two frontiers, an inner and an outer. The latter was the limit, sometimes fanciful, of Chinese influence or, as in the steppes of central Asia, indicated the limit of temporary Chinese occupation. The outer limits of Chinese influence did not necessarily imply that the Chinese had the intention of occupying the territory up to this frontier. It was a conception of the boundaries of 'the Chinese world'. This conception influenced such 'modernizing' figures as Sun Yat-Sin, the first president of a Chinese republic in 1911 and, at least until the late 1930s, Mao-Tse-Tung.[43]

Pressure from militarily and commercially superior powers forced a change in deeply embedded attitudes. The Chinese were compelled to accept European imperial powers into the Chinese world, to allow direct trading, diplomatic contacts and permanent trading establishments on Chinese soil, and finally to negotiate treaties which defined China's frontiers. The Russian empire was the largest gainer of territory at the expense of China; in 1864, when the Chinese pressed the case for regarding the outer frontier as the mutually acceptable frontier between Russia and China, the Russians successfully imposed the inner frontier, much further to the south and east. This effectively put an end to the

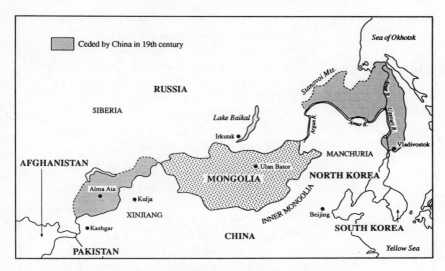

Map 14   Areas seized by Russia through the 'unequal' treaties

notion of the two frontiers in northern Asia. However, it survived to colour Chinese attitudes towards Tibet and towards the controversial agreement, in 1914, of the MacMahon line as the frontier of British India. It remained in the background of the Chinese Communist regime's drive to overturn the 'unequal' treaties, imposed from the eighteenth to the twentieth centuries.

The Chinese government produced maps in 1954 showing the extent of the influence of the Chinese empire at the time of the Opium Wars in 1840.[44] The publication of these maps was taken, by the Indian government as well as by the United States, to reveal the expansionist plans of China.[45] Until the death of Mao, the ambitions of China to dominate the region, to redraw frontiers to its own advantage, to repress any secessionist attempts by non-Chinese peoples within its frontiers[46] and to lead the Third World caused considerable alarm to her neighbours as well as to the US-led coalition of western powers. This resulted in two costly American interventions in Asia; the first, in Korea, led to a direct military confrontation between the United States and the People's Republic of China, the second, in Vietnam, concluded with the first defeat in war in American history.

The confrontation with India showed, however, that although the Chinese were determined to gain advantages, they were cautious in their methods. They also pursued different frontier policies depending on the threat to Chinese interests posed by the neighbour across the frontier. The People's Republic found it easy to adopt normal bilateral

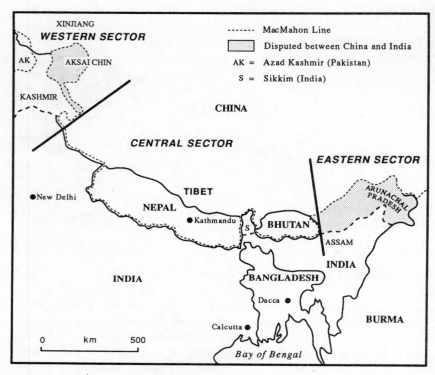

Map 15 The Himalayan frontier between India and China

relations with small and non-threatening states. Treaties were concluded with Burma and then, in 1960, with Nepal. The Chinese also concluded frontier agreements with Bhutan, Pakistan and Mongolia. Relations with the USSR, India and Vietnam have been, and to a degree remain, difficult. In all three cases, there has been armed conflict with loss of life, the most serious being the conflict with Vietnam in 1979 which cost an estimated 50,000 lives. The Chinese grievance related to the imposition by the French of the frontier, agreed by a Franco-Chinese commission in 1885–7 and demarcated five years later.[47] Border skirmishes and modest territorial claims were a part of a wider struggle for influence in the region. The close relations between Vietnam and the USSR, ancestral tensions between the Chinese and the Vietnamese people and the belief that China should be the dominant power in south-east Asia contributed to the conflict.

China's rejection of the Soviet Union's pretension to lead the world Communist movement and China's bid to become leader of the Third World formed the background to the territorial issues which divided them. China's claim for a triangular 125-square-mile island between the Amur and Ussouri rivers was the territorial dispute which provoked armed clashes, but Soviet anxiety concerned much larger questions. The Russians had reached the Pacific as early as the seventeenth century; huge territories to the north and east of China were later seized by tsarist Russia (confirmed by three 'unequal treaties' between 1858 and 1881). Although the northern and north-eastern borderlands were not under effective Chinese control at the time, they were regarded as part of the Chinese sphere. Underpopulated, and of potentially great economic significance, these territories were the focus of Russian anxieties about renewed pressure from the billion-strong Chinese population. The consequence was that a large Soviet army with theatre and battlefield nuclear systems was stationed on the Chinese border, provoking considerable Russo-Chinese tension. Russian intransigence in the 1990s over Japan's claims to some of the Kurile Islands, seized in 1945 by the Soviet Union, is partly to avoid renewed Chinese claims on the territories annexed in the nineteenth century.

Excluding Taiwan, which Beijing has consistently regarded as part of China, and also excluding the propagandist allusions to 800,000 square kilometres of the Russian Far East, India is the only state against which China has pressed a large territorial claim, comprising in total 140,000 square kilometres. This claim was advanced in 1959 when the Chinese denounced the MacMahon line, drawn by Sir Henry MacMahon at the Simla Conference of 1913–14 as the frontier between India and China/Tibet.[48] In the west there were sectors of Aksai Chin, which is 5,400 metres in altitude and has no economic value. The occupation of this territory was important to the Chinese who, between 1954 and 1957, built a military road through it linking Xinjang to Tibet, skirting the impenetrable Kulun massif. Aksai Chin is, according to the Indians, historically part of Ladakh, a region of Kashmir. It is also close to the sensitive Karakorum pass which marks the frontier (the 1949 ceasefire line) of India and Pakistan. The military road was not only strategically important to the Chinese but also an affirmation of Chinese sovereignty over Tibet.

The Chinese achieved their objective in Aksai Chin because the *de facto* frontier remains the line established by Chinese troops at the end of the India–China war in 1962. In the middle and eastern sections of the frontier, the Chinese again seemed to achieve their objectives but attempts to reach a permanent settlement have foundered because India will not settle for less than a substantial reacquisition of territory in the eastern section of the frontier. In the central sector, the Chinese position in Tibet has not been fully resolved. The Chinese trace the origins of their protectorate over Tibet from the thirteenth century and have good arguments for their claim of suzerainty over Tibet. International opinion remains uneasy about Chinese behaviour in Tibet. The exiled Buddhist leader, the Dalai Lama, has remained, as a consequence, a symbol of the Tibetan people, respected in many international circles; the Chinese have engaged in repeated acts of repression against the Buddhist monks of Tibet. During the fortieth anniversary in 1991 of the 'peaceful liberation' of Tibet by China, a formidable stream of Chinese propaganda aimed to convince international opinion of the legitimacy of the Chinese presence. Chinese propaganda has been racist – the Chinese made the biological argument that the blood groups of the Tibetans are closer to those of the Chinese than of the Nepalese and, in an apparently contradictory assertion, that the Tibetans are innately primitive and superstitious.[49]

In 1949 Formosa became the place of refuge of the Kuomintang government, led by Chang Kai Chek, after its defeat by the Chinese Communists. The Kuomintang regime, under American protection, retained the objective of the reunification of China under its leadership, while the Communist government consistently adopted the position that Taiwan was part of the territory of the People's Republic of China. *De facto* and then *de jure*, the international community recognized them as two separate states. The economic and social development of the two countries diverged, with Taiwan participating fully in the dynamic economic growth of the Pacific rim. With the opening of China to foreign trade and investment in the 1980s, Taiwan became a trading partner and a source of investment funds for mainland China. But the democratization of Taiwan placed an additional barrier to the reunification of the two states. Reunification can now only be seen as a long-term prospect.

On the maritime frontier, China has traditionally claimed the whole of the China Sea, its islands, islets, sand banks and even submerged reefs. A situation has arisen, rather like that in the Antarctic, but without the benefit of an overall system of cooperation such as the Antarctic Treaty System.[50] In the China Sea, no country recognizes the claims of the other five countries involved, but no one challenges occupation by force of arms (although in 1988 there was a naval clash between China and Vietnam). There is a *de facto* acceptance of the presence of neighbouring countries on some of the islands, but not in the Spratleys group nor on Mischief Reef close to Borneo, where real tensions persist.[51] The delimitation of the continental shelf in the South China Sea is emerging as a serious issue, following, in 1994, contracts for oil exploration between both China and Vietnam with major American companies.

In the 1980s tension over Chinese frontiers, in general, diminished.

The incidents between Chinese and Russian frontier guards which provoked serious animosity in the 1960s and 1970s petered out. By 1983, China had put into abeyance claims on territory of the USSR. Negotiations were resumed in 1987 and a commission of experts was established for the Amur–Ussouri river to determine the *Thalweg* (median line) of the principal channel which would become the frontier between the two countries. Some frontier posts, closed since 1962, were reopened and normal transfrontier relations were resumed in the border region. On 16 March 1992 the two countries ratified a treaty bringing to an end their outstanding frontier disputes. As well as formal recognition of existing frontiers, transfrontier 'cooperative development zones' were to be established between Siberia and the Chinese provinces of Inner Mongolia and Heilungkiang. Economic cooperation was envisaged between three Russian cities and Harbin (the capital of Heilunkiang) and Shanghai. Another project in transfrontier economic cooperation was a multinational venture at the junction of the Russian, Chinese and North Korean frontiers at the estuary of the Tumang river. In April 1992, experts from the three countries met with the UN Development Programme to engage in detailed planning but, apart from engaging a Finnish consulting firm, no progress has been reported.

On the Vietnam frontier, tension eased in the 1980s without any resolution of the issues in dispute. Successful negotiations in the 1980s ended the Portuguese occupation of Macao, and other negotiations planned, with some difficulties, the end of the British lease of the New Territories, due to expire in 1997, and the transfer of Hong Kong to China. Despite occasional flurries, the Himalayan frontier has been quiet. This calming of frontier tensions has coincided with a Chinese government drive towards reintegrating the country in the world economy. The priority given to economic development, trade and international economic relations means that frontier disputes have become second-order questions, deliberately played down to avoid interfering with the new priorities.

Other Asian Problems

The Russo-Japanese quarrel over the Kurile Islands, the creation of Bangladesh, the Kashmir dispute, the Iraqi frontier disputes with Iran and Kuwait, the Kurdish problem and the Arab–Israeli dispute illustrate the wide variety of Asian territorial disputes. They demonstrate many of the characteristics of territorial disputes in Europe during the high tide of 'balance of power' politics. They mask struggles for regional dominance between competing powers.

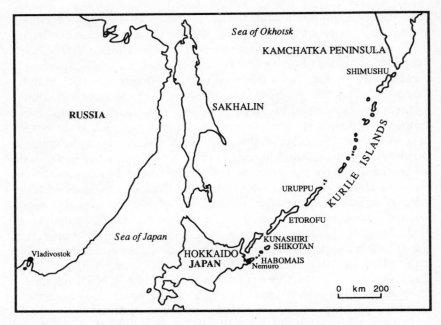

Map 16   The Kurile Islands

The Russo-Japanese dispute over some of the Kurile Islands is the only remaining territorial dispute between two major powers. The dispute has resulted in the virtual absence of relations between the two states and has had a serious economic impact on the Russian Far East. The Japanese claim the Habomais group (one of whose islands is only 5 kilometres from Hokkaido), together with Shikotan, Kunashiri and Etorofu. The other eighteen islands running north from Uruppu to the Kamchatka Peninsula are not disputed. The southern islands have been important to Russia for strategic reasons, giving ice-free deep-water access to the Pacific from the Sea of Okhotsk, as well as providing some natural harbours and tracts of land suitable for military bases.

The origin of the dispute was the seizure by the USSR of the Kurile Islands and the southern half of the large island of Sakhalin in the last days of the Second World War.[52] Both sides claim historic rights to the islands by virtue of being the first to occupy them. The first recorded Russian presence in the islands was in the first half of the eighteenth century, and the Japanese had visited the islands at least 100 years before. There was no internationally recognized sovereignty over them until the Treaty of Shimoda in 1855, in which the Russians apparently recognized Japanese suzerainty over the islands. The Soviet Union claimed that this treaty was signed under duress by a Russian diplomat held as a hostage by Japan during the Crimean War. Moscow also argued that the 1875 agreement, in which Japan renounced a claim to Sakhalin in exchange for all the Kurile Islands, was never ratified.

After the Soviet seizure, sanctioned by the 1951 Treaty of San Francisco, there was an attempt to efface the Japanese presence and, until 1989, no foreigners were allowed in the islands except former Japanese residents and their relatives to tend graves. In 1956 the USSR offered to hand back two islands of the Habomais group and Shikotan, but the Japanese, under American pressure, rejected this offer. Negotiations between the USSR and Japan over establishing economic relations in 1984 broke down over the islands. Russia did not feel able to make concessions in the Kuriles in case other territories were called into question (particularly by China). Immediately after the failed coup against Gorbachev in August 1991, the Japanese prime minister wrote to the Soviet president saying that the time had come to normalize Soviet–Japanese relations and that the first step would be the return of the Kuriles. President Yeltsin failed to make conciliatory moves. The weakening of the Russian position as a result of the secession of the Muslim Republics in central Asia and the 1994 electoral success of the extreme Russian nationalists led by Zhirinovsky[53] made concessions even more difficult.

The separation of Bangladesh from Pakistan in 1972 involved a large population but did not have important repercussions outside the immediate region. Pakistan was created in 1947 with an unusual geographical configuration, giving to Pakistan those regions of the Indian subcontinent with a majority of Muslims. This created a country with a large territory in the north-west and a smaller area, with almost the same population, in the east (Bengal) separated by about 2,000 kilometres of Indian territory. The new state was dominated by the soldiers and the great families based in the capital, Islamabad, in West Pakistan, while the marginalized East contained one of the poorest populations in the world. According to one author, the relationship between West and East Pakistan was 'an unmistakable pattern of colonial exploitation'[54] – a view which was widely shared.

The crisis between the two halves of Pakistan was triggered by a natural catastrophe – the flooding of the low-lying area around the Ganges delta which claimed, according to unofficial estimates, between 1 million and 1.5 million lives. The aid, provided by the central authorities and distributed by the military, was both grudging and incompetently administered. By coincidence the first elections, after many years of military government, were held immediately after the catastrophe; the separatist Awami League gained three-quarters of the

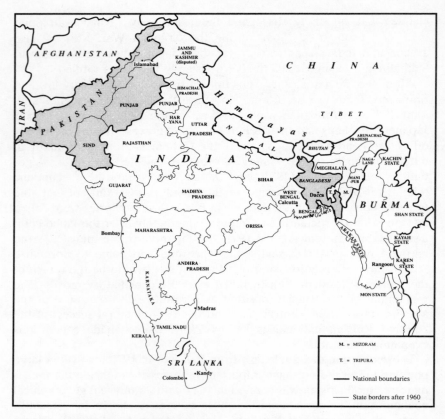

Map 17 The Indian sub-continent

seats in the East, giving it an overall parliamentary majority with the support of minority parties in the West, thus provoking a constitutional crisis.[55] The leader of the Awami League in the East, Sheik Mujibur Rahman, declared independence in March 1971. The army immediately arrested him and proceeded to shoot large numbers of demonstrators on the streets of the capital, Dacca. Soldiers of eastern origin deserted and formed the core of an armed resistance movement. After further repression, the Indian government, led by Indira Gandhi, which had never wholly accepted the legitimacy of Pakistan,[56] seized the opportunity to intervene. After a short campaign, Pakistan capitulated and, in January 1972 Mujibur Rahman was released and proclaimed the independence of Bangladesh.

The deep divisions in the international community were important to the secession's success. Indian intervention was in flagrant violation of the principle of non-intervention in the UN Charter as well as recently voted UN resolutions which India had supported.[57] China and the United States had established close relations with Islamabad, and in August 1971 the USSR had signed a treaty of friendship and cooperation with India.[58] In these circumstances, no great power consensus over the crisis could emerge. Many Third World countries did not want to see a successful secession but had little sympathy with Pakistan, considered a client state of Washington.[59] There was, therefore, neither a majority in the Security Council nor in the General Assembly of the United Nations to prevent Indian intervention and the setting up of the new state.

Kashmir, the other major territorial dispute between India and Pakistan, has lasted since 1947. The ruler of Kashmir initially acceded to the Indian state on independence, and successive Indian governments have been unwilling to concede a referendum to allow self-determination on the grounds that territories which are already part of a state do not have such a right.[60] With a Muslim majority in Kashmir, the result would be a foregone conclusion. India, with a large Muslim minority and various other religious communities, cannot accept religion as a valid basis of state legitimacy. After the partition of 1947, the conflict quickly reached such an intensity that neither side could make a concession which satisfied the other without major humiliation.

The dispute became enmeshed in Cold War politics, with Pakistan aligning with the United States and India supported by the USSR. After the ending of the Cold War, the long-standing dispute shows no sign of resolution. Both sides have encamped behind what was originally intended to be a temporary ceasefire line. Sporadic violence, which India claims is fomented or supported by Pakistan, and continuing skirmishes between Indian and Pakistani troops on the Karakorum glacier maintain tension. The conflict is intractable because the cohesion of both the Indian and Pakistani states seems to depend on having an immediate threat across the frontier.

In the 1980s and early 1990s, the two most bloody and dangerous Asian frontier disputes to date have arisen on the borders of Iraq. One centres on Iranian access to the sea through the Shatt al-Arab and the delta – the confluence of the Tigris and Euphrates. The other is over the delimitation of the Kuwait–Iraq boundary and, indeed over the very existence of the state of Kuwait. A third, which is less likely to provoke inter-state warfare, is the conflict with the Kurdish minority which has stubbornly refused to integrate into Iraq and has links, not always amicable, with Kurds living in Iran, Syria, the ex-USSR and Turkey.

An apparently small territorial issue concerning the Shatt al-Arab was the cause of a major and bloody war, lasting for eight years, between Iran and Iraq. This frontier was first delimited by the 1847 Treaty of Erzorum between the Ottoman empire and Persia. The Ottoman empire retained the waterway of Shatt al-Arab because of the importance of the port of Basra and the river as a means of communication, whereas, at the time, it was of minor importance to the Persians. The origin of the recent difficulty was the discovery of oil on the north bank of the Shatt al-Arab in 1908 and the consequent development of the Persian port of Mahammarrah; the ships carrying oil had to sail through Turkish waters and therefore pay dues. At this time the Shatt al-Arab was effectively under British control. According to the 1913 Protocol of Constantinople, part of the frontier was to follow the *Thalweg*, but the waters of the lower part of the river and the estuary remained Turkish.

The Shah of Iran refused to regard Iraq as the successor to the Ottoman empire, and claimed, according to international custom, the *Thalweg* for the whole length of the river where it formed a common frontier, from Khorramshar to the Persian Gulf. Iraq responded with the argument that the river was its only access to the sea whereas Persia had many other ports. Another compromise in 1937 accepted the *Thalweg* for the section of the river facing the Persian port of Abadan. In 1969 the Shah denounced the 1937 compromise, accusing Iraq of failing to use the dues levied on Iranian shipping to maintain the river, and refused to accept the Iraqi flag and Iraqi pilots on Iranian ships in the Shatt al-Arab. The Shah went further and sent troops to occupy three strategic islands in the straits of Ormuz, leading to a break in diplomatic relations between Iran and Iraq.

The 1975 Algiers agreement, between Saddam Hussein and the Shah, surprisingly gave Iran most of its demands. But the fall of the Shah and the 'fundamentalist' Shia revolution in Iran offered an opportunity to Iraq to reverse the position. In 1980 Saddam Hussein abrogated the Algiers agreement and launched a military offensive against Iran, occupying Khorramshar and encircling Abadan; the Iraqis claimed that Iran had not fulfilled the terms of the Algiers agreement by failing to give up about 1,000 square kilometres of strategically important territory. Iraq subsequently laid claim to Khuzistan, sometimes known as 'Arabistan', an oil-rich province inhabited by 2 million Shia Arabs, but this claim was dropped when in 1982 Iran regained the military initiative.

The territorial dispute between the two countries was of secondary importance in triggering the long war which claimed at least a million lives. The Iraqi leadership felt threatened by the Iranian revolution because of its possible effects on the Iraqi Shias, a majority of the population. The desire to limit the religious–political impact of the

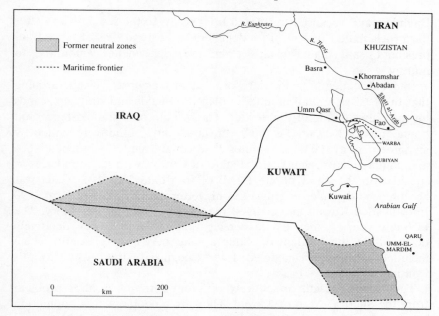

Map 18   Iraq's south-eastern frontiers

Iranian revolution was not limited to Iraq. Iraq benefited from the
sympathies, and substantial financial support, of its Arab neighbours to
the south, and from access to arms supplies from the USSR and the
west. A radical revision of the frontier was improbable, but any
readjustment symbolized victory or defeat. The military balance moved
strongly towards the Iraqis in 1988, and the Iranians had to accept Iraqi
terms. The situation was soon reversed when, in order to ensure Iranian
neutrality in the Gulf War of 1990, the Iraqis conceded a return to the
Algiers agreement. The Iranians reasserted a dominant role in the
region, although in a more restrained and subtle way.

  The 1990 Gulf War was provoked by the Iraqi invasion of Kuwait.
Kuwait emerged in 1913 as an entity, recognized in international law as
a British protectorate. The British supported the el-Sabah family, who,
under the Ottomans, had been recognized since the eighteenth century
as the local rulers. The autonomy of Kuwait was guaranteed by the
British in return for support of the el-Sabahs against the Ottomans
during the First World War. The Kuwaiti frontiers were extended and
delimited in 1922, at the same time as Iraq was founded under British
protection. Kuwait became independent in 1961, but the Iraqis were
reluctant to accept its existence because they considered it part of an
Ottoman province (the vilyat of Basra) which was administered from

Baghdad, and because it restricted Iraqi access to the sea. Six days after the proclamation of Kuwaiti independence General Qassem, the Iraqi president, said that Kuwait's claim to independence amounted to mutiny.

Iraq subsequently made territorial claims against Kuwait, arguing that the 1922 delimitation unfairly placed oil-fields and strategic islands on the Kuwaiti side of the border. The dispute over the existence and boundaries of Kuwait was, however, apparently definitively settled by an agreement of 1963, the minutes of which affirmed 'the independence and complete sovereignty of the state of Kuwait with its boundaries as specified in the letter of the P. M. of Iraq date 27.7.1932 which was accepted by the ruler of Kuwait in his letter dated 10.8.1932'.[61] In 1990 Iraq invaded Kuwait and claimed the whole of Kuwait's territory. The UN intervened under US leadership and the Iraqis were decisively defeated on the battlefield. After a long period of pressure, which included economic sanctions, Iraq recognized, in 1994, Kuwait's frontiers.

The Kurds present an entirely different form of frontier problem from the Shatt al-Arab or Kuwait. They are a people with a population greater than the majority of the members of the United Nations – estimates of the number of Kurds vary greatly but they are generally thought to be between 12 and 20 million (maximum figures are 10 million in Turkey, 6 million in Iran, 3 million in Iraq, 800,000 in Syria and 350,000 in certain republics of the ex-USSR).[62] But the Kurds suffer, in an extreme form, from all the disadvantages of a linguistically and culturally distinctive population which has not possessed political autonomy, unity or independence since biblical times.[63] Moreover, they have been used in the complex rivalries between Iraq, Iran, Turkey and Syria. From the beginning of the twentieth century, some Kurds have campaigned for an independent Kurdistan. But mass mobilization for independence and unity was made impossible by traditional clans which lacked any sense of national political cohesion. Notwithstanding the lack of a developed sense of nationhood among the Kurds, the principle of an autonomous, potentially independent, Kurdistan was imposed by the victorious allies on Turkey at the 1920 Treaty of Sèvres but revoked by the 1923 Treaty of Lausanne negotiated with the resurgent Turkey of Kemal Ataturk.

In contemporary Kurdistan only the PKK (the Marxist-Leninist Workers Party of Kurdistan based in eastern Turkey) continues to fight for complete independence. The PKK have created serious problems for Turkey both inside and outside the country. For example, on 24 June 1993 PKK activists occupied Turkish consulates in Munich and

Marseilles, provoked a violent confrontation outside the Turkish embassy in Berne and attacked Turkish premises in Stockholm, Copenhagen and London.[64] But the Kurds of Iraq, although subject to savage repression by Saddam Hussein after the United States failed to support their revolt in 1991, claim only autonomy in a federal state;[65] they have helped the Turks to remove PKK bases from Iraqi territory so that Turkey will maintain supply lines to Iraqi Kurdistan. Iranians have attacked Iranian Kurds on Iraqi territory – only a minority of Iran's Kurds support Kurdish independence. The Kurds of the ex-USSR and Syria are too few in numbers to have a genuinely independent political voice. The Kurds of Iraq, benefiting from international sympathy, are protected by the UN against Iraqi air strikes while the Kurds of Turkey remain an international embarrassment and a considerable cost in security operations to the Turkish government – compounded by the 1995 Turkish invasion of north-eastern Iraq to seek out PKK bases.

The Arab–Israeli dispute seems the most intractable of all territorial disputes; it has resulted in four regional wars, terrorism and counter-terrorism, unprecedented international attention and fears that the conflict could directly involve the USA and the USSR. The dispute has unique characteristics, the first of which is the history of the Jews – a tenacious religious tradition going back to Abraham, Moses and the Old Testament prophets has been wedded to the strong sense of identity as a 'chosen people'. The tragic peculiarity of Jewish history is that centuries of discrimination and persecution culminated in the Holocaust when, during the Second World War, the Nazi regime made a deliberate attempt to exterminate them. This history has created a special attitude, amongst Jews and Gentiles, regarding the right of the Jews to a national home. An additional complicating factor in the Arab–Israeli dispute is that a substantial Jewish community lives within the frontiers of the two superpowers; in the case of the United States, Jews occupy an influential place in the political system; in the former Soviet Union they were a captive people, exposed to traditional forms of anti-semitism.

Initially both Israelis and Palestinian Arabs believed that they had the sole historic right to all the lands formerly called Palestine. For many Jews, Israel is the promised land of the Old Testament, theirs by God-given and historic right (and recently by effective occupation); for the secular Zionist, Palestine is the only conceivable national home for the Jews, and a national home is necessary to make the Jewish people safe from persecution. The Arabs claim effective occupation from the eighth-century conquest of Jerusalem to the mid-twentieth century when they were wrongfully dispossessed. There are many examples of mutually exclusive territorial claims but no other has equivalent clarity.

Extremists on both sides have sought the other side's complete exclusion from the territory; moderates are willing to countenance the presence of the other side only as a subordinate minority group.

The development of Israeli territorial ideologies concerning the geographical limits of the state and Palestinian territorial strategies concerning the effective occupation of the territory are more complex than those found elsewhere. The Israeli 'territory-forming ideology' (the phrase of Baruch Kipnis) is composed of three elements. First, a pattern of settlement (which in other contexts would be called colonization) gives priority to agricultural settlements and control over useful resources, the most important being the waters of the Jordan.[66] Second, a balanced population spread, partly by the establishment of new towns, throughout the national territory should ensure a Jewish majority everywhere.[67] Third, the 'deterritorialization' of the Palestinians should be promoted by isolating the Arab settlements and in some cases removing them, making resident Arabs dependent on Jewish institutions and the Israeli economy.[68] The Palestinians have adopted defensive strategies to secure as much of their territory as possible through 'sedentarization' of nomadic Bedouins, land reclamation and planting of olive trees, illegal housing construction and the like. The only Palestinian strategy which brought Israel to the negotiating table after a long stalemate in the 1980s and early 1990s was the *intifada* (uprising) on the West Bank of the Jordan and the Gaza Strip. The Israelis accepted the principle of territorial concessions ('land for peace'). A peace process was initiated by the 1992 Madrid conference and culminated with the September 1993 Washington agreement between Israel and the PLO.

The crux of the negotiating problem between Israel and the Palestinians (and the neighbouring Arab states) is that any compromise position is likely to be seen as victory for the other side by influential hardliners on both sides. The minimum an Israeli Labour government and the PLO would accept is no longer certain. Israeli moderates would accept something like the 'Allon Plan' of the late 1960s – Israeli sovereignty over Jerusalem, the Jordan Rift Valley and a few pockets on the West Bank, with the remaining areas of of the West Bank ceded to the Palestinians; for the Arab moderates, a return to the pre-1967 frontiers and the setting up of an independent Palestinian state would probably suffice. The 1993 Washington agreement on autonomy for the Palestinians in the Gaza Strip and Jericho was an interim agreement which left the main lines of a definitive agreement deeply disputed. Intractable issues remain – the rest of the West Bank, the Golan Heights, management of the Jordan river and, above all, Jerusalem, regarded as a holy city by Jews, Christians and Muslims alike.

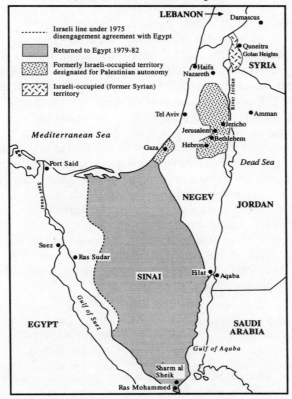

Map 19 (*a*) Changes in Israeli territory 1975–93; (*b*) an Israeli view of the future

The establishment of a state by force of arms in territory previously occupied by another people and defending the new frontiers by military means has been a common occurrence throughout history. Revolutionary states have, from the French to the Chinese revolutions, challenged the territorial status quo and the norms of international society with some success.[69] Since 1945, force of arms and displacement of populations have ceased to be acceptable to the 'international community' as legitimate ways to establish a new state. The UN became the arbitrator of the legitimacy of new states and of their behaviour. The majority of its Third World members have considered that Israel was either a colonial power or an instrument of imperialism. They sympathized with the view of Israel's neighbours that the new state was an unacceptable intrusion into the Palestinian Arab or Muslim world. In western countries, Israeli policy towards the Palestinians was regarded as destabilizing and dangerous because the Palestinians had the support of the oil-rich Gulf states. The Arab–Israeli dispute has therefore remained at the centre of international attention in a way which has no parallels with other territorial disputes.

Conclusion

During and immediately after decolonization, the rival hegemonic powers – the United States and the Soviet Union – maintained an environment hostile to secessionist movements and to the acquisition of territory by violent means. Both superpowers became involved in disastrous wars, but the US over Vietnam and the Soviet Union over Afghanistan could both argue that they were attempting to preserve a territorial and political status quo. The changed international situation following the collapse of Communist power has resulted in great uncertainty. The UN has extended its peace-keeping operations, conducting more simultaneously since 1989 than at any previous period.[70] But the situations it has confronted (with the exception of the Iraqi invasion of Kuwait) have arisen from the collapse of governments (as in Somalia and Rwanda) rather than inter-state warfare. The capacity of the UN to continue to engage in intervention in anarchic situations is doubtful because the aims of UN missions cannot be clearly defined and the results of intervention are unpredictable.

A wide range of factors – demographic pressures, great disparities in wealth and natural resources, the ready availability of weapons and the renaissance of militant ideologies – encourage territorial conflicts. The nineteenth-century distinction between 'satisfied' and 'unsatisfied' powers could acquire a new relevance in Africa and Asia, in situations where territorial adjustments seem possible. These situations may occur in areas in which there is no major American strategic or economic interest and where there is no strong regional power to keep the peace. In Africa, there are few states with sufficient internal cohesion to create the military and political organization required to challenge the existing frontiers, but disintegration of states may occur. Strong regional powers in Asia undoubtedly have the capacity to engage in major military campaigns and may, in certain circumstances, be tempted to do so. The degree to which frontiers remain stable depends on whether the states in both continents are integrated into a world order which offers some hope of solutions to their problems and in which there are effective sanctions against those who challenge the territorial status quo. The prospects are poor in both cases. The pauperization of large populations, social and economic circumstances which result in despair and the lack of political will and imagination by the rich countries make global territorial stability improbable.

4

Boundaries within States: Size, Democracy and Service Provision

The purpose of this chapter is to examine the nature of boundaries of territorial units below the national level. The main argument is that the clear distinction between international frontiers and boundaries within states in Europe is weakening. But the characteristics of these sub-state boundaries vary greatly. Sometimes ancient origins have etched them deeply into the cultural landscape; in other cases they are of recent origin and easily changed. Their functions are inseparable from their location and changing their location is usually associated with a change in function. They frequently have a direct effect on the composition of governments and the balance of forces within legislatures. But these effects are not uniform. Great changes, such as the drawing of entirely new regional boundaries as in post-Franco Spain, can be carried through with minor political difficulties, whereas small changes may threaten cataclysmic effects, as in the case of Les Fourons.[1]

There are connections between state boundaries and boundaries of sub-state jurisdictions. Boundaries within states have, in the past, sometimes been frontiers between states. The boundary may correspond exactly, as in the case of the Scottish border, or be approximate, as in the cases of Tuscany and Bavaria. The micro-states of Europe remain as testimony to a history in which small jurisdictions were common. One of these small jurisdictions, Luxembourg, has survived to become a full member of the European Union. But most small European kingdoms, duchies, principalities, bishoprics, republics and free towns, which enjoyed sometimes long, sometimes transitory, political independence, were integrated into larger political entities. Occasionally their frontiers remain, in whole or in part, as local government boundaries. Most have been effaced by war, social upheaval and turbulent political change. Conversely, boundaries within states sometimes become boundaries between states. For example, the present Northern Ireland border with the Republic of Ireland was, until 1921, made up of three county boundaries within a single sovereign jurisdiction, while Slovakia[2] and Slovenia were formerly provinces or states of a federation but never, prior to the 1990s, independent states.

Boundaries within states are both reflections of, and an influence on, the distribution of power in the state. Changes in territorial arrangements, often presented as technical adjustments to promote efficiency of administration, are never independent of changes in power relationships. Sub-state boundaries have a determining, if frequently obscure, effect on the results of elections. The boundaries of regional and local government are the 'building blocks' of electoral constituencies and thus bias the outcome of elections. The location of international frontiers also has this effect, rarely perceived except after the creation of a new international frontier. An example is the establishment of the Northern Irish border in 1921, which transformed a minority of Protestant unionists in the island of Ireland into a permanent majority in the Province of Northern Ireland. The break-up of Yugoslavia and the Soviet Union has had a similar effect of transforming former minorities in a large political system into new majorities within new and smaller boundaries.

Boundaries within states have often been based on military or security needs. These security considerations may be distant and obscure, such as those underlying the English shires, lost in the mists of feudal military organization, or they may be recent, as is the case with the German *Länder* which were the result of the security needs of the western partners in the victorious coalition after 1945 to ensure that there was no strong German central government. The internal security dimension is never wholly absent from internal boundary-making. The requirements of policing certain areas as well as who controls the police and how this control is exercised is a – sometimes hidden – element in considerations about territorial organization. Governments may sometimes keep debates about the territorial organization of policing separate from debates about local and regional government in order to retain control over internal security services.

Boundaries within states may mark the limits of political identities or may create new political identities. Catalonia, Alto Adige, Bavaria and Flanders are examples of strong political identities, with deep historical roots. Like international boundaries, some sub-state boundaries are the outcome of long historical processes of conflict and adjustment between competing interests. Some newly established regions such as Midi-Pyrénées and Centre in France or Castilla-la-Mancha in Spain had no pre-existing political identities but a sense of identification tends to emerge once the regional government (as in some Italian regions from the 1970s and Spanish regions in the 1990s) acquires significant control over resources. The geographical division of labour within states may result in inter-regional conflicts or sharpen differences in political outlooks. These are sustained by different cultural forms and language use.[3] When this occurs, inter-regional boundaries can become the analogues of international frontiers. Local 'nationalism' can have many of the characteristics of state nationalism and produce similar sensitivities about boundaries.[4]

But the limits of territorial entities vary in their importance and the ways in which they influence political behaviour. The external environment, the different size and resources of local and regional government, the history of the relationships between the various levels of government which make up the states, constitutional provisions, and the norms and practices in the political struggle to acquire power are all part of a complex pattern.[5] Sidney Tarrow severely castigates the authors of the considerable literature on intergovernmental relations (between central, state/regional and local governments) as being 'all too often . . . limited to seeing the pirouettes of pettifogging bureaucrats fighting apparently abstract battles'.[6] This deficiency reflects the difficulty of linking the conflicts between levels of government with the political battles which directly involve the social and political forces based on social classes, political networks and economic interests. These are the major influences on whether the frontiers of local and regional governments are the limits of strong political authority or drawn merely for administrative convenience, and therefore easy to change.

The Origins of 'Rational' Boundaries

Many attempts have been made to establish more rational principles on which to base the drawing of boundaries within states. The first of these attempts, the establishment of the *départements* in France has been a notable success; the *départements* became part of the republican tradition and the basis of local political identities. They have survived into an age when the axioms on which they were based have ceased to correspond to social conditions and new technologies.

Decisions about territorial divisions have seldom been purely arbitrary and have usually been designed to achieve certain objectives, such as military security and revenue-raising. At their inception, rationality has never been wholly absent from boundary-making and, in this sense the territorial divisions of the Carolingian empire or the Italian communes at the end of the Middle Ages were no more or less 'rational' than the boundaries of modern local authorities. The crucial difference lies in what is expressed by the French word *finalités* (the ultimate objectives) of political organization. When the object of government ceased to be securing links of personal fealty in favour of loyalty to an abstract conception – the state – then territorial divisions were justified (on the relatively rare occasions when they had to be) in terms of an ultimate objective of the state.

The beginnings of this can be seen in the Roman empire. In Roman law, a concept of depersonalized authority (*imperium*) underpinned the territorial organization of the Empire. The purpose of the Roman administrative system, with its territorial hierarchy of *pagi* and *provinciae*, was to place military and fiscal matters securely, at least in principle, under the control of the *imperium*. All succeeding empires, from Charlemagne to Charles V and to the Russian tsars, established internal boundaries on the basis of military requirements, the state of military technology and the fortunes of war, but their origins and justification were contingent and ultimately justified in terms of some divine plan. Boundaries were established pragmatically in order to control, in particular circumstances, territory and peoples. As a result, the territorial organization of feudal Europe became a complex patchwork of different jurisdictions which often remained fossilized into the eighteenth and even the nineteenth century. Under the *ancien régime* in France, territory was divided into *généralités, gouvernements, élections, sénéchaussées, bailliages, jurisdictions parlementaires, marches, départements de l'impôt, villes royales* and many other units, with resultant confusion of powers, administrative inefficiency and the proliferation of sinecures.

The first thoroughgoing, systematic, uniform and 'rational' reorganization of internal boundaries after the Romans took place during the early stages of the French Revolution of 1789. The Constituent Assembly received a report in September 1789 from Jacques-Guillaume Thouret on behalf of the Committee on the Constitution, saying: 'We have come to the conclusion that the organization of each district in the Kingdom should be constituted in such a way as to serve as a basis for the formation of the legislature as well as the various classes of administrative assembly ... in other words, to define the basis – political, electoral, judicial, ecclesiastical – of the new France.' He proposed eighty *départements*, whose boundaries would be defined by population, territory and wealth (established by tax revenues). The abolition of the old territorial units met an urgent practical need to find a basis for constituencies from which to elect a new National Assembly. Place names and maps were radically changed by the proposed reform.

The break with the past was as clear as the change in the status of individuals from subjects of the king to citizens.

Like most apparently novel revolutionary ideas, it had antecedents. The term *département de l'impôt* was already in common use. In the 1780s Robert de Hesseln had published a map which divided France into eighty-one *contrées* – a map which greatly influenced the Constituent Assembly. The canton had also already been proposed as an administrative unit by the physiocrats. The guiding principle of the *département* was that the capital of the most important administrative unit should be within a day's journey from its outer limits, and the subdivisions, the cantons, within half a day, on the grounds that all citizens should have convenient and, as far as possible, equal access to central government. Arguments about local autonomy and local control, although advanced by some federalists, were not influential.[7] Objectors also talked in terms of 'geographical rationality', particularly stressing the geography of communications, and opposed particular boundaries on the grounds that they would 'break up' communities.

Edmund Burke, the most acerbic foreign critic of the project of the revolutionaries, accused them of believing that their country was a blank sheet of paper on which they could draw anything they chose. Some argued in favour of retaining the boundaries of the historic provinces; the comte de Mirabeau suggested that the dismantling of the old provinces would divide people united by customs, language, manners and economic activity.[8] Some historic boundaries of large provinces were more or less retained although they were subdivided into *départements* – Provence into three *départments*, Brittany and Normandy into five each, and some small ones became *départements* – Aunis et Saintonge. But the restoration of the historic provinces remained part of a reactionary dream until the mid-twentieth century and led to the 1941 restoration of the regions by the Vichy regime. The *départements*, however, remained the most durable legacies of the Revolution, maintained by the Bourbon restoration of 1815 and never seriously threatened thereafter.

The core of the argument in favour of the *départements*, and its subdivision the canton, was size. Although the purposes of territorial units below the national level have been conceived in increasingly complex ways, the issue of scale has remained at the heart of the debate. Particularly in the English-speaking world, democratic, practical and technocratic arguments have been advanced in favour of or against proposed territorial reorganizations, but it is the size of the proposed units that has been the basis of disagreements. Earnest attempts have been made to remove the prejudices and value judgements which have clouded and envenomed the exchanges between different protagonists by using the formal techniques of rational choice.[9] These, in turn, have been attacked as obscuring the value judgements which have to be made.[10] Formal techniques can be used in order more effectively to achieve certain ends, but they cannot determine the nature of those ends.

Size, Democracy and Efficiency

Questions about the relationship between size of territory, type of government and social organization were first raised in classical Greece but have still not been adequately answered. The success in the recent past of the smaller European countries such as Switzerland, Austria, the Netherlands and Finland in combining highly democratic practices, corporatist economic decision-making and a high degree of adaptability to the changing economic and political environments has been widely admired and analysed.[11] Smallness does not necessarily offer these advantages in other circumstances and it does not guarantee them in the long term. But small political entities have shown a remarkable capacity to survive; there is little evidence that there has been variation in the relative size of polities over a long period.[12] This general observation holds good for units of government below the national level.

The relationship between size, form of government and effectiveness of government has been little explored since the rise of the large nation-state in Europe.[13] But the relationship was central to Aristotle's political thought and his ideas continued to exercise a powerful influence until the eighteenth century. Aspects of his thinking have informed discussions about local government in the nineteenth and twentieth centuries. Aristotle's contention was that an essential precondition for a balanced constitution, a polity, was the possibility of an assembly of all citizens. The *polis* (roughly translated as city-state), with its limited size and population, was the geographical unit suited to the best form of government. The small population made it possible for citizens to know one another and appreciate each other's problems; it also implied a frugal life because a small population could not generate great wealth and inequalities would therefore be limited.

The impossibility of all citizens participating in the affairs of large states led democratic theorists to consider local government as an arena where democratic values could be sustained. The nineteenth-century liberal, John Stuart Mill, was concerned at the prospect of extending the franchise to people who lacked a civic education. Since, in representative systems of government in countries with large populations, active participation at the national level was limited for the overwhelming majority to the simple act of voting, Mill was led to propose that local government had a vital role in political education.[14] Many more people could participate in an informed way in local government; this made local government an essential instrument for political education. It followed from this that the territories of local government should be sufficiently small to allow for the maximum participation by the people. There is some support for Mill's position in recent research. Dahl and Tufte report comparative findings which support the contention that despite a low turnout in elections, citizens feel they can affect decisions at the local level more than the national level.[15] The size of English local authorities, the result of 'the single-minded pursuit of criteria related to service delivery',[16] has probably made it difficult for the public to identify with them.

Dahl and Tufte also put forward the familiar argument of Mill in the language of the late twentieth century: 'If the great units are needed for the handling of transnational matters of extraordinary moment, very small units seem to be necessary to provide a place where ordinary people can acquire the sense and the reality of moral responsibility and political effectiveness in a universe where remote galaxies of leaders spin on courses mysterious and unfathomable to the ordinary citizen.'[17] The boundaries of government areas should therefore be drawn to maximize effective participation and do this in a way which would help to sustain representative democracy. Boundaries should, according to this view, pay due attention to the aspirations and wishes of the population they enclose; they should in principle correspond to 'self-determining communities'. This position has seemed particularly persuasive in either large states or divided societies (with deep cleavages of religion, language, race and culture).

Questions about what ought to be the proper size of the territory of governments below the level of the state and what ought to be the boundary functions of these governments are linked to three types of theory – constitutional theory about the distribution of power, theories about the relationship of government to economic performance and propositions about the capacity of government below the national level to deliver services. Most federalist thinking holds that, to have a properly functioning federation, rough similarity of area between the federated states is necessary, a proposition for which there is empirical evidence. Debates have taken place between the various schools of thought concerning the relationship of territory to power in unitary or non-federal political systems. These schools have rather obscure titles – neo-colonialist theory, territorial systems analysis, diffusion theory, territorial dependency theory and administrative/political brokerage hypotheses.[18] A more practically orientated discussion has been about how territorial organization affects economic performance. The central proposition around which this debate revolves is very simple – too much centralization in government inhibits economic development. Political discussion revolved around this question during the regionalization debate in Britain in the 1960s and in France from the first effective regionalization measures in 1956 until the Common Programme of the left (radicals, socialists and Communists) espoused the cause of regionalism in 1973. It was also evoked, with a different focus, in the 'post-Fordist' debate about the impact of new technologies on industrial processes; some authors considered that new possibilities of dispersal of economic activities and 'flexible specialization' could effectively revive hitherto depressed and peripheral regions.[19]

The other practical debate has concerned what is sometimes termed 'system capacity', that is to say the limitation of government units of a particular size, in terms of human and financial resources, to tackle various problems or to supply certain services. Discussion of optimal boundaries for the provision of services is, almost inevitably, restricted to specialized political, administrative and professional groups. The majority of the electorate are excluded except when some particular measure offends a sectional interest and provokes vociferous opposition. Redrawing boundaries according to some criterion of efficiency is regarded as a technocratic exercise, and one of the reasons for the alienation of British opinion from local government has been excessive concentration on this form of argument.

European Regional Reform

As Yves Mény writes, 'In Italy, France and Spain, the regional question has been on the political agenda almost without interruption since the Second World War, albeit in very different forms.'[20] Regionalism ceased to be associated with political reaction and became linked with ideas of reform of the state and economic modernization. The detail of territorial reform in western Europe is extremely complex because of the diversity of territorial units used for different purposes. But one driving force behind administrative reform and territorial reorganization was changes in transport and communications technology which have opened up new possibilities in providing public services. The post-1945 reforms of territorial organization were influenced by urbanization and industrial location, occasioned by a long period of economic growth.

France, Spain and Italy attempted to reform a centralized 'Napoleonic' state. In all three, local government was, as British local government is now, severely constrained by central guidelines concerning local services; providers of these services had the role of agents, or were under the tutelage of central government. Moreover, they could not usually acquire strategic control over decisions because the area of their competence was too small. The system was inefficient in a period of rapid economic change and it had insoluable informational and decision-making problems when detailed policies were required concerning matters such as land use, infrastructure development and local economic planning. In all three systems central government was, or came to be regarded as, oppressive for contrasting reasons. In France, excessive centralization had resulted, so it was argued, in a dynamic capital and a provincial desert; in Spain a dictatorship had ruthlessly and wrongly suppressed regional authorities as dangerous for the unity of the country; in Italy, central government was considered ineffectual, bureaucratic and corrupt, whereas local government (in the north) was regarded as being relatively efficient and honest.

France

When, in the 1950s, moves towards territorial reorganization commenced in France, they were partly inspired by a wish to bring some order into the central goverment field services and partly by considerations concerning economic development. Many central government services used a regional level of organization but their boundaries did not coincide, leading to problems of administrative and policy coordination. The imbalance between a prosperous and congested capital, and economic backwardness and depopulation in many parts of provincial France was thought to be the result of the drawing off of talent from the provinces to the capital. Reactionary nostalgia played some part in supporting regionalism – its earliest and most eloquent propagandist, Jean-François Gravier, had a neo-monarchist and Vichyite past – but the measures introduced were essentially technocratic. Some regions, however, retained a distinctive regional identity. For example, despite the fact that 'Brittany has neither physical, human, linguistic nor economic unity',[21] the region retained an identity strong enough to be the basis of mobilization of a coalition of interests, particularly through the Comité d'Études et de Liaison des Intérêts Bretons (CELIB) in the post-1945 period.

The move towards greater regionalization in France began in 1956 and resumed in 1965, when regional Economic Development Councils were put in place. The socialist government elected in 1981 took up the issue of regional reform in the loi Defferre of 1982, which instituted directly elected regional assemblies with a degree of financial autonomy. Another initiative, the Joxe bill, espousing the principle of subsidiarity and published on 1 August 1990, marked a decisive break with the deeply entrenched tradition of Jacobin centralization in France. It stated that central government should only be charged with those tasks 'having a national character' and whose 'execution cannot be delegated to a territorial level'. A framework for inter-regional communities involving a maximum of three regions[22] for the purposes of regional development was established and the territorial collectivities could enter into agreements with local and regional governments in other countries, within the limits of their competences. The regions, at least at the level of principle, became autonomous entities for certain purposes; the central authorities of the state had divested themselves of some powers which could thereafter be exercised at a lower level.

Spain

The relationship between central authority and provincial societies in Spain is in marked contrast to that in France, a difference which originates in the early history of state formation.[23] Spain was formed by a union of the crowns of Aragon and Castile and by the reconquest by Christian forces starting from the remote north, rolling back, then finally driving the Moors out of the southernmost region of Andalusia. Catalonia had a prosperous independent existence before becoming part of Spain. Regional societies were not fully integrated because of a range of factors – ineffective central government, very different rates of economic development and a topography which made communications difficult. Throughout most of the nineteenth and twentieth centuries, the unity of the country was considered to be at risk and there were bitter differences of view about how Spain could best be preserved, through either federalism or centralization.

National unity was one of the issues over which the civil war (1936–9) was fought. Franco and the nationalists alleged that the country was in danger of disintegration under the republican regime, especially after autonomy had been granted to Catalonia and the Basque provinces – a Basque republic had a brief existence (1936–7). When the nationalist forces were victorious in 1939, Franco imposed rigid centralized rule and harshly repressed the Basque and Catalan languages. On Franco's death in 1975 the demand for autonomy was renewed. The former government of Catalonia, the *Generalidad,* in office in 1939, was restored in 1977. The 1978 Constitution provided the framework for the development of a semi-federal state. The Constitution was vague on the limits of the autonomy which could be granted to the regions but the right of secession was not included.[24] Four regions, Andalusia, the Basque Country, Catalonia and Galicia, for historical, cultural and political reasons, took a fast route to autonomy, with the other thirteen taking a slow route, leaving them, at least until the financial reforms of 1993, with significantly less power. Some of these other regions, like Rioja, had a certain economic unity but others – Castilla-la-Mancha, Castilla-Léon, Cantabria and Madrid – were arbitrary territorial entities. However, the conferring of genuine political authority seems to be generating new regional identities.

Disparities remain between the four leading autonomous regions and the thirteen others in sensitive fields such as taxation, policing and use of regional languages. In the thirteen regions, there was at first little demand for autonomy; they did not always use the modest powers which they were granted. However, by 1991 all the regions were demanding more power and more money from the central government. Politicians of all major political parties realized both that a strong political base could be built in the regions and that they had a socialist government willing to expend large sums in order to buy internal peace and tranquillity.

Italy

Italy has similarities with Spain; in both countries some regions retained a high level of distinctiveness, others manifested little desire for devolved powers and some were poorly integrated into national economic and political life. The 1947 Constitution of the Italian Republic provided the framework for devolution of power to the regions to break with the authoritarian Fascist past. Initially, however, only four out of the five peripheral, so-called 'special', regions in which there were considerable 'non-Italian' features were established – these were the two large islands of Sicily and Sardinia, the formerly French-speaking region of the Valle d'Aosta, over which there had been the possibility of a territorial claim by France in 1944–5, the Trentino–Alto Adige (see chapter 2), and Friuli–Venezia–Giulia, with Friulan and Slovene minorities. By giving them control over some aspects of their own affairs, it was hoped to bind them more closely into the Italian political framework – also, particularly in the case of the German- and French-speaking minorities, to persuade international opinion of the good intentions of the new regime.

In the two years following the 1970 establishment of the ordinary regions, an initial transfer of power and personnel from the centre to the regions took place. A new coalition of opposition parties of the left, with elements of the ruling Christian Democratic Party, pressed for further regionalization. The coalition built on the realization that the newly established regions could be the source of genuine political power. In 1973–8 the mobilization of this regionalist front led to a marked expansion of the competences of both regional and local government. The arguments used were technocratic, economic and democratic – the first was mainly concerned with land-use planning, the second was based on the contention that new regional structures would lead to more regional economic development and better regional balance, and the third was that strong regions would allow more participation by citizens in decisions which affected them.[25]

A *de facto* federalism, still in embryonic form, is developing at different speeds in France, Italy and Spain. The general European environment favouring regional initiatives, and sometimes specific transfrontier factors, influences this trend. The frontier regions of France experience pressure from neighbouring countries, notably Alsace, where proposals have been made to amalgamate the two *départements* of the Bas Rhin and the Haut Rhin to produce a coherent and strong regional tier with equivalent autonomy of action to the *Land* of Baden-Württemberg across the Rhine and the Swiss canton of Basel Stadt. But central government dominance remains strong in France because of the persistence of a centralizing republican political tradition and mentality. Already, the financial autonomy acquired by the Spanish and Italian regions inhibits effective central government intervention in regional policies. But financial autonomy is not the only factor – the more the regional level is used for implementing labour market, education and training, internal security and social policies, the more the regions are able to impose their own priorities. One factor driving federalization is a reluctance of the rich regions to carry the 'burden' of subsidies for poorer regions. However, even in Italy, despite the 1994 electoral successes of the Northern League, this revolt is unlikely to be carried to the ultimate limit – that of secession of the rich regions.

The United Kingdom Debate

The unsuccessful movement to set up regional authorities in England and Wales is, at least at the level of theoretical debate, as instructive as the successful establishment of regional governments in other west European countries. The debate, begun in the immediate post-Second World War period, continued for more than thirty years, mainly focusing on how large conurbations should be governed and, more briefly, on the requirements of land-use planning and economic development. Arguments about the government of conurbations are very similar to those about the government of regions in general.

The history of practical reforms of units of government below the national level is, however, one of false starts. The short-lived Local Government Commission (1945–7) addressed the question of city government but was dissolved because it overstepped its powers. The Local Government Commission set up by an Act of 1958 led to some reorganization of local government areas, but it was abolished in 1967 before it had finished its work. In the meantime Regional Economic Planning Councils, on the French model, had been set up in the early 1960s. Partly because of the French example, the stage was set for a comprehensive regional reform when the Royal Commission on Local Government in England and Wales (1966–9) was appointed. The report was comprehensive in its coverage of issues and gave an unusual amount of consideration to the size of regions. But its recommendations were rejected and its impact was negligible.[26]

The starting-point of the Royal Commission was that local government must provide services efficiently, attract the interest of the public, be sufficiently strong to relate effectively to central government and be able to adapt to changing patterns of everyday life. Attention was then turned to the question of the size of authority which would enable these objectives to be met. The Commission's view was that the basic unit should be a city-region centred on a large town and including the allegedly interdependent surrounding communities. The government of this territorial unit should be responsible for environmental services (economic and land-use planning, transportation and public protection). Personal services (housing, education and the social services) had, the Commission argued, specific population requirements. The population had to be above a certain threshold (estimated at a quarter of a million) to maintain the necessary technical, financial and staff resources and below another threshold (estimated at a million) in order to ensure a proximity to users and to citizens. Splitting local government into two levels leads occasionally to overlapping or poorly coordinated functions but it was, in the thinking of the Commission, a necessary compromise. The main recommendation of the Commission was that most of the country should have single-tier regional authorities while the largest conurbations should have two tiers. On the drawing of boundaries the Commission again proposed a compromise between the requirements of economic and social geography and respect for historic boundaries. A minority report by one commissioner, Derek Senior, suggested that the Commission paid insufficient attention to social and economic geography; on the basis of evidence collected in this area, he proposed thirty-five city-regions.

The Conservative government, elected in 1970, rejected the idea of regions in England and Wales, but not in Scotland where, in 1974–5, regions were set up. The government maintained two-tier local government and respected, where it could, historic boundaries of the counties of England. A handful of new counties were established and six metropolitan counties were introduced for the major conurbations. The detail of these reforms is of transitory interest, since the metropolitan counties were swept away in 1986, along with the regional government of the capital, the Greater London Council; Scottish regions were abolished in 1995. The Conservatives showed an active commitment to overhauling the system every few years both in terms of local government functions and of the boundaries of those governments. There is no evidence that these changes have produced financial savings or an improvement in the delivery of services.

These two tendencies, frequent radical change in territorial organization and rejection of regional government, distinguish the United Kingdom from the rest of western Europe.[27] Even with radical change in the powers of regional governments in France, Italy and Spain, territorial boundaries have been respected. In these three countries there has been limited controversy over the drawing of regional boundaries. Some Bretons, for example, were opposed to the exclusion of the *département* of Loire Atlantique from the Brittany region but boundaries have changed little. The problem is to explain why there has been a particular, steady development of policy in these three countries and oscillation of policy in Britain.

Broad historical and cultural factors are involved in this 'British exception,' but three political factors are the immediate causes of it. First, the Conservatives were unwilling to see their opponents in charge, on a continuing basis, of an influential layer of government. Second, the subordinate position of local government, lacking any constitutional protection either in law or traditional practice, and relying on central government grants for about half of its expenditure, made impossible any protracted resistance by local government to central government plans for reorganization. Third, tight party organization and discipline prevented the growth of the local electoral 'fiefdoms' dominated by strong local notables, which characterize the political structures of many other European countries. Local power bases of national political figures, absent from politics in the United Kingdom, are a countervailing force to the unilateral imposition of central government dictates.

Transfrontier Cooperation and the Erosion of the
International Frontier

The international frontier is still regarded as different in kind from intra-state boundaries in that the former is the limit of a sovereign jurisdiction whereas the latter is merely the limit of a subordinate jurisdiction. But the exercise of sovereignty, in practice, varies; sovereignty does not have the same meaning and significance for all states throughout the world. The states of the European Union have lost their legal autonomy to act in economic and social matters and they have, therefore, become in some respects more like governments below the state level, since both are restricted in law and in practice by a higher level. Also, regional and local governments have become actors in the international system, which conflicts with the doctrine of sovereignty in its pure form, in which external relations are a monopoly of the state.

The last two major revisions of the Rome Treaty, the 1985 Single European Act and the 1991 Treaty of European Political Union enhanced the position of the regions as an important political layer in a more integrated Europe. The EU promoted inter-regional networking,[28] advancing arguments that strong regional structures promote democratic participation, economic development and administrative efficiency, and help to promote European integration by eroding the importance of frontiers between states. The development of European citizenship rights,[29] including the right of resident non-nationals to vote in local (and European) elections, the direct application of European law to the environmental and social services provided by regional and local authorities, direct contacts with the Commission, since 1975, through the European Fund for Regional Development (FEDER), all helped to give a European dimension to their activities. Organized lobbying developed, including the maintenance of permanent offices in Brussels; the local authorities initiated the Consultative Council of Local and Regional Governments of the EC member States, various more specialized associations were founded for frontier regions, mountain regions, peripheral and maritime regions (CPMRE), and in 1979 these were grouped in the Bureau of Liaison of Organizations of Regions of Europe (BLORE). The representation of local authorities through the Council of the Regions established after the Maastricht Treaty and through the consultative committees of the European Union all helped to erode the previously clear distinction between the national and sub-national levels of government.

Regular cooperation between local and regional governments straddles state frontiers within the EU and frontiers between the EU and its neighbours, particularly Switzerland, Austria (now a member of the EU), Slovenia, Croatia, Poland and Hungary.[30] Transfrontier associations of regional and local authorities have been promoted by the Council of Europe, which has sponsored a model agreement to regulate relations between members.[31] Transfrontier relations between local and regional governments predate the Maastricht Treaty by forty years. The first forms of transfrontier cooperation between local governments across the Rhine originated in the early 1950s as part of a movement for Franco-German reconciliation. In the early 1960s the focus changed to overcoming difficulties created by the international frontier for land-use planning.[32] For example, the requirements of the Basel economy and the lack of suitable room for expansion in Switzerland prompted the setting up of a planning office, the Regio Basiliensis, which analysed the infrastructure and labour market requirements for the wider Basel region, including southern Alsace in France and the south-west corner of Baden-Württemberg in Germany.[33] Co-operation between frontier towns (Strasbourg–Kehl, Mulhouse–Freiburg) also became well established. Eventually two official forums for transfrontier cooperation were established by an agreement reached in 1975 – a tripartite commission for the Basel region, and a bipartite commission for the Strasbourg region. These commissions discussed projects such as the upper Rhine high-speed rail link, on which work began in 1992, and a second Rhine bridge at Strasbourg. Interest in the work of these commissions increased through involvement in the EC programme, Interreg, and by the dismantling of frontier controls on the Rhine frontier.

The upper Rhine, comprising Alsace, Baden-Württemberg and Basel, is one of the most intense areas of transfrontier cooperation. It involves the universities, transport (Basel airport is in France) and the banking sector, as well as consultative committees of central and local government officials which frequently develop working parties in which private sector interests participate. Direct transfrontier investment also plays an important role. According to local Chamber of Commerce estimates, in the district of Germany immediately adjacent to the frontier as much as 80% of the direct investment is Swiss. According to the Association pour le Développement Industriel de la Région d'Alsace, there is a heavy concentration in the south of Haut Rhin in the immediate frontier area. A transfrontier labour market has developed. In the early 1990s, about 53,000 French workers commuted daily to Switzerland and Germany to work in administration and research as well as in manufacturing. In some firms transfrontier labour plays a crucial role; the Basel firm of Sandoz employs 1,700 Alsatians and 500 Germans out of a total workforce of 7,400. In tourism and leisure the great gainer from transfrontier business was the Black Forest, but Germans and Swiss are very important for the Alsatian restaurant, hotel, food and wine industries. In the 1970s, the buying into hunting syndicates in Alsace by Germans and Swiss caused considerable bad feeling,[34] demonstrating that not all intrusions across the frontier are welcome.

There are parallels to this in other regions. There has, for example, been negative reaction to the increase in Spanish investment in the French Basque Country, and to the numbers of Spanish tourists in the Pyrenées Atlantiques. The Chamber of Commerce in Bayonne stated that in 1991 over forty firms in the town had Spanish capital in them. The greater entrepreneurial dynamism on the Spanish side of the frontier created some fears of domination of areas of French territory close to the frontier. On the other hand, French Basque nationalists and others objected to the growing number of tourists across the frontier on the grounds that this was distorting the regional economy and making it excessively dependent on the fragile base of tourism.[35] Frontier towns such as Hendaye in the south-west corner of France and Irun, the Spanish town immediately across the frontier, were very heavily orientated towards activities which entirely depended on the frontier – transport services, customs, police, goods not easily available or differentially priced across the frontier.[36]

The immediate impact on the two towns was negative but the longer-term perspective was considered more favourable because the frontier, as a barrier to cooperation, disappeared and relations between the two municipalities became close. François Jacqué, the president of the Chamber of Commerce of Bayonne, said: 'Hendaye, Irun, Fontarabia should become the unified centre of a conurbation which stretches from Bayonne to San Sebastian. It is the only way of being on equal terms with the great European metropoles.'[37] On the Italian–French frontier similar views have been expressed. After the establishment of the consultative group[38] Alpazur on the Franco-Italian frontier little happened (with the exception of the establishment of the Mercantour transfrontier natural park) until the approach of '1992'. Menton and Ventimiglia signed a protocol in April 1991 establishing cooperative ventures. By 1993, a number were under way, including a university institute in medical biotechnology, a joint industrial zone, a waste disposal plant and a master plan for urban development covering both municipalities.[39]

Some transfrontier institutions have enjoyed, for limited periods, considerable political influence. Examples are ARGEALP for the Alpine region, stretching from Tirol and Bavaria in the north to Lombardy in the south and Croatia in the east, and including the Swiss canton of Graubünden, and Euregio on the Dutch-German frontier. But most are struggling for national as well as European Union recognition. An example is the Community of the Pyrenees, which brings together three French regions, Aquitaine, Midi-Pyrenées and Languedoc–Roussillon, and four autonomous Spanish regions, the Basque Country, Navarre, Aragon, Catalonia with the Principality of Andorra. It has conducted campaigns for the extension of the French high-speed railway system through both ends of the Pyrenees and it claims paternity of the controversial tunnels of Puymorens and Somport. But, apart from a few university exchanges, seminars and some tourist brochures, little can be directly attributed to it. It attempted to become the coordinator of projects for the EC Interreg programme but, of seventeen proposals made by the Community of the Pyrenees, none was accepted by the French government for transmission to the EC.[40]

The position of transfrontier workers was the focus of particular interest in the 1970s. Transfrontier commuting was of considerable proportions where dynamic centres of activity such as Baden-Württemberg, Basel or Geneva were located close to a frontier.[41] In the stagnating conditions of the late 1980s and early 1990s, this topic was submerged by more pressing matters but it returned to prominence in the 1990s. An influential report under the direction of André Vernier was published in 1993 under the auspices of the French Confédération Française des Travailleurs Chrétiens on land-use planning in frontier regions.[42] After comparing economic and administrative structures in the frontier regions of France and her neighbours, the report analysed the agreements on the status of frontier workers and the tax regimes which applied to them. These revealed inequitable situations and perverse effects which distorted the labour market. The three most important recommendations of the report were: a redrawing of the boundaries of the communes to create administrative territories of similar dimensions to those found in Belgium and Germany; the setting up of task forces for the frontier regions between the Meuse and Haute-Savoie, with financial authority for defined areas of expenditure; and a European Social Security Card in order to do away with the 'infernal' formalities required by local and national administrations.

Activities on the territory of one state often create nuisance or harm in another state; a contentious example is the pollution of the Rhine by the potash mines of Alsace. In 1976, the states bordering the Rhine reached an agreement to permit the French to find a solution to the problem of saline waste other than dumping it in the Rhine. The Netherlands, the Federal Republic of Germany and Luxembourg ratified the agreement and eventually (in 1983), after one failed attempt, France also ratified. The original agreement envisaged a subsidy to the mining company, 34% paid by the Netherlands,[43] 30% by Germany, 30% by France and 6% by Switzerland so that the saline waste could be dumped in disused mines in Alsace and Lorraine. The mayors of the communes of regions affected rebelled on the grounds of damage to the water table. French governments felt unable to confront this opposition. In 1986, nine years after the first Dutch payment, the French minister of the environment gave details of a French plan for tackling the problem to be put into effect in the following two years. It envisaged a progressive slowing of the rate of dumping of salt in the Rhine until it ceased completely when, in 2004, the mines were closed. The plan included the continuation of a much reduced flow of waste matter into the Rhine with dry storage of salt in flat piles not higher than 20 metres and some dumping in the North Sea.

Many other issues of transfrontier pollution remain. Although the EU has developed an environmental policy with relatively high standards, particularly for water pollution, the difficulty of access across member-state frontiers to legal redress for harm is one of the weaknesses of the integration process. Transfrontier cooperation between local and regional authorities can help to reduce the number of incidents of transfrontier pollution but they can overcome neither the problem of different legal systems and regulatory regimes nor the clash of major national interests such as the siting of nuclear power stations. One example is the French Cattenom station to which Luxembourg and the German frontier regions took strong exception. The influence of transfrontier coalitions, even when backed by one central government, is clearly limited.[44] For the most part governments resist arguments about transfrontier harm resulting from nuclear installations and systematically contest the evidence on transfrontier air pollution. Without the cooperation of governments effective remedies will either not be available or will take a long time to enforce.

Transfrontier consultative institutions were established to resolve the practical difficulties encountered by people affected by the frontier, to develop good neighbourly relations between people, to obtain remedies for harm and to gain information about decisions and developments which may affect the material interests of neighbouring regions. In some cases a relationship of dependence of one region on the activities, or the economic power of a region on the other side of the frontier, makes the dependent region seek access to the decision-making processes of the stronger region. The dormitory towns in France, for example, are in this dependent relationship with the Swiss cities of Basel and Geneva; most regions in the Alpine arc in Switzerland and Austria, which have small populations, are exposed to overwhelming economic and social influences from densely populated and highly industrialized regions in the surrounding plains of Lombardy, Bavaria and Rhône–Alpes.[45] With increasing openness of frontiers, the political conflicts which these imbalances engender will be difficult to manage in the absence of a constitutional framework regulating inter-regional relationships.

Conclusion

The aspiration of Denis de Rougemont for a 'Europe of the Regions'[46] with the dissolving of the nation-state and the strengthening of European institutions seems unlikely, although the regional tier of government is becoming more important in Europe. *De facto* federalism within European unitary countries is likely to emerge, perhaps even in the United Kingdom. Such federalism will allow regional governments to develop the access to the European institutions which is already available to them. The more densely populated regions with a strong sense of identity, coupled with entrepreneurial leadership, will have considerable advantages in the more open and fluid politics which are developing within the European Union. The obvious examples are Bavaria, Lombardy and Catalonia; Bavaria has a larger population and a stronger industrial base than half the member states of the European Union. The old regions may be joined by newer ones with strong elites such as Rhône-Alpes and North Rhine-Westphalia. These regions will take on the characteristics of mini-states with whom central governments will form negotiating partnerships. Regionalization may not be helpful for weaker regions, even with European Union programmes to help them, unless they can form alliances and associate with others in 'regional communities'. Sparsely populated and maritime regions, through, *inter alia*, the Committee for Peripheral Maritime Regions (CPMRE), are developing in this direction.

Those states of the European Union with a strong regional level of government are likely to maintain the stability of internal boundaries. The exceptional case is the United Kingdom, which does not have this strong regional level and which is proceeding to dismantle the Scottish regions and English counties in favour of smaller single-tier local authorities. The absence of regional authorities which can negotiate with the European Commission or be democratically represented in the Council of the Regions means that all business has to be channelled through agencies controlled by central government. This is unlikely to be a sustainable position in the long run, if the EU institutions maintain or increase their authority.

In the rest of the EU the distinction between the international boundary and other kinds of political/administrative boundaries no longer has the clarity which it possessed in the immediate post-Second

World War period. The growing number of transactions between regional and local governments is not unique but it is more advanced in Europe than elsewhere.[47] Similar initiatives have been taking place in other continents, including Africa,[48] North America and South America. Among the many examples, the June 1963 Treaty of Caracas between Venezuela and Colombia set up three institutions for transfrontier cooperation on the Colombian–Venezuelan border. A 1966 Colombia –Ecuador accord set up a similar array of institutions; a lighter structure was put in place by an agreement of July 1971 between Ecuador and Peru.[49] The United States–Mexico frontier region is developing intense transfrontier cooperation; a population with distinctive characteristics is emerging in this region with interests, cultural characteristics and outlook which differ from those of the populations of the heartlands of the two countries, with complex patterns of transfrontier interaction.[50] On the United States–Canada border a transfrontier economic region, encouraged by the signing of the agreement on the North American Free Trade Area, is emerging between Seattle/Everett and Vancouver. The examples could be multiplied.

Frontiers, whether they be international or sub-state boundaries, are the outcome of political processes, the clash and compromise between values and interests. However, within the European Union, there are now pressures to arrive at more coherent frontier region policies. Also, the connection between internal boundaries and external frontiers is becoming more explicit as the external frontier of the EU has to serve purposes which were previously under exclusive state control; frontiers between the member states are being dismantled for certain purposes, and some policy areas and the local and regional governments are more and more involved in transfrontier and European Union affairs. The frontiers between member states of the EU, however, remain the limit for most purposes of judicial systems, police powers and administrative and executive authority, as well as of the patriotic loyalties of citizens.

5
Frontiers and Migration

Three questions are paramount in the contemporary discussion of frontiers and migration. First, do contemporary state frontiers exist primarily to control the movement of people? Second, are frontier controls effective in stopping migration? Third, whether, and to what extent, are frontiers the instruments of oppression and injustice? No simple answers can be given to these questions because the circumstances in which migration takes place vary very widely. The purpose of this chapter is, therefore, to review some of the arguments relating to these questions and to summarize some of the varying circumstances in which contemporary migration takes place.

To exclude or to accept immigrants raises fundamental philosophical issues about the relationship of the individual to the state.[1] According to one basic position of principle, membership of a state, now usually called citizenship, is a primary good and those in possession of it rightly control entry to this club. Citizenship is a primary good in that some degree of closure is necessary for a state to preserve local identities, cultures and most stable features of human life. Citizens have the right and duty to control entry because uncontrolled entry would make it impossible to deal justly with individuals, valuable cultural characteristics of the group would be eroded and stable institutions would be impossible. The 'nation-state', although admittedly never ethnically homogeneous, is the best defence of these values because, so it is argued, there is no viable alternative to it.

A distinguished exponent of this view, Michael Walzer, takes a strict view of how states should treat immigrants. He suggests that a state which admits migrants, because it needs their labour, should grant them full citizenship on the grounds that 'Men and women are either subject to the full force of the State's authority or they are not, and if they are subject they must be given a say and, ultimately, an equal say, in what that authority does.'[2] Walzer's position accords with American historical experience as a country built on immigration and, therefore, with a different construction of cultural identity to that of European countries or, to take a more extreme case, Japan. If the trend towards an increasingly integrated global economy persists, admitting only those individuals to whom it is intended to give citizenship may result in a rigidity in the labour market which is to no one's advantage.

A second position, defended by Elsa M. Chaney, is that, although states have the right to set admissions policy (and *de facto* they obviously have the power to do so), there are fundamental moral obligations to the migrants, both on the part of the sending countries and of the receiving countries. These obligations ought to be recognized and, if possible, enforced by international treaties to ensure proper treatment of migrants.[3] In an implicit extension of this view, Thomas Pogge argues that sovereignty can be divided vertically and some decisions be authoritatively made at a global level, others at the regional, others at the state and still others at the sub-state level.[4] It would be complicated and confusing for all these levels to have an equally important role in formulating policies on migration, but authorities at all of them clearly have something to contribute. There is no compelling reason why the state should be the sole arbiter of immigration, and some matters may be regulated by international organization. In practice, states are losing their ability to control the problems which migration causes.

A third, and truly cosmopolitan, view is that our obligations extend to the limit of the effects of our actions; in an interdependent world with rapid communications and an integrated world economy, these effects extend over the entire planet.[5] The implication of this position is that states should not refuse entry to migrants if, as a consequence, migrants would suffer harm. Economic migrants, seeking to escape penury and hunger, should be admitted by rich countries, as well as those suffering persecution for religious, political or ethnic reasons. To exclude people in desperate need because they originate from across an arbitrarily delimited frontier is to deny them justice.

The implications of the first position are that citizens have a right to bar immigrants; they should be careful about admissions policy because once immigrants are established in a country they must be given full citizenship. This position has a narrow, xenophobic version if, as the Japanese have believed, the requirement of preserving a culture is the total exclusion of persons belonging to other ethnic groups. But an open version, proposed by Daniel Cohn-Bendit,[6] the head of the Department of Multicultural Affairs for the city of Frankfurt, in his jointly authored book *Heimat Babylon*,[7] is that immigration enhances diversity and enriches societies. In an argument which is not necessarily related, he suggests that immigration policy be removed from the member states to the European Union, now the only authority in Europe capable of formulating and enforcing a coherent immigration policy.[8] He seeks to replace the homeland of the homogeneous nation-state with a cosmopolitan Europe.

The second position is accepted, at the level of principle, by governments of the highly industrialized countries. However, governments prefer to regard undertakings in international agreements on refugees, asylum-seekers and migrant labourers as norms which can be ignored if they are, in certain circumstances, not in the 'national interest'. No government, and only small minorities of citizens, in the European Union accept the third position of allowing entry for those who would suffer harm if entry were denied them. The consequences of adopting the third position are wholly unpredictable. Although a headlong rush from the poor to the rich countries might not, for reasons of cultural difference, take place, it is inconceivable that rich countries would take the risk of this happening. Most citizens of these countries would regard the adoption of such a policy as an act of foolhardy irresponsibility. The widely held image of immigrants as poor and needy is a major block to obtaining the acquiescence of west European electorates to such a policy.

Entry and Exit Controls

In the contemporary world, the ability to control frontier crossings is universally regarded as an essential attribute of sovereignty and the right to refuse entry to aliens is a stable principle of international law. The exclusion of would-be immigrants (or the prevention of emigration) is sometimes regarded as a central function of frontiers and at other times may be subordinated to other objectives such as economic development or national security; controls may concern only the passage across the frontier of certain categories of persons such as criminals and those who are considered a threat to rulers, or there may be a stringent control on everyone who wishes to leave or to enter a territory. Beliefs, prejudices, contingencies and calculations of interest determine the way in which governments use frontier controls.

Checking every individual who crosses a frontier is formidably difficult but it has been attempted at frontiers, and even internal borders, by authoritarian regimes such as tsarist and Communist

Russia.[9] In the period of liberal optimism after the collapse of Communist governments, a greater freedom of movement across international frontiers appeared certain to many. But there is little basis for this optimism. Frontier controls of persons are likely to affect increasing numbers of people because these controls, in Zolberg's words, 'serve to maintain global inequality',[10] in a world of rapidly increasing populations. In the past, the rate of global population increase has regularly been underestimated, but the current consensus, despite recent signs of populations stabilizing in some countries, is that strong growth is likely in South America, Africa and Asia.[11] With the inexorable increase in population and the increasing amount of information available, more people will seek to move from the poor 'south' to the rich 'north'.

Although control of entry dominates contemporary debate, control of exit has been of historical importance. Compelling people to leave a country has been regarded as a punishment, particularly severe for peoples like the Greeks of the classical period whose personal identity was bound up with membership of a *polis*. The exile of a contemporary, such as that of the Nobel Prize-winner Alexander Solzhenitzyn from the USSR, is also considered a severe punishment; in Solzhenitzyn's case, he was cut off from cultural roots which were supremely valuable. Communist governments were the last major category of regime to exercise control over exit; the USSR exacted payment from Jews wishing to leave the country, as did the GDR from Germans, and all Communist countries either forbade or strictly controlled emigration. As late as the mid-1980s, eastern bloc countries had tight control over emigration with the exceptions of Poland and Hungary, which exercised partial and limited controls.[12]

Although Nikita Khrushchev, after he lost office, came to have doubts about 'fencing people in',[13] the control of exit was justified by Communist regimes on the grounds that contribution to the collective good was supremely important. In Marxist theory, the objective interests of the proletariat and the promotion of world revolution took precedence over the rights of the individual; those who wished to emigrate were often designated enemies of the proletariat, and enemies of the proletariat were not regarded as having rights. The consequence of this Communist view was intensively policed frontiers. The Soviet Union invested heavily in border controls, promulgated elaborate legislation about the border[14] and punished attempts to escape to capitalist countries with the death penalty. The German Democratic Republic erected what has been described as 'the most inhumane border in the world'[15] to prevent its citizens escaping to West Germany. The Communist position was regarded, in the rich western countries, as repugnant, at least in principle. The issue of poor countries attempting to limit emigration of those with professional and technical skills in order to prevent loss of human capital is easier to justify in terms of the costs of investment in education rather than in terms of political ideology.

The Basis of the Freedom of Movement

In the liberal tradition, emigration has been regarded as a basic freedom, and a 'natural' or fundamental right. In the seventeenth century Samuel Pufendorf, while rejecting the right of individuals to secede from polities, upheld their right to emigrate from them. Since Pufendorf, all liberal theorists have supported the freedom of exit from, if not of entry to, state territory. Pufendorf added an important proviso which, in practice, has been accepted by liberal governments; he considered that the right to emigrate could be withheld at the discretion of the ruler.[16]

For John Locke and his liberal successors, since government was based on the consent of the governed, the most peaceful way of withdrawing consent from rulers was to leave the territory which they governed. Locke assumed that the act of leaving was a legitimate option for the dissatisfied. Indeed, it may be suggested that the whole of Locke's political philosophy rested on the availability of empty lands into which people could move. He suggested that people acquired property by mixing their labour with natural resources, and that they entered civil society in order to preserve their liberty and property. If they emigrated they would lose property and therefore must have the opportunity of reacquiring it. The existence of America was essential to the imagining of Locke's system.

A difficulty with Locke's position is that those regimes which Lockean liberals find most objectionable are the ones most likely to prevent exit as a form of withdrawal of consent. Albert Hirschman argues that authoritarian states cannot tolerate the right to emigrate; they are compelled to repress attempts both to change the system from inside *and* the right to leave if change is not accepted.[17] Hirschman's observation seems empirically correct, although authoritarian regimes have shown an inclination to allow emigration to those who can find money to pay for exit visas. However, from Locke's death in 1704 until the First World War, emigration, provided transport could be found, was easy. It was indeed encouraged by governments, including the British government,[18] who saw it as a way of removing indigent and trouble-some populations. For many, it was a genuinely 'liberal' exit in that migrants were escaping from oppressive European political and social systems to the freer society of North America. The great movement of

people in the nineteenth century across the Atlantic, and their subsequent prosperity, linked emigration with emancipation in the popular
mind.

Freedom of movement was eventually included in international
covenants. The liberal belief is stated in its simplest form in Article 13
(2) of the Universal Declaration of Human Rights: 'Everyone has the
right to leave any country, including his own, and return to his own
country.' The major difficulty, both in principle and in practice, is that
the right of governments to restrict access to their territories has never
been contested. A right of exit is empty if there is nowhere for the
migrant to go. The United Nations High Commission for Refugees
(UNHCR) constantly confronts this problem when trying to find
receiving countries for displaced persons and the response of the rich
countries is evasive. Within these countries the liberal debate has
tended to shift away from the desirability of accepting all victims of
oppression towards how immigrants, once accepted into a country,
should be treated. International agreements exist on treatment of
refugees, asylum-seekers and immigrant workers, but conforming with
these is voluntary[19] – no authority can punish a state which does not
comply with them.

The Characteristics of International Migration

Although anti-immigrant governments and political movements in
contemporary Europe propagate an image of international migration as
deviant and aberrant, human beings throughout history have been
highly mobile. Even in prehistory, before the rise of literate civilizations,
in the Mesolithic and Neolithic periods, there is evidence of migrations
over vast distances. When changing technologies led to the development
of agriculture and the growth of the first urban settlements, more stable
patterns of human settlement resulted. But lack of adequate food
supplies, fear of pestilence, the prospect of a better life elsewhere and
population pressures on existing resources remained great driving forces
behind population movements.

In historical times migration could still take the form of movement of
people into previously empty spaces, although the most desirable
territory was increasingly occupied. By the end of the nineteenth
century, no uncolonized habitable land was left. Even before then,
European emigration mainly involved moving into already occupied
territory. Settlers, in an argument first made by Hobbes in the seventeenth century, were thought to have a 'right' to develop land and
resources if they were under-utilized by the original inhabitants. In the

middle of the twentieth century, some Israeli arguments ('making the desert bloom') come close to this colonialist view. Quebecois arguments concerning hydro-electric development in territories recognized as the traditional hunting grounds of the Cree Indians are similar. There are many other examples, but these arguments are, in the late twentieth century, unlike the seventeenth century when Hobbes was writing, almost invariably contested by the indigenous inhabitants.

Population movements across the surface of the globe have been complex and are well described elsewhere.[20] In Europe, the largest movements of population, between the fall of the Roman empire and the sixteenth century, were the result either of conquest and the displacement of populations through military action, or population pressures compounded by natural disasters such as famine and plague. From the sixteenth century, the technological advantage and military superiority of the European powers allowed the development of global empires. The imperial expansion of Europe took place against the background of the turmoil of the religious and trade wars of the sixteenth and seventeenth centuries, which initiated a seemingly permanent struggle for power and influence between the European states. Behind the struggle for mastery in eighteenth- and nineteenth-century Europe lay a rapid increase of population. Urbanization, industrialization, growing requirements for food supplies and the extension of the market economy transformed European society.[21]

The states of the Atlantic seaboard – Britain, France, Spain, Portugal and the Netherlands – acquired empires by using sea power; the Russians conquered lands to the south and east of their original heartland of the Duchy of Muscovy. This 'expansion of Europe' was accompanied by large-scale migration. In the period 1821–50, migrants from Europe to other parts of the world averaged 110,000 a year, increasing to 900,000 a year from 1881 to 1915. By the second half of the nineteenth century no major European state, with the exception of Russia, controlled migration. Mass migration also took place within Europe, often within states, from the rural to urban areas. The 'internal' migration was an essential part of building the modern, highly integrated nations of Europe. The decline or disappearance of particularist local societies with their own dialects, and sometimes their own languages, accompanied this rural emigration.

In the first half of the twentieth century war and changes in frontiers, remained the central causes of migration and population change. Between 1914 and 1921 European Russia lost a third of its population as a result of casualties in the First World War, revolution, frontier changes, famine and disease. Others were affected on a similar scale, such as the 1,250,000 Greeks and 400,000 Turks who were obliged, by the terms of the 1923 Treaty of Lausanne, to migrate from their place of birth to their respective mother countries as a consequence of the newly drawn frontiers. Forcible transfer of populations and redrawing of boundaries was, after the Nazi accession to power in 1933, a major aim of German policy. Under the slogan of *Heim ins Reich,* the Nazis concluded a series of eleven agreements between 1939 and 1943 with eastern European countries to repatriate ethnic Germans to Germany or to establish them in newly annexed territories.[22] Nazi policies of expansion to the east and massacres of Slavic people brought speedy retribution. In 1944–6, 10 to 12 million Germans were driven out of the eastern territories – Brandenburg, Pomerania, Silesia, East Prussia, the Memel territory and scattered pockets elsewhere – which had been occupied by Germans, often for many centuries.

After the Second World War, a modest increase in the populations of the highly industrialized countries was accompanied by relatively little migration between them. Displacement of populations, involving large numbers of people, through military action, political persecution, lack of the means of subsistence or a combination of these factors, remained a common phenomenon in the less developed world. In the second half of the twentieth century, the preferred destinations of emigrants escaping poverty and persecution in the less developed world were Canada and the United States, the countries of the European Communities and the oil-rich Gulf states – but there have been many others, particularly for temporary migrant labour, in Africa and South America (at one point there were up to 2 million Colombian illegal immigrants in Venezuela despite the avowed opposition of both governments to this migration). All booming economies since 1950, excepting Japan,[23] have attracted significant numbers of migrants, with the flow being stemmed during periods of economic downturn. Frontiers quickly close against immigrants when there is no demand for their labour. Since the first oil shock of 1973 the west European countries have moved towards tight control of immigration,[24] although the United States and, to a lesser extent, Canada continued to receive large numbers.

Immigrants from poor countries are often desperate to gain entry to the rich countries to escape intolerable social and economic conditions in their own countries. Their persistence in trying to gain entry, despite the obstacles put in their way, is evident in both Europe and North America. At the El Paso and San Diego sections of the United States–Mexico frontier would-be immigrants will try again, and again, when caught trying to cross illegally. European Union countries have virtually banned immigration and have made their frontier controls more effective; the criminal activity of smuggling illegal immigrants into the European Union, particularly via the southern European countries, has grown in the 1990s. Tolerance or rejection of immigrants has depended on a wide variety of factors, including economic conditions, size of the influx, availability of unutilized resources, demand for labour, cultural proximity of the host community and the immigrant group, and historical patterns of immigration and emigration, to mention only the most obvious.

Immigration Regimes: Similar and Contrasting

All European Union countries now adopt restrictive immigration policies, partly because of popular conceptions of immigrants and partly because of depressed labour-market conditions. However, it is difficult for them systematically to exclude all migrants from outside the EU and to revert to the attitude encapsulated in a Dutch administrative circular of 1938, in which all foreigners were regarded as 'undesirable aliens' and a refugee was defined as 'a foreigner who has left his country under pressure of circumstances.'[25] Apart from humanitarian assistance, the cyclical variation in European economies provides the best explanation of the rate of migration to these countries.[26] The completion of the Single European Market and freer world trade may eventually stimulate economic growth in Europe. If this is the case, immigration will be economically advantageous both to the receiving countries and to the immigrants.

A common European Union policy on entry visas, control of temporary residents, granting of citizenship and treatment of asylum-seekers and refugees which goes beyond general statements of principle is difficult to achieve. The Schengen Agreements, the Draft Convention on the External Frontier of the European Union, and the Maastricht Treaty are silent on the substance of immigration policy, merely providing a context in which one may be developed. European Union immigration policy development is hindered by the absence of a framework for considering immigration in the context of other policies – external and security policy, trade and aid policy, and internal labour market, social services and equal opportunities policies. Weakness in policy planning reflects political volatility; considerable risks are involved for the Commission of the European Union in taking an active role in this field. Challenging state sovereignty in an area in which nationalist and xenophobic movements have shown both the ability to disturb public order and make electoral gains has the potential to provoke an unmanageable conflict.

Individuals are treated in a variety of ways in the EU member states.

The belief that states should decide who is to be admitted as a resident and to citizenship, and according to what rules, is still deeply ingrained in European national parliaments and public opinion, despite strong practical pressure, caused by the free movement of citizens and the existence of rights of residence in the EU, for common European rules.[27] The scale of migration into western Europe has been charted with anxiety.[28] Evidence from surveys shows racial bias behind this anxiety since host populations systematically overestimate the numbers of coloured immigrants in their countries.[29] According to a survey of summer 1993, a majority of people in the EU, for the first time, were of the view that there were too many foreigners in their countries.[30] Apprehension about the electoral impact of immigration has been felt in virtually all west European countries (including those outside the EU), and anti-immigrant measures have been taken to counter it.

Germany

Of the larger countries, Germany, from the 1950s to the 1970s, accepted more immigrants on a temporary basis than other European countries to provide labour for its booming industries. Germany made agreements with a number of Mediterranean countries (Greece and Spain 1960, Turkey 1961 and 1964, Morocco 1963, Portugal 1964, Tunisia 1965, Yugoslavia 1968) to attract labour on a temporary contract basis. Temporary immigration, the 'guest-worker' system, did not function as intended; it was based on the assumption that mainly male immigrant workers would come to West Germany for contracts of specified length, which might be renewed once or twice, and that they would then return to their countries of origin. But immigrants were frequently joined by their families, and many children of immigrants were born in Germany.

When Germany decided to close the door on further immigration, immigrants already there remained, although they had no established right to permanent residence. The German government was reluctant, because of memories of Nazi treatment of foreign labour, to engage in mass expulsions. After the 1989 unification of Germany, Turks (with non-white asylum-seekers and Gypsies) were the target of increased racism and violence in Germany,[31] causing much introspection among liberal Germans. One target of criticism was the apparently racist assumptions underlying German immigration law which was based on *jus sanguinis*. Ethnic Germans from eastern Europe are allowed, according to Article 116 of the Basic Law, an automatic right to citizenship. The conditions of access to citizenship for non-ethnic Germans were subject to draconian restrictions – continuous residence in Germany for at least ten years, a 'positive attitude' to German culture and a knowledge of the German Constitution. These conditions were made less severe by a law passed on 1 January 1991 which applied to the children of immigrants. A major problem remained the necessity of renouncing one's previous nationality, which posed a dilemma for most Turks. Only about 10,000–12,000 non-Germans per year acquire German citizenship compared to approximately 120,000 acceding to citizenship in France.

The United Kingdom

British immigration policy has been a series of *ad hoc* responses to political pressures. The 1905 Aliens Act, restricting immigration, was passed in response to the influx of Jews from central and east Europe. This law was made more restrictive just prior to the First World War, giving the Home Secretary and the immigration service discretion to exclude any alien without having to offer an explanation. Citizens of the Commonwealth countries, colonies and dependencies were regarded, for most purposes, as subjects of the British Crown and had unrestricted right of entry and abode, and full civic rights in the United Kingdom until the Commonwealth Immigrants Act (1962). This Act was a response to the growing public hostility to non-white immigrants, but it applied indiscriminately to all Commonwealth citizens.

When, in 1968, the Ugandan dictator Idi Amin summarily expelled Asians holding British passports, legislation was passed by the UK parliament in less than a week to withdraw the right of abode of British passport-holders. Only British passport-holders resident in, or who had close connections with, the UK had the right of unrestricted entry to the UK. Subsequent legislation attempted to bring some order into citizenship and immigration rules which had been enacted piecemeal. According to the Immigration Act (1971) British passport-holders were divided into patrials and non-patrials. The category of patrial was established on a notion of proximity to the United Kingdom. To qualify, there had to be a link: either personal through, for example, adoption and naturalization, or by descent through birth and parentage. British subjects who did not fulfil any of these conditions were treated as 'other immigrants'. A major breach in the principle of giving pre-eminence to the closeness of the link between the individual and the UK was made by granting the right of abode to citizens of other European Community countries when Britain acceded in 1973 to the Treaty of Rome.

The term 'patrial', criticized because of its allegedly racist connotations, was removed from the terminology of the Immigration Act

(1981), in favour of the notion of the right of abode. British subjects were divided into three categories: first, citizens of the United Kingdom and the colonies corresponding to the patrials of the 1971 Act; second, citizens of dependent territories (such as Hong Kong or Gibraltar) who did not have an automatic right of entry to the UK;[32] third, overseas citizens who were holders of British passports who fell into neither of the first two categories and whose British nationality had been withdrawn by legislation in 1968 but who held no other passport. The law also put an end to the automatic acquisition of citizenship by birth on British soil – only those children qualify who have at least one parent who is either a British citizen or a permanent resident in the UK. The administrative rules applying the 1981 legislation and ensuing judicial decisions severely limited the rights of the intending immigrant.

United Kingdom controls on immigrants (like those in other EU countries) are exercised in three ways: in the countries of origin through the issue of entry documents; by transporters (mainly airlines) who were made responsible by legislation in 1987 for people who travel without proper documentation; at the frontiers by immigration officials. Immigration from the 'new (i.e. non-white) Commonwealth' has been reduced to a trickle. Despite the absence of some internal controls (the UK does not yet issue identity cards) compared with the countries of continental Europe, increasing numbers of undocumented immigrants in Britain are located and deported. There remains strong support in the electorate for tight immigration controls and little support for effective measures to oppose discrimination by race.

France

The French legislation on citizenship and immigration has much greater consistency than that of the United Kingdom. It builds on ideas of the eighteenth-century Enlightenment and the French Revolution – the nation was conceived as a political association rather than a group defined by kinship and blood.[33] Subsequently, anxiety about the demographic weakness of France in the late nineteenth and first half of the twentieth centuries led to favouring immigration of foreigners intending to stay for a long period on French soil and to their eventual naturalization. By 1930 France had a higher proportion of immigrants in its population than the United States. The main principles governing French citizenship have been maintained since legislation in 1889 stipulated that citizenship may be acquired by descent, by place of birth and by residence. These principles were confirmed in 1927 legislation and included in a 1945 *ordonnance* (executive act), with tidying-up amendments passed by the National Assembly in 1973. The changing composition of the French population and tensions in areas with large immigrant populations provoked the former president of the republic, Giscard d'Estaing, to suggest the adoption of the principle of *jus sanguinis* and in 1987 led the minister of justice, Albin Chalandon, to propose that the automatic acquisition of citizenship to those born on French soil be abandoned in favour of an acquisition by individuals when they reached the age of majority, a proposal eventually passed in 1993 (the loi Pasqua) under a new right-wing government.

Policy concerning the entry of temporary immigrants wishing to work in France has undergone important changes. According to the 1945 *ordonnance*, temporary immigration is a matter for administrative action, and not legislation.[34] In the early 1970s labour shortages in France disappeared, and the first important decision to stem immigration was taken in July 1974. Controls preventing immigration never wholly succeeded.[35] Jean-Claude Barreau, president of the Office des Migrations Internationales, suggested in 1991 that immigration, despite its virtual banning, was still running at about 100,000 a year.[36] Alarm at the implications of Muslim fundamentalism, individual acts of violence by and against immigrants, and civil disturbances in the dilapidated suburbs with high concentrations of immigrants made immigration the most sensitive and tense political issue in France. All major parties were affected by it, and campaigns by left-wing groups against racism were directed at protecting French residents rather than promoting liberalization of immigration rules.

Italy

The Italian law on acquisition of citizenship was very similar to the French, based on a mixture of *jus sanguinis* and *jus soli*. In other respects, until the end of the 1980s, the Italian position sharply contrasted with that of its northern neighbours, because Italy, traditionally a country of emigration, did not have any immigration legislation. Italy's position was made untenable by the approach of the Single European Market and Italy's membership of the Schengen group. Both required a control of immigrants from non-EC countries satisfactory to Italy's partners. Also hostility towards immigrants began to emerge within Italy – the large numbers of black street-traders were found particularly objectionable in some cities, and the increasing incidence of petty crime and drug-trafficking was associated in the public mind with immigrants. While the lack of controls meant that the number of immigrants, mainly African, was unknown, it was variously estimated at between half a million and 2 million.

The Italian government eventually acted by executive decree in December 1989. Immigrants already in Italy were required to regularize their position with the police. If they were in Italy before the end of 1989 and registered within a limited period, they were granted rights of residence, and equal rights to employment, health care and education. The legislation also put in place a system to control future immigration, especially difficult because of Italy's long coastline. These measures were approved by both houses of the Italian parliament in February 1990. The Italian determination to enforce strict limitations on immigration was demonstrated by the forcible repatriation of thousands of Albanians, escaping penury in their homeland, who attempted to gain entry in 1991 through the port of Brindisi. Italian control of its external frontier did not entirely satisfy its European partners and Italy was not accepted in the first group of countries implementing the Schengen Agreements in March 1995.

The United States

The US and the EU are exposed to similar pressures of immigration from the south: large poor populations live south of the Rio Grande and on the southern shore of the Mediterranean, and there are analogous stark contrasts in culture and economic development between sending and receiving countries.[37] Immigration has played a contrasting role in American history to the one it has played in European countries.[38] The United States was established as a great power by large-scale migration – from 1820 to 1987 the United States took in 54 million individuals and, despite the imposition of immigration controls, has maintained its well-established record in recent years as the world's major recipient of immigrants. An awareness that the nation was founded by immigrants is widespread and, despite all the pressures felt in the twentieth century, the benefits of immigration are still defended in the United States in a way which is rare in Europe.[39]

Nevertheless anti-immigrant sentiment in the United States has a long history. In the late nineteenth century, various restrictive measures were passed, some on racial criteria (against Chinese in 1882), some on social and political grounds (against anarchists, polygamists, criminals, prostitutes, beggars), and others on health grounds (against epileptics, mental defectives and those suffering from tuberculosis). After the First World War the rise of isolationism, and beliefs that immigrants coming in vast numbers from southern and eastern Europe would bring with them anarchism, socialism and Communism, created an overwhelming movement of opinion in favour of the restrictive legislation of 1921–4. A ceiling of 158,000 per annum was imposed, and immigrants were admitted in accordance with national quotas based on an estimate of the countries of origin of the existing population. The Immigration and Naturalization Service (INS) was created in 1933 to assist in the enforcement of immigration rules. The INS remained seriously under-resourced and large numbers of illegal immigrants were never traced.

The passage of the McCarran–Walter Act (1952) discriminated against immigrants of Asian origin, strengthened powers of expulsion of aliens (particularly Communists) and restricted immigrants to 150,000 per year. Legislation in 1965 and 1978 abolished national quotas, but no country could send more than 20,000 migrants per annum. The influx of refugees (who had never been counted as immigrants), became a serious issue in the 1970s; the refugees originated mainly from Cuba, Haiti and Vietnam, and a ceiling of 238,000 per annum was imposed in 1980, subject to revision according to circumstances. The main continuing problem were the large numbers of illegal immigrants crossing the Mexico–United States border. The official Bracero programme in the 1940s, allowing the temporary migration of agricultural labour into the border states, was completely submerged by illegal entrants. In the celebrated Operation Wetback in 1954, 1.3 million illegal immigrants from Latin America were sent back to their countries of origin.

Controlling the flow of immigrants across the southern border required more resources and a more authoritarian stance by the US authorities than the US Congress or public opinion were prepared to allow. As V. H. Palmieri wrote, more effective control involved 'more planes, more helicopters, electronic devices and, of course, armed patrols – as well as a major step up in apprehension activity in the workplace, requiring that the INS (notoriously understaffed, under-financed, and overwhelmed) be reborn as an enforcement agency'.[40] Illegal immigrants were, in principle, subject to fines, short periods of imprisonment and expulsion, but very few prosecutions were brought and employers were not penalized for employing them. The INS tried ineffectually to stem the flow at the Mexican frontier through the border patrol.

In 1986, after long discussion, Congress passed a new Immigration Reform and Control Act (IRCA). Mexican opinion was, for the most part, hostile to this legislation, believing that the pre-1986 regime served both countries well,[41] but US anti-immigrant groups argued that large numbers of Hispanics would replicate problems associated with Black Americans.[42] The Act granted an amnesty to the illegal immigrants already in the country, established quotas of immigrants for seasonal employment and, for the first time, penalized employers who took on illegal immigrants. More resources were given to the INS so that it could seek out illegal immigrants in agricultural and industrial enterprises. Fines ranging from $250 to $10,000 for each worker illegally employed, followed by terms of imprisonment for repeated offences, were directed at closing down the market for illegal immigrants. Congress required the administration to prepare reports and updated statistics.

Early studies of the effect of the 1986 Act suggested that its effects were limited, even though from the legal standpoint it marked a radical change. The amnesty in the Act was a failure – illegal immigrants often considered that the amnesty was a method of identifying them and deporting them. Employers did not drastically change their ways (partly because they were not required by law to verify the authenticity of documents presented to them by immigrants), immigrants did not fear the new legislation, and the INS, partly because of lack of resources, did not engage in the mass expulsion which would have been necessary to make it effective. Up to 1991 about 6,000 employers had been fined for employing illegal immigrants, but the fines were relatively low.

Another immigration law, signed by President Bush in November 1990, raised the quotas on both ordinary immigrants and asylum-seekers for a temporary period and discriminated heavily in favour of those bringing either capital or skills with them.[43] But the continuing large flows across the Mexican frontier threatened to trouble the closer relations between Mexico and Washington after the signing of the North American Free Trade Treaty in 1993. At the beginning of October 1993 the border patrol engaged in 'Operation Blockade' at the El Paso end closed the frontier.[44] In principle, the 1993 treaty establishing the North American Free Trade Area has no consequences for the movement of people between Mexico, the United States and Canada.[45] In practice, it becomes more difficult, within the framework of close economic cooperation, for the United States to adopt strong repressive measures against migrants on the US–Mexico frontier.

The practice of all the rich countries in recent years has been a tight control of immigration. The relative openness of the United States is a contrast only with the contemporary practice of other rich states – it is illiberal compared to the practice prior to 1914. Restrictions have been complemented in some cases by efforts to integrate immigrants already in the country. For example, in 1989 a Consultative Council for Islam in France (CORIF) was established to counter the deeply rooted beliefs that Islam is not a religion like other religions, but a sinister and reactionary force linked to hostile foreign powers, and that Muslims refuse to accept the norms of the host society in education and on the issue of the status of women.[46] In March 1990 a 'High Council for Integration' was also established in France, which published a series of measures on 18 February 1991 aimed at establishing better integration of immigrants, adapting administrative organization and behaviour to take account of their problems, improving their housing and living conditions and giving them better access to social security.

The Pattern of Migration in America and Europe

Between the 1950s and the 1970s, there was a radical change in the origin of immigrants to the United States: the proportion coming from Europe declined, while numbers of immigrants of Asian and Third World origin increased rapidly.[47] In Europe, individuals coming from Africa and Asia were tolerated in small numbers while the colonial empires lasted; European hospitality towards these immigrants declined rapidly after the colonies became independent states. Migration of white people between highly developed countries tended to be uncontroversial.[48] Movement of individuals within the European Union was uncontroversial, although the French National Front attempted to create hostility towards British purchasers of houses in France. The largest migrant population within the EU was Portuguese moving to France – but they were accepted, for reasons of cultural proximity, as industrious and law-abiding residents.

A major change threatened when the Communist regimes in central and eastern Europe collapsed. From April 1987, the Trevi group (of ministers of the interior and justice) returned to the topic at regular intervals; the Hanover European Council in July 1988 gave priority to developing a common approach to immigration and asylum.[49] In 1993 the signatories of the Schengen Agreements (1985, 1990) agreed on a common visa policy and a common principle on illegal immigrants (*personae non gratae* in one country were unacceptable in all signatory countries). There is also an increasing number of 'readmission' agreements between EU countries and their eastern neighbours, allowing the immediate return of an illegal immigrant. Poland, the Czech Republic and Hungary reinforced, as a consequence, their own frontier controls.

Western countries condemned Communist bloc countries for infringement of human rights when they prevented freedom of movement, and European and North American countries had insisted that the Communist bloc should accept freedom of movement in the 1975 Helsinki Final Act. But the European Union countries became acutely concerned when restrictions on emigration were eased and eventually removed.[50] While migration westwards had seldom been more than 100,000 people per year throughout the 1970s and most of the 1980s, in 1989 there were 1.3 million; the flow threatened to grow exponentially as authoritative reports (*inter alia* from Morgan Stanley bank in 1991) predicted unemployment would reach 14 million in eastern Europe and between 30 and 40 million in the USSR by the mid-1990s. In 1990 the Soviet Union officially warned the EC Commission that Soviet emigrants could total 3.7 million; this was revised upwards to 7 million at the 1991 Vienna conference on east–west migration after the Soviet emigration law had been approved in spring of that year and unofficial estimates were as high as 10 million.[51] The emigration of Soviet Jews reached a level which made the USA increasingly reluctant to accept them, in practice compelling most of them to go to Israel. In 1990 over 200,000 reached Israel,[52] creating tension between the USSR and the Arab states and fuelling still further tension between Israelis and Palestinians.

The significant change in migration to the highly industrialized countries has been the rapid increase in the number and countries of origin of people claiming the status of political refugees.[53] Until the 1970s, the great majority of refugees were east European; since the collapse of Communist regimes in eastern Europe, they have become almost exclusively non-European, with the exception of people from ex-Yugoslavia. The 1951 Geneva Convention on Refugees and the 1967 New York Protocol place an obligation on signatory states to give asylum to those escaping from political persecution. However, there is an increasingly difficult problem of distinguishing 'true' political refugees from those who are escaping penury. In many cases, the distinction is virtually meaningless – people are both starving and persecuted.

Increased numbers of asylum-seekers have created strains in all the main receiving countries. In Germany, the number of asylum-seekers was more than the entire number arriving in all other European countries.[54] The liberal nature of German asylum rules allowed a huge increase in asylum-seekers (from 121,000 in 1989 to nearly a quarter of a million in 1992), after Germany closed the frontiers to foreigners seeking work. Until 1992, anyone who arrived on German soil had the constitutional right to start proceedings for asylum. Although fewer than 10% per annum were granted it, the process of examining applications was so slow that many established themselves in Germany, since they were allowed to work and enjoy welfare rights, pending the outcome of their appeal.[55] Even if their appeal was rejected, they often stayed. Finding this situation intolerable, in May 1990 the federal government and the *Länder* governments controlled by the CDU–CSU declared that nationals from a series of countries did not qualify for the status of political refugees. These included Afghanistan, Iran, Sri Lanka and Ethiopia; all nationals of these countries were threatened with instant expulsion if they appeared in Germany asking for asylum.[56] In 1992, the Basic Law was amended in a way which allowed the severe restriction of the right to asylum, bringing the Federal Republic close to British practice.

By German standards, the UK numbers of asylum-seekers from the Third World (5,000 in 1988, 30,000 in 1990 and an estimated 50,000 in 1991) were small. In the 1980s, refugees and asylum-seekers were accused of trying to evade the effects of immigration legislation. The government introduced new measures on 3 July 1991 further restricting the right of entry of those claiming refugee status. Britain would not accept a refugee who had previously entered another country which could be regarded as a safe haven. The 1991 measures were a continuation of previous practice – they gave little right of judicial review to those refused entry – expulsion was a discretionary administrative act. In this, the UK acted against the spirit and the letter of the 1951 UN Convention on Refugees and the 1967 New York Protocol.[57]

France had a tradition of taking in refugees from political persecution but became less willing to do so. The number of refugees dropped from 61,000 to 56,000 between 1989 and 1990 because of the increased resources given to the Office de Protection des Réfugiés et Apatrides (OFPRA).[58] Prior to a 1989 computerization and increase of personnel for OFPRA, refugees could (as in Germany) usually count on administrative delays to allow them to find a job and housing, so that it became less acceptable, and perhaps less necessary, to deport them. The speed of the new procedures opened the way to arbitrary decisions and caused complaints from civil liberties groups.

The personal circumstances of many refugees are desperate – some have been tortured and killed on return to their native lands. But the French, German and British governments (as well as others such as Austria, whose 1992 asylum legislation resulted in an 80% reduction of asylum applications in the first six months of 1993) are confronted by public opinion hostile to the presence of increased numbers of non-Europeans, whatever the reasons for or causes of their migration. Any liberalization of the regime of asylum is likely to increase the flow of refugees but any toughening of it produces extremely hard cases and appears inhumane.

Refugees and Migrants in Other Regions

Migratory flows with a different pattern take place in other parts of the world. Oil-producing countries, particularly in the Middle East, have attracted migrant labour. Most of the migration in the Third World is a result of famine, war and persecution. There is little reason to believe that the situation will change. Poverty, hunger and population pressures are likely to increase.

The Middle East

The largest peaceful flux of migrant labour outside the highly industrialized countries in the late twentieth century has been to the oil-rich states of the Middle East. The pattern of migration to the Middle East is unlike that to the highly industrialized countries. Since the First World War, the great oil companies have imported labour to assist in the construction and operation of oil extraction and transportation facilities.[59] The first wave of immigrant labour revived the free circulation of people between the different provinces of the Ottoman empire, and along the old merchant routes and the pilgrimages to the holy places. It seemed to presage a common market for labour in Arab countries which would have helped to redistribute wealth between the rich and the poor, and could have become a concrete expression of solidarity of 'the Arab nation'. This migration supported those who believed that frontiers in the Arab, or the Muslim, world were the unfortunate legacy of western domination and ought to disappear.

By 1972 there were about 800,000 immigrants in the region (often on short-term contracts), including small numbers of professionals and technicians and a large number of unskilled labourers.[60] A rapid increase of immigration followed the 1973 oil price rise, when immigrants arrived in large numbers both in the sparsely populated countries, Saudi Arabia and the Emirates, and the relatively densely populated Iraq. Palestinians had come to Kuwait as early as 1948–50, followed by the Yemenis and Egyptians, the latter being particularly important to the Iraqi economy in the long war against Iran which began in 1980.[61] But on the outbreak of the Gulf War Egyptian and other migrant workers in Iraq were brutally expelled. The prospect of an Arab common market for labour vanished.

Industrial development and the great public works of the Gulf states required more labour than other Arab countries could supply. A stream of immigrants came from the Indian subcontinent as well as the Far

East (particularly from Thailand, South Korea and the Philippines). By the mid-1980s, Asians represented 45% of the immigrants in the Gulf, against 20% in the mid-1970s.[62] The original attitude towards the Asian immigrants was that they were less desirable than Arabs, who were closer to the cultural values of the host countries. After various political and social conflicts at the end of the 1970s and beginning of the 1980s, the Asians came to be preferred as a more docile and easily managed labour force.[63] A strategy to resist the creation of a permanently resident working class was pursued[64] – a prudent strategy since the proportion of immigrants in the working population became very high: it passed 50% in the mid-1970s and reached 75% (90% in the United Arab Emirates) in the 1980s.[65] The ability of the Gulf states to pay most of their own nationals from oil revenues without requiring them to work, the age structure of the population in which almost 50% are less than 15 years of age and the presence of small indigenous populations made it impossible for the Gulf states to dispense with immigrants.

Eastern Europe

There are parallels, on a smaller scale, with the Middle Eastern labour markets in South Africa from the 1950s to the 1970s and in Venezuela, but large movements of people elsewhere have usually been caused by violence. In eastern Europe, ethnic tensions, which Michael Walzer has characterized as the 'new tribalism',[66] have led, after the collapse of Communism, to migrations of minorities. Ethnic cleansing and flight of populations from the states established in ex-Yugoslavia are the best-known example in the 1990s, but there are many others. Another east–central European example is the Hungarians – between a quarter and a third of the Hungarian population lives in neighbouring countries – the Ukraine, Slovakia, Austria, Serbia (Vojdovina) and Romania. Tensions arise because of the Hungarians' wish to retain a distinctive cultural identity as well as to reside in lands which have been their home for generations; this desire to retain a cultural identity sometimes appears to the host states as disloyal and the basis of irredentist claims. The systematic destruction of Hungarian villages in Transylvania, which began in 1985,[67] led to the flight of Hungarians to the mother country. Ethnic Hungarians were severely punished for attempting to emigrate by the Ceausescu regime (1965–90) in Romania, as well as being regularly subjected to other forms of discrimination. Although suffering discrimination elsewhere, Hungarians have not been subject to the same level of persecution as in Romania.

The Turks of Bulgaria were repressed in a similar fashion. Numbering between 900,000 and one and a half million in the south-east of the country, the Turks became a vulnerable minority after Bulgarian independence in 1878. But Turks and Bulgarians lived in relative harmony until the Communist takeover in the closing stages of the Second World War. Discrimination started in the educational system with the closing of Turkish schools in 1947; in 1958 lessons in Turkish in the schools were suppressed. Subsequent discrimination, harassment and violence caused large numbers to seek refuge in Turkey.[68] By the 1980s, although Turks still comprised about 10% of the population, less than 1% of university students were Turkish, there were no Turks in senior government positions, there was no Turkish press, no Turks were allowed to carry arms during military service and Turks lost their jobs if they practised Islamic rites. In 1985, compulsory name changes, stripping and rape of Turkish women, the removal of children from Turkish homes and their dispatch to Bulgarian boarding schools, and dozens of deaths were reported.[69] Turkey offered, in January 1985, to repatriate the Turkish minority, but to no avail. The decline of the Bulgarian Communist Party in the late 1980s made the situation worse, with 300,000 Turks fleeing across the border after indiscriminate killings. Anti-Turkish feelings, deeply embedded in the population, were revealed by the anti-Turkish riots when the authorities in one region, Kurdzhali, trying to promote greater toleration, restored religious rights to the Turks.[70]

The problem of refugees in eastern Europe was small by comparison with Asia and Africa. An estimated 10 million people fled East Pakistan to India during the secession crisis which led to the creation of Bangladesh in 1971. Over 2 million people fled from Afghanistan to Pakistan during the Soviet intervention in the 1970s and 1980s.[71] 'Ethnic cleansing' on a vast scale has taken place in Africa and Asia, sometimes creating refugee camps more populous than the largest cities in the region. An example is the expulsion of ethnic Nepalese from Bhutan where the refugee camp at Beldangi in eastern Nepal has housed 85,000 Nepalese, compared with only 30,000 inhabitants of Thimpu, the capital of Bhutan.[72] When the Khmer Rouge took power in 1975 in Cambodia, Thailand received 1,191,000 Cambodians, of whom 660,000 departed to other countries but almost 360,000 remained in camps on the Thai border. Over a third of a million Laotians also fled to Thailand after the Communist takeover in the early 1970s, and 64,000 remained in 1991.[73]

Africa (excluding the states bordering the Mediterranean) was the continent with the largest number of refugees by the later 1980s; one calculation suggests that at this time more than 13 million people were denied safe domicile.[74] In the 1990s further problems have arisen, such as the mutual massacres of Hutsi and Tutsi in Rwanda–Burundi, the flight of hundreds of thousands of people to neighbouring Zaire, and the displacement of up to 4 million people. An international double standard was established in the post-colonial period: discrimination, violence and even ethnic massacre did not delegitimize governments in the Third World (because a change of government was unlikely to result in an improvement in behaviour) whereas the same acts would result in the ostracism of developed states by the international community.[75]

Conclusion

Hostility to one people intruding into another's territory is an almost universal phenomenon. Individuals and temporary residents may be tolerated, even welcomed, but the arrival of large numbers of people, with a sense of identity and solidarity, is usually regarded as a threat. Frontiers have been established and clearly marked in order to prevent such intrusions; they have always had the general purpose of controlling or preventing the movement of people. Frontiers have had other exclusionary purposes as well – keeping out goods or taxing them, preventing the circulation of ideas and proselytizing for unauthorized religious beliefs and, above all, serving as lines of military defence. These purposes still exist but, in the highly industrialized countries, have become relatively less important.

Migrations have been a repeated feature of human history and, in the contemporary world, affect virtually all societies. European political rhetoric on immigration frequently presents it as a recent, undesirable and 'unnatural' development. Public opinion in all the highly industrialized countries expresses the desire to control, restrict and even exclude immigrants; controlling immigration is a necessity if their inhabitants are to preserve their systems of government and justice, rights, privileges, access to resources and cultural characteristics. The problems of rich and poor societies faced with unwanted immigrants are not strictly comparable. The goods which inhabitants of poor countries seek to defend against unwanted immigrants are often more basic – physical security, cultural–religious practices and food supplies. Survival and Hobbesian problems of order are their first priorities.

In terms of ability to control their frontiers, states vary widely. Highly industrialized countries have the technical capacity to prevent people entering their territory, but for various reasons may not be in a position to use that capacity effectively. Sealing frontiers is expensive, particularly if technologically advanced surveillance equipment is used for long and difficult frontiers, and other policy priorities may have first call on resources; the commercial interests of the state usually require, in contemporary circumstances, that very large numbers of people legitimately cross the frontier with ease and the minimum of delay – thus creating conditions in which illegal immigrants can cross as well; important interests inside the country may have a use for illegal immigrants and find them valuable; the amount of force required to stop people coming in may cause political difficulties both internally and externally; liberal beliefs in a basic right to freedom of movement may be so widespread that they undermine the determination to keep people out; the foreign policy interests of a state may conflict with legislation restricting rights of entry.

For less developed countries, such as those of sub-Saharan Africa, frontier controls are rudimentary and inefficient. Trained personnel, communications equipment and transport facilities for border guards are lacking. Large stretches of frontier are undemarcated, let alone policed. People separated by the frontier are ethnically either the same or similar. Those who wish to cross the frontier are often highly motivated by the prospect of criminal profits, by the possibility of food supplies if they are starving or by the chance of employment in some oasis of prosperity in a poverty-stricken continent. Preventing movement of individuals across their frontiers is a near impossibility for many African states. Sporadic and often violent attempts are made to keep out undesirable intruders, but these have only temporary deterrent effects.

Whether by restricting the movement of people, frontiers are used as instruments of oppression depends on what entitlements individuals are thought to possess. The frontier controls of the German Democratic Republic between the building of the Berlin Wall in 1961 and the collapse of the Communist regime in 1989 prevented the East Germans from enjoying freedom of expression and of movement, regarded as fundamental rights in neighbouring countries to the west. Restricting the rights of refugees to enter countries is sometimes to refuse them the right to life: an example of this was the action of western liberal democracies in limiting the numbers of Jews fleeing from Nazi Germany. The assumptions of the western liberal tradition suggest, as Onora O'Neill writes, some boundaries 'systematically inflict injustice on outsiders'.[76] Boundaries are used to deny them the right to asylum, travel, abode, work, settlement or citizenship. Liberal theories of justice are, however, held by a small proportion of the world's population, and sometimes by a minority in the highly industrialized countries.

6
Uninhabited Zones and International Cooperation

Uninhabited spaces, and the activities which take place in them, affect thinking about frontiers for two main reasons. First, by using uninhabited spaces, states and powerful private interests can gain access to the territory and inhabitants of another state in ways which were not possible earlier in the twentieth century. Conflicts arise over uninhabited zones, and have resulted in many international treaties and conventions. Second, arrangements and agreements have been reached about uninhabited spaces which set aside the concept of territorial sovereignty. International regimes are proposed because spaces which 'belong' in a legal sense to no one or for which no one feels responsible, offer temptations to plunder, exploit or misuse, without regard to the interests of others or to the longer-term consequences of activities.

New concepts have been developed: some, such as 'the common heritage of mankind', derive from ordinary language and some are novel, such as the notion of 'an international regime', and have analogies with the concept of private property rather than with the absolute territorial control implied by the notion of sovereignty. According to one influential view, private property is a bundle of relationships between individuals, involving rights, duties and obligations;[1] by substituting the term 'state' for 'individual', this may also describe some of the regimes for uninhabited spaces, because states do not claim absolute territorial dominion over them.

However, the analogy presents difficulties, for two main reasons. First, as Jeremy Waldron has written about private property: 'If [property as a bundle of rights] were all, there would be no problem about definition: ...if [the bundle] remained constant for all or most cases that we want to describe as private property, the bundle as a whole could be defined by its contents. The problem is, of course, it does not remain constant, and that is where the difficulties begin.'[2] Waldron's statement applies *a fortiori* to regimes for uninhabited spaces. Second, the regime for each category of empty space is specific to it; no regime, with the exception of aspects of maritime law, has remained stable for long periods. Although concepts associated with environmental protection are forming a link between different kinds of empty space, no rights and obligations common to all uninhabited spaces are even hypothetically suggested. But the argument in this chapter is that states attempt, as far as they are able, to acquire rights analogous to property rights in order to facilitate exploitation or use of the resources of these spaces. Mutual recognition of states' rights is usually necessary to achieve this end.

The Case of Antarctica

From the eighteenth to the twentieth centuries land areas regarded as uninhabited gradually diminished in number and area. Claims to territory based on discovery (and even effective occupation) have disappeared. The Empty Quarter of Arabia, and the great deserts of Africa, Asia, Australia and North and South America, are now regarded as being under the effective occupation and control of states. The vast, sparsely populated Arctic tundra, with its scattering of perhaps forty indigenous peoples across Europe, Asia and North America, now outnumbered locally by incomers from the south, is under the effective sovereign control of the states.[3] The single great wilderness remaining is Antarctica.

The Antarctic continent, like oceans, seas and estuaries, is uninhabited in the conventional meaning of the term – all inhabitants are temporary residents. A few hundred people stay in the various scientific stations throughout the winter; in the summer months, several thousand arrive, supplemented by a few tourists. Recent international interest in Antarctica has been based on the belief that it contains valuable mineral resources;[4] it is also a focus of scientific interest as a unique natural environment, rich in research possibilities, especially concerning evidence on climate change. Whether Antarctic resources are exploited depends on the availability of resources elsewhere, commodity prices, technological progress and the political regime agreed for the continent.[5]

The inhospitable climate and terrain of the continent make virtually inapplicable the usual bases of claims to territory in international law – discovery, occupation, historic rights, proximity and geographical conti-

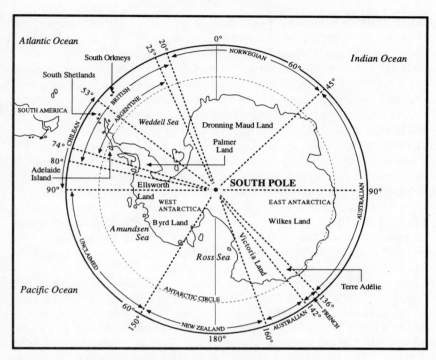

Map 20   Existing territorial claims in Antarctica

guity. Nonetheless, seven states have formal claims; these are Argentina, Australia, Chile, France, New Zealand, Norway and the United Kingdom. Australia has the largest claim (2.4 million square miles) and France the smallest (150,000 square miles). About one-sixth of the continent, between 90 degrees and 160 degrees west, remains unclaimed; the USSR and the USA, however, reserved their right to make claims and scrupulously avoid any action which might implicitly involve the recognition of the claims of others. As Peterson writes: 'The compromise on sovereignty, forming the basis of the Antarctic regime, was not the first choice of most participants. The claimants would have preferred acceptance of their claims.'[6] A situation has arisen in which 'Antarctica is unique – an entire continent of disputed territory.'[7] No established rules of international law uphold claims to sovereignty in it.[8]

The claims have echoes of the early period of European imperialism when explorers and monarchs claimed vast territories which they had never visited and of whose characteristics they were only vaguely aware. Indeed, Chile and Argentina have based their claim to Antarctic territory on historic rights, going back to the earliest period of European imperialism – the papal division of the western hemisphere between Spain and Portugal – and, as successor states, claim *uti possidetis*. They also engage in symbolic acts of occupation, enacting laws relating to their Antarctic territories, making governmental visits, establishing post offices and issuing stamps.[9] In August 1973, President Lastili of Argentina and his cabinet visited the Marembio base and declared it to be the temporary capital of Argentina. The first childbirth in 'Argentinian' Antarctica took place in the Esperanza base in 1978. President Pinochet made visits to Territoria Chileno Antarctico, and families resident in Antarctica for two-year periods were intended to demonstrate, at least symbolically, Chilean occupation. Argentina and Chile are the only two claimants who have integrated Antarctic territory with their sense of national identity.[10] The others make claims, hoping to gain advantage or prevent others from gaining advantages.[11] Their assumption is that economic benefits would be gained from claims to sovereignty if exploitation of mineral resources occurs in the future.[12]

An unstable stalemate has been established in the framework of the Antarctic Treaty System (ATS). With the exception of Norway, no state has considered unilaterally renouncing its claim; however, all would encounter fierce opposition from the other participants in the system, and in the United Nations, if they tried to enforce their claims. The Antarctic Treaty System is based on the 1959 Antarctic Treaty, which was signed by twelve states, including the USSR and USA, as well as those with territorial claims.[13] The thirteen original 'consultative parties' were subsequently joined by other states as participants or observers until, by 1991, a total of forty-one states were associated with the system. The signatory states accepted responsibility for the continent on the basis of each conducting scientific enquiry in it; they agreed to differ on conflicting territorial claims; they aimed at continuing international harmony in Antarctica, specifically by excluding the presence of military bases and military forces. Four other major agreements have been successfully negotiated on the basis of the treaty: Agreed Measures for the Conservation of Antarctic Flora and Fauna (1964); Convention for the Protection of Antarctic Seals (1972); Convention for the Conservation of Antarctic Marine Living Resources (1980) and the Protocol on Environmental Protection (1990).[14]

Until the late 1980s, any attempt to renegotiate the basic framework risked provoking unresolvable conflict; but a low level of governmental and public interest in the continent was the prerequisite for the maintenance of the regime. The increasing national and international importance of the ecological movement has caused tension in the ATS. In 1988 Australia and France refused to ratify the Convention for the

Regulation of Antarctic Mineral Resources Activities (CRAMRA) which contained a conditional ban on exploitation, instead jointly proposing an international natural park, preserved in perpetuity.[15] The notion of Antarctica as a natural park, the common heritage of mankind, goes back to the 1950s; it was championed by the World Conference on National Parks in 1972 and by Greenpeace (using the phrase 'global commons') and other environmental groups; and it was revived again at the close of the 1982 United Nations Conference on the Law of the Sea.

Increased awareness in sections of public opinion, the activities of Greenpeace and the defection of France and Australia from the consensus of rich countries have changed the political environment of the ATS.[16] Non-Governmental Organizations and Third World countries, particularly Malaysia, alleged that the Antarctic Treaty System was a 'secretive club'. The lack of effective policing and enforcing of agreements has been exposed and signatories to agreements have been accused of ignoring their spirit. For example, there is no definition of 'significant harm' contained in the 1980 Conservation Convention. France, in constructing an airstrip at Pointe Géologique, blasted a number of small rocky islands which had been designated as a protected breeding ground for Adélie penguins. This was regarded as 'significant harm' by Greenpeace and wildlife protection groups.[17] Both its permission of prospecting and the non-integration into national laws of the provisions of the unratified Convention on Antarctic Mineral Resources raised suspicions among environmental groups that signatory states were preparing the ground for mineral exploitation.

There are other general reasons for the vulnerability of the ATS.[18] Its legal basis is in dispute.[19] Traditional international law could not supply any precedents which could help to provide a regime for the continent. The system appears to its critics as a neo-colonialist intrusion of highly industrialized countries into a potentially rich wilderness. The ATS lacks a sound moral and environmental justification. A new nationalist mood carries the risk of more irresponsible behaviour in the region;[20] an example is the increasing human activity in the continent which creates a problem of pollution because, in the frigid conditions of the continent, waste matter neither degrades nor disperses. Suspicions are repeatedly voiced by Greenpeace about the motives of leading members of the ATS – suspicions which are increased by the refusal to allow Non-Governmental Organizations and the United Nations into the ATS.

Replacement of the Antarctic regime is unlikely until a new factor emerges (such as a rogue state engaging in mining or the South American states attempting to enforce their claims to sovereignty).

States with territorial claims are unlikely to give them up voluntarily and the international community is unlikely to recognize territorial claims in return for a stringent regime of environmental protection. The continuation of the present regime remains the second-best choice of most states and probably the majority of all interested parties.

Sea and Ocean Boundaries

Customary law of the sea has been a highly developed and relatively stable branch of international law, much of it codified by the 1982 UN Convention on the Law of the Sea.[21] One important principle of customary law of the sea is the right of innocent passage through territorial waters, although states continue to enjoy 'sovereignty' over these waters. The principle may eventually be applied to the territory of states because it has already become difficult to deny, without good cause, the right of innocent passage over land. In the last thirty years, the delimitation of sea boundaries has been highly controversial, but the principles are now broadly agreed. The main issues have been the boundaries within which states may claim the exclusive use of the resources of the sea and the sea bed.

Current sea-boundary disputes occur because valuable resources are at stake, because problems of drawing boundaries in coastal waters can be intractable and because a sea boundary is sometimes part of a series of interlocking disputes between neighbouring states. According to one recent estimate,[22] there are 300 bilateral delimitation issues outstanding, and other estimates put the figure even higher. The extension of the territorial rights of states beyond the old 3-mile limit and the concept of the Exclusive Economic Zone have been sources of new disputes in the last thirty years.[23] These new disputes have sometimes stimulated creative solutions – joint development or management zones which cross hypothetical boundaries have, in some cases, been adopted.

Although, prior to the 1960s, there had been attempts to extend territorial waters to protect resources (particularly fisheries), the great impetus for renewed interest in maritime boundaries was the discovery and exploitation of offshore oil and natural gas reserves after 1945. In the United States, offshore exploitation in the Gulf of Mexico led, in the late 1940s, to the 'Truman Declaration' which claimed the continental shelf as the natural extension of national territory for the purposes of exploiting resources. The precedent was followed in the Persian Gulf and in the North Sea where the continental shelf was shared by the riverine states. The delimitation of the North Sea boundaries was achieved without serious disputes because the interested states wanted to reach a speedy conclusion in order to exploit the oilfields. Mediterranean sea boundaries were also relatively easy to settle, with the notable exception of Libyan claims and the conflict between Greece and Turkey in the adjacent Aegean Sea. At the global level, the poorer countries of the world, represented by the Group of 77 in the United Nations, became particularly concerned that they would be excluded from the profits derived from mining the deep ocean bed, beyond the continental shelf, because the rich countries would have a monopoly of the necessary technology. The extent of the recoverable resources on the ocean bed has not yet been accurately surveyed, partly because the concept of a 'recoverable' resource depends on market prices and on rapidly changing technologies, and partly because commercial secrecy screens the results of prospecting activities by major corporations. Uncertainty about the medium- and long-term future makes any stable framework very difficult, if not impossible, to negotiate.[24]

The third United Nations Conference on the Law of the Sea (UNCLOS III) successfully negotiated the 1982 Convention which came into force in November 1994. An amending protocol was to overcome the last great obstacle to ratification by the United States and other major industrialized powers – the exploitation of the deep-sea bed. The convention established three maritime zones to which states could lay claim: the territorial sea (up to 12 nautical miles), the contiguous zone (another 12 miles), and the Exclusive Economic Zone (200 nautical miles), all distances measured from the low-water mark. The Convention (Article 15) also re-enunciated a traditional principle of international law regarding neighbouring states – 'Where the coasts of two states are opposite or adjacent to each other, neither of the two states is entitled, failing an agreement between them to the contrary, to extend its territorial sea beyond the median line, every point of which is equidistant from the nearest points on the baselines from which the breadth of the territorial seas of each of the two states is measured. The above provision does not apply, however, where it is necessary by reason of historic title or other special circumstances to delimit the territorial seas of the two states in a way which is at variance therewith.' This left existing disputes between states exactly where they were and established no principle which might help to resolve them.[25]

In addition states may, according to the Convention, claim jurisdiction over the continental shelf, which varies in extent and often has to be partitioned between neighbouring states. The implications of claims to the continental shelf and to the EEZ vary from one region of the world to another, and some regions have been intensively studied.[26] States composed of groups of islands, which meet with certain criteria, can claim archipelago status and measure their zones from the outer islands.

The problem here is that the zone often contains islands which belong to other states. When one state's zones overlap with another state's, then 'lateral' delimitation is necessary, arrived at by negotiation, by arbitration or by another judicial process.

France sought to apply the principle of a 200-mile EEZ for its scattering of islands, thus claiming a large maritime empire. An illustration of the problems caused was in the north-west Atlantic, where the eighteenth-century struggle between England and France for control had left a trace in a minor but troublesome conflict between France and Canada. The French claim for a 200-mile EEZ to the south of the archipelago of Saint Pierre et Miquelon was rejected by Canada. A second conflict over fishing quotas for French vessels operating in Canadian waters complicated the dispute. In 1991, hearings before an international tribunal in New York to arbitrate the dispute ended with a compromise largely favouring the Canadian position.

The principle that the high sea and the deep-sea bed form part of the common heritage of mankind is embedded in the 1982 Convention. The less developed countries at the United Nations take the view that the rich countries should not exploit sea-bed resources, by using advanced technologies, to their own exclusive advantage. Another concern, especially for Greenpeace and environmentalist groups, has been the dumping of nuclear waste and other noxious materials in the deep sea. Before the 1980s, most nations which had nuclear power stations and nuclear weapons routinely dumped at sea. Even a landlocked state such as Switzerland hired ships to take its nuclear waste to be dumped in the north-east Atlantic. In response to public pressure, a Convention was signed by the 'nuclear powers' in London in 1983 for a ten-year moratorium on dumping. The facts of dumping were, however, hard to establish. There were suspicions, but little evidence until 1993, about Russia's dumping activities. When the countries involved in the 1983 Convention reassembled in London ten years later, Russia revealed extensive and potentially dangerous dumping north of the Arctic Circle and in the Sea of Japan; Russia agreed to a permanent ban, provided it could be delayed in order to overcome intractable short-term problems. Making the ban on dumping permanent in 1993 showed that the rich countries were prepared to support an international regime for the protection of the high seas. The agreement is, however, virtually impossible to monitor. Moreover, the problem of dumping at sea is much wider than that of radio-active materials: the dumping of munitions, dredged material, often heavily contaminated, from rivers and estuaries, and chemical wastes also results in damaging pollution.

Some sea-boundary disputes are difficult to resolve because they are enmeshed in several interlocking disputes. An example is the Aegean Sea conflict between Greece and Turkey, whose origins lie in the 1923 Treaty of Lausanne.[27] The treaty confirmed Italian sovereignty (through conquest in 1911) over islands close to Anatolia and the Dodecanese; after the Second World War, because they formed part of classical Greece and the majority of their populations were Greek, the islands were awarded to Greece. Some small ones were within a few hundred metres of Anatolia. The Turks objected in general terms, but the first specific dispute arose over airspace, because Greece unilaterally increased its airspace to 10 miles in 1931, when the usual limit was the 3 nautical miles of territorial waters.[28] The claim has never been recognized by Turkey and the dispute over airspace reached crisis proportions in the period 1974–80.[29] Infringements of airspace have been the subject of repeated complaints and counter-complaints.

The next two disputes concerned the sea bed and territorial waters. There was a coincidence, in 1973, of a world energy crisis and the discovery of oil in commercially exploitable quantities off the island of Thasos (in the north of the Aegean). The Turkish government issued licences to the Turkish state oil company to drill off the islands of Lemnos, Lesbos and Chios in international waters which Greece regarded as its section of the continental shelf by virtue of the presence of the islands. Turkey's position was that the waters in which it was drilling formed a natural extension of the Anatolian continental shelf. The Greek position was in accord with the 1958 Geneva Convention on the continental shelf which Greece had signed but Turkey had not. In May 1974, Turkey declared that any extension of Greek territorial waters beyond 6 miles would be regarded as a *casus belli*. The Turkish government argued that an extension to the more normal 12 miles would increase Greek control of the Aegean from 44% to 71%, in effect turning it into a Greek lake. There have subsequently been naval incidents and Greek threats to sink Turkish exploration vessels.

The Aegean dispute has also been enmeshed with the Cyprus dispute, the treatment of Greek and Turkish minorities and North Atlantic Treaty Organization politics. Greece withdrew from the military structure of NATO in 1974 because the Greek government believed that the western allies favoured the Turkish position (the Turkish government believed the opposite). The result was that NATO reorganized the command and control system in the Aegean, giving a greater role to Turkey (to which Greece objected strongly). The Aegean and Cyprus dispute affects NATO in many other ways.[30] Probably before, but certainly after the 1983 declaration of the Turkish Republic of North Cyprus (recognized only by Turkey), Greece remilitarized some of the

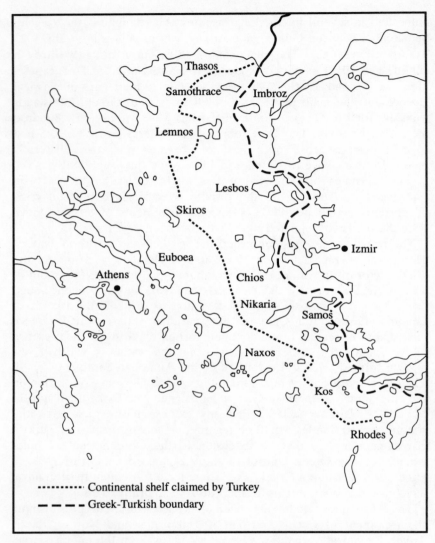

Map 21   The Aegean Sea

key Aegean islands in violation of undertakings in the 1923 Lausanne
Treaty and the 1947 Paris Treaty. Turkey protested vigorously against
this remilitarization.[31]

A meeting in 1988 between the Greek and Turkish prime ministers,
Papandreou and Ozal, at the Davos World Economic Forum gave rise
to a brief period of optimism. But personal goodwill between leaders

cannot resolve complex disputes of this kind. Indeed, the return to office of Papandreou in 1994 ushered in a period of increased tension, for reasons of internal Greek and Turkish politics. Furthermore, Turkey entered a coalition with Italy, Albania and Bulgaria to open up a land bridge to Macedonia (Skopje) after Greece had closed the frontier because the Skopje government refused to give way to the demands of Greece concerning the name, constitution and flag of the newly independent republic (see the Conclusion).

When a series of interlocking disputes occur between countries with a long history of mutual distrust, some overwhelming common interest (such as fear of the Soviet threat which brought both countries into NATO) must emerge to trigger a process of compromise. The Aegean can be partitioned only as part of a complex agreement in which a compromise is reached on all the problems of *voisinage*. The resolution of difficult sea-boundary disputes therefore goes far beyond the simple acceptance of the principles in the 1982 UN Convention on the Law of the Sea, which offer no guidance on the basis of compromises between neighbouring states.

Disputes over Rivers and Estuaries

Rivers and estuaries, although uninhabited, are considered for most purposes as the sovereign territory of states. They are less theoretically interesting than other categories of uninhabited space considered in this chapter, but vital interests are often at stake in conflicts over them. When great rivers pass through several states and are heavily used for the transportation of goods, treaties between states regulating their use have long been regarded as essential. The nineteenth-century international river commissions which managed traffic on the Rhine and the Danube were the first timid steps towards supranational authorities – although a recalcitrant riverine state could *in extremis* block their decisions. As concern for environmental protection increased, regimes governing 'international' rivers have been increasingly subject to critical scrutiny by governments and pressure groups. The use of rivers, for example to generate hydro-electricity or cool nuclear power generators can result in serious tension between states.

For example, the Danube, the estuarine waters between Colombia and Venezuela, the upper waters of the Tigris and the Euphrates, the Shatt al-Arab between Iraq and Iran, all demonstrate the gravity of river and estuarine conflict. In 1989 a dispute broke out between Hungary and Czechoslovakia over management of the Danube, which marked the common frontier between the two countries for most of the territory between Bratislava and Budapest.[32] In 1977 the governments of the two countries had signed an agreement for a joint programme of control and development of the Danube, which involved the construction of two dams and the canalization of the river.

The disintegration of the Communist system altered the political and economic calculations of the countries concerned. The non-governmental but influential Vienna-based Danube Circle denounced the canalization and diversion of the river as an ecological disaster, adding its support to economists who doubted the economic viability of the hydro-electric scheme. In Hungary the issue divided the political parties, and there were demands for a referendum on the question. The dispute became entangled with the treatment of the Hungarian minority (because it directly affected their lands[33]) in Slovakia and a general deterioration in relations between the two governments resulted. Although armed conflict between the two states remained a remote possibility, harassment of the Hungarian minority in Slovakia increased tension. In May 1989 the Hungarian government ordered a cessation of work because it could not provide the necessary financial guarantees. The Czech government complained about the violation of international law and demanded compensation for Hungary's action.

Some disputes seem to provoke tensions out of all proportion to the interests at stake and which, at the end of the twentieth century, seem anachronistic. For example, in 1994 the estuarine waters between the Colombian peninsula of Guajiri and the Venezuelan peninsula of Paraguana have resulted, because of the absence of agreement on a maritime boundary, in an incident redolent of nineteenth-century disputes; Venezuela charged that a Colombian corvette was trespassing in Venezuelan waters. The Venezuelan government closed the frontier and both sides dispatched military reinforcements to the frontier zone. President Raoul Alfonsin of Argentina and the Secretary General of the Organization of American States intervened and pressure was applied to take the matter to the International Court of Justice for arbitration. These disputes are becoming less numerous as equitable agreements are implemented, such as the one between the former German Democratic Republic and Poland over the mouth of the Oder.

In other disputes the vital importance of the interests at stake is clearly apparent. The most disastrous recent conflict (discussed in chapter 3), the Shatt al-Arab dispute between Iran and Iraq, occurred because of the inequitable drawing of the boundary on the Iranian bank rather than the *Thalweg*, or the median line between the two banks. This dispute was, however, a proxy in a struggle between Iran and Iraq for regional dominance, first over the Gulf states and then the whole of the Middle East. In the other disputes, utilization of the river water itself is a matter of life and death. Conflicts over the Jordan, Euphrates and Tigris are struggles for survival.[34] Of these the Euphrates conflict is probably the most immediately dangerous; the series of dams built in south-east Anatolia, culminating in the huge Ataturk dam, finished in 1992, and the Tabqa dam, threaten to deprive Syria, and above all Iraq, of essential water supplies. Other serious political issues divide Turkey, Syria and Iraq and, despite various attempts at negotiation on water resources, no resolution is in sight. Other disputes present similar, if less dangerous problems – examples are the Indus river system which spans China, Afghanistan, India and Pakistan and the Nile river system which spans nine states and is the only source of water for consumption in northern Sudan and Egypt.

Boundaries in the Atmosphere

Airspace boundaries are normally regarded as coextensive with land boundaries, although there is some technical dispute about exactly what that means. A line drawn vertically from the outer territorial limits of the state, extending to the limits of the atmosphere, defines what is within the sovereign jurisdiction of that state. At what altitude airspace ceases is uncertain, and has never been defined in an international treaty. The conventional limit is the so-called von Karman line where aerodynamic flight becomes impossible.[35] This is about 80 kilometres up, but varies according to conditions.

Although there had been previous reference to the notion, establishing national claims to airspace did not become a pressing matter until the military use of aeroplanes during the First World War. The first international agreement on airspace was the 1919 Paris Convention, which came into force three years later, and which embodied the principle that each state has complete and exclusive sovereignty over the airspace above its territory. The 1944 Chicago Convention on International Civil Aviation, in its first article, confirms the same principle. There are difficult points of law and of fact, and occasional disputes where states are separated by straits, or in archipelagos, where claims for airspace sometimes exceed the limits of the territorial waters of states.

Sovereignty over airspace has, in the twentieth century, been important for two main reasons. The first is military; any armed intrusion into airspace is regarded with almost the same seriousness as a terrestrial intrusion. During times of international tension, approaching and infringing the airspace of opposing states has been regarded as a method of showing determination to pursue the quarrel. The principle that countries may respond to intrusions with force, such as the Russian shooting down of the American reconnaissance aircraft, the U2, in 1957, is universally recognized. Overreaction, such as the bringing down of the South Korean airliner in the Soviet Far East in 1983, is the subject of considerable international outcry and, in this case, allegations of Russian inability to distinguish a military from a civilian plane.[36] But no one contested the right of the Russians to defend their airspace. Depriving a state of the right to use its airspace for military purposes is a sanction which is applied to a power defeated in war, as in the case of Iraq deprived of its right to fly over territory occupied by Kurds after the Gulf War, or as a sanction approved by the United Nations to dissuade aggression, such as the exclusion of fixed-wing aircraft over Serb-occupied territory in Bosnia.

The second reason for the importance of sovereignty over airspace is commercial. With the associated, but distinct, right to control landings, it has been used as a powerful means of protection of national airlines. The ability to restrict overflying rights and landing rights for foreign airlines has allowed national airlines to benefit from a monopoly rent and to enter cartel agreements with other national carriers to share lucrative routes. The resulting excessive cost of air travel led to an assault on this practice through 'deregulation' by the Reagan and Thatcher administrations, supported by influential economic interests and by most of the travelling public, incensed by high travel costs. But, without the protection which sovereignty over airspace and landing rights provide, the national carriers of the smaller and poorer countries could not survive.

Two pressures have challenged the clear principle on which sovereign airspace is based. The first is the technical requirements of air traffic control in congested airspace adjacent to international frontiers and the second is concern about atmospheric pollution. All states are bound by air traffic control arrangements, negotiated through the International Civil Aviation Organisation, from which they can only withdraw at the cost of damaging their own interests. For example, under a 1952 ICAO decision, virtually the whole of the airspace of the Aegean was placed under the Athens Flight Information Region. A few days after the coup against President Makarios in Cyprus and the retaliatory Turkish invasion of Cyprus, Ankara challenged the 1952 decision by issuing NOTAM 714, requiring all air traffic to report to Turkish air traffic control on crossing the median line between the Greek mainland and the Turkish coast. Greece retaliated by issuing NOTAM 1157 which declared the whole of the Athens FIR to be a danger area, with the effect that all direct flights between the two countries were cancelled. After holding out for six years (a record for withdrawing from ICAO arrangements), the Turkish government decided such a condition was not in the Turkish interest and unilaterally rescinded NOTAM 714.

The ICAO acts as an arbitrator and does not, in principle, infringe state sovereignty. But an agreement for European airspace, Eurocontrol, established in 1961, contained elements of supranationality. Although members of Eurocontrol became dissatisfied and reduced its supranational aspects in a revised Convention in 1981, the supranational principle may be necessary in very busy airspace in order to achieve the necessary coordination of air traffic.[37] In practice, although the principle of sovereignty over airspace is not denied,[38] the large number of aircraft on international routes has effectively removed the option of closing airspace in all but the most unusual circumstances.

Extra-Atmospheric Space

Although five significant agreements on the law of outer space have been reached,[39] issues relating to outer space have, with the exceptions of satellite broadcasting and observation satellites, been pushed down the international political agenda. The collapse of superpower rivalry, the partial abandonment of the American 'star wars' project, the marginalization of outer space as an arena of superpower competition, the declining governmental and public support for manned space flight, epitomized by the Russian abandonment of the Energia rocket and the Bourane shuttle projects and the cutting back of the NASA budget by the US Congress in 1993, and the general scepticism that outer space can be exploited for significant economic gain in the foreseeable future, have all removed the urgency from the need to regulate human activity outside the earth's atmosphere.

In the 1980s, despite the outlawing of the military use of space by the 1967 'Outer Space Treaty', concern grew about the militarization of space, prompted by the development of anti-satellite and anti-missile technology.[40] According to the treaty, although defensive action was permissible,[41] nuclear and other offensive weapons were banned. The Strategic Arms Limitation Agreements (SALT) of 1972 and 1979 and the Anti-Ballistic Missile Treaty of 1972 banned interference by the Soviet Union and the United States with each other's satellites engaged in the monitoring of these agreements. In 1983, the Strategic Defence Initiative (SDI) was launched by President Reagan, who defended this 'star wars' initiative as defensive – incoming Soviet missiles would be destroyed by lasers in space. But the allegedly defensive system threatened to transform the strategic balance from MAD (Mutually Assured Destruction) to one in which the USA had a decisive strategic advantage. Whether the laser-beam weapons stationed in space would have functioned effectively remains an unanswered question, but the USA partially abandoned the programme as a result of arms limitation agreements with the Russians and the virtual disappearance of a direct Russian military threat.

Nonetheless, difficult issues of the military use of outer space remain. The most obvious is the development of high-resolution observation satellites for commercial purposes by a French–Belgian–Swedish consortium. In 1986 SPOT 1 (Satellite Pour l'Observation de la Terre), and in 1990 SPOT 2, broke the superpower monopoly on this technology; although ostensibly developed for civil surveying purposes, it became available for military objectives.[42] A number of other countries such as Japan and India were capable of developing this technology without external assistance. This created four tiers of states – Russia and the USA which had the highest grade of surveillance satellites; those who had, or were about to develop, SPOT technology; those who enjoyed secure access to it; and those for whom it was potentially useful but who had no access to it. Whether the spread of this technology will affect the stability of the international system is a matter of speculation, but it is certain that more states will be able to see more clearly what is occurring on other states' territory, further eroding the protection provided by territorial sovereignty.

The pollution of outer space by the debris of space vehicles potentially threatens the safety of satellites. Governments are unlikely to regard it as a matter of urgency until there are proven dangers on a scale similar to those posed by meteoroids to functioning satellites.[43] The responsibility for 'clean-up' costs of debris from satellites which damage private property on re-entry to the atmosphere or to another state's territory is a practical legal issue (regulated in principle by the 1972 Convention on International Liability for Damage Caused by Space Objects), which will increase in importance if schemes for hundreds of low-level satellites for multi-media communications come to fruition. In general, space law is a creative domain for speculation over possibilities such as competition for space resources, rescue of space craft, governance of space societies and contact with extra-terrestrial beings. One possibility which is difficult to imagine, despite the Bogotá Declaration of Equatorial States,[44] is the delimitation of boundaries in space and territorial disputes between states.

The political problem of extra-atmospheric space is analogous to the problem in Antarctica – how to establish a regime where state sovereignty cannot be exercised. The 1967 Treaty governing the activities of states in exploration and utilization of extra-atmospheric space, including the moon and other celestial bodies (which by 1990 had been ratified by ninety-two states) recognized that territorial rivalries could not be transposed from the earth to outer space. Article I sub-section 1 established the principle that the exploration and utilization of space was the 'province of all mankind' and thus equivalent to the principle adopted by the United Nations Conference on the Law of the Sea, which accepted that the seas were 'the common heritage of all mankind', a notion which rejects sovereignty.[45]

The 1967 Treaty also affirmed the principle that states bear international responsibility for their activities in outer space. In the absence of a doctrine of sovereignty this raises interesting legal issues of jurisdiction, civil responsibility, intellectual property rights for technical and scientific discoveries and copyright.[46] It is difficult to envisage how these problems can be solved to the satisfaction of all without the establishment of a genuine international jurisdiction. In the short term, the states which have the technological superiority have an overwhelming practical advantage in any disputes which arise.

Intrusions into State Territory

Three intrusions across frontiers have the potential to cause a radical change in perceptions of territory in and the significance of frontiers. The first, already discussed, is the availability to a significant minority of states (and private corporations within them) of high-resolution observation satellites which make it difficult for one state to hide from other states any economic or military activity, even in remote and inaccessible locations. The second is transfrontier pollution and the harmful, potentially disastrous, effects of economic activity on the citizens of other countries. The third is the use of international telecommunications (including computer networks). Frontiers and sovereign control of territory provide, at best, very limited defences against the social, economic, cultural and security impact of these intrusions.

Scientific knowledge of the environment is still limited, and there is no definitive answer yet to the basic question of why the biosphere needs protection. There is, however, agreement that much of the effort of environmental protection must be based on international cooperation. Any measure of environmental protection inevitably promotes some interests and harms others. A state which unilaterally protects the environment runs a risk of damaging its competitive interests, although it may gain short-term protectionist advantages by banning the impact of manufactured goods which do not meet its standards.[47]

The first 'environmental' treaty, the 1902 Convention for the Protection of Birds Useful to Agriculture, had a strictly utilitarian motivation.

The second, the 1911 Washington Treaty for the Protection of Seals, had a similar rationale but arguments were introduced about the proper treatment of wild animals.[48]After the Second World War, the United Nations and its specialized agencies, took the lead in putting environmental questions on intellectual and political agendas.[49] The UN was flanked by others: the World Meteorological Organization, the International Maritime Organization, the International Civil Aviation Organization[50] and the International Atomic Energy Agency have played influential supporting roles in specialized areas. Regional organizations – the Organization for Economic Cooperation and Development,[51] the European Community/Union,[52] the Council of Europe[53] – have given an increasingly central place to environmental issues in their deliberations and decisions.

Non-governmental organizations such as the International Union for the Conservation of Nature and its Resources, established in 1948, and its better-known progeny, the International Wildlife Fund (1961), have mobilized public opinion and private interests. The Worldwatch Institute, with its widely noticed reports and studies, and, above all, Greenpeace, with its spectacular campaigns of direct action, have helped to stimulate interest in environmental issues. Pressure groups and voluntary organizations with international membership and a global outlook have been influential in establishing international environmental regimes.

A mixture of environmental catastrophes and of international initiatives has popularized certain ideas or concepts. The first key date was the 1967 wreck of the oil tanker *Torrey Canyon* on the Scilly Isles, which resulted in major pollution of the beaches of Cornwall and Brittany. The impact was great because it affected two countries, Britain and France, simultaneously, and because both regions were tourist destinations and sites of great natural beauty. More than thirty major spills have taken place since the *Torrey Canyon,* but perhaps only the 1989 *Exxon-Valdéz* spill in the ecologically fragile Alaskan fjords has made a comparably great impact, because of massive US and international media coverage.

The second key date was the 1970 major report on *Man and the Biosphere* by the United Nations Educational, Scientific and Cultural Organization (UNESCO), which popularized the view that all aspects of the environment are interdependent. In 1972 a Convention was negotiated through UNESCO concerning the protection of the global cultural and natural patrimony. At the same time, the UN Economic and Social Council initiated the 1972 Stockholm Conference which produced a series of resolutions which became the UN Programme for the Environment. Under this programme, the UN Fund for the Environment, which sponsors an annual theme and supports research projects in general environmental modelling, was established. These UN initiatives made familiar the idea of the interdependence of environmental issues – in the most extreme cases, such as the prospect of the destruction of the ozone layer, environmental catastrophe could occur which would make human life unsustainable. The concept of interdependence helped to promote the ideas of the common heritage of mankind and global stewardship. These are now an integral part of thinking concerning Antarctica, the seas and oceans, the atmosphere and outer space. Its potential long-term influence on state sovereignty is radical.

The next important date was the catastrophic 1984 explosion of the Union Carbide plant at Bhopal in India, which resulted in many casualties (4,000 dead and 20,000 injured) and serious damage to the health of survivors. The export of hazardous materials and processes from the highly industrialized to less developed countries became a growing concern of international agencies and environmentalist groups. The export took two major forms. First, the export of toxic waste materials from industrial processes: poor African countries, and even the People's Republic of China, were willing to receive dangerous waste matter in return for hard currency; in addition, waste matter was sometimes dumped without the knowledge of the authorities who lacked the inspectorates and technical knowledge to control it. The second was the export of manufacturing processes some of which were eagerly sought by the poorer countries, but which became dangerous where less stringent health and environmental protection standards were applied. The 1965 *maquiladora* programme to attract US industry into the frontier region of Mexico explicitly stated that in northern Mexico US firms would face both lower labour costs and less exacting health and environmental regulations.[54] The savings increased as more stringent health and environmental rules were enacted in the United States and the *maquiladoras* flourished. The US Congress has opposed both the export of hazardous waste (although the outright ban was rescinded by an executive order of President Reagan) and dangerous manufacturing processes; both prohibitions have met with some success.[55] The states of the European Union have taken a more complacent view, despite pressure from European Community institutions and environmental groups. In Europe, the problem is not limited to export to poor Third World countries. Illegal transfrontier disposal of dangerous waste within the European Union comes to light from time to time; relatively poor European countries have been prepared to accept less strict environmental protection regulations in order to attract large-scale manufacturing plants to their territories. One of the comparatively rich countries, with a declining industrial base, the United Kingdom has been willing to accept an activity, nuclear waste reprocessing, which most other countries regard as too hazardous.

The export of waste and hazardous manufacturing procedures present difficult problems of definition, of conflict of interest, and of coordination of national and international regulatory regimes. Action to safeguard the environment, so that measures can take effect in time, may have to be based on suppositions and precede definitive scientific evidence of danger. Governments faced with serious economic problems are reluctant to take such action. Conflicts of interest in environmental protection are legion within and among rich countries as well as between poor and rich. The imposition of the high standards of rich countries on poor countries risks being even more ineffective in relation to the environment than in the field of human rights, and the attempt to do so has been stigmatized as a new form of domination by the rich over the poor.

The rich countries, it is argued, have become rich by plundering the environment, especially the environment of the poorer peripheral countries; environmental protection is now a method of preserving the material superiority of the rich. In banning products like the CFC gases,[56] rich countries also had easy access to alternative products and technologies which poor countries lack. The cooperation of poor countries may only be acquired by financial aid to implement changes required by environmental regulation and by the stringent application of national legislation against firms in their countries of origin for their activities in the poor countries. The problem with stringent national regimes, as well as with detailed and restrictive international regimes, is that they encourage evasion because of the large illegal profits which can be made. The illegal dumping of toxic waste has been an important criminal activity both in Europe and North America.

The most recent landmark environmental catastrophe was the explosion, in April 1986, of one of the four Soviet (now Ukrainian) nuclear reactors at Chernobyl, 120 kilometres north of Kiev. The catastrophic consequences illustrated dramatically that state frontiers afford no protection against a major incident, and international cooperation of a systematic kind is necessary to control the consequences. The immediate casualties at Chernobyl were relatively modest according to official figures (thirty-two dead and 499 seriously injured) but over 4 million people in the USSR were subjected to radiation, and the incidence of cancers increased significantly. Within two days Sweden reported high levels of radioactivity (the first indication outside the Soviet Union that the accident had taken place), and within a week the whole of France and parts of Britain were affected. The radioactive cloud went round the world, with damaging effects in Poland, Scandinavia, Germany, Austria, Switzerland, France, the Netherlands and Britain. The international impact persisted for several years: in 1992 600,000 sheep in Scotland and Wales still had excessive levels of radioactivity.

The Soviet Union initially released information slowly but eventually it called in international experts and accepted help from the International Atomic Energy Agency (IAEA). The explosion was an economic catastrophe, with the estimated direct cost of decommissioning and making safe the installation (as well as providing an alternative source of energy to the three remaining reactors which western countries wished to see closed) considerably in excess of the financial resources of an independent Ukraine. In July 1994 a financial plan of action by the international community was proposed by the European Union and accepted by the G7, with Italy being charged with conducting the sensitive technical, financial and political negotiations with Ukraine to ensure that all the reactors were decommissioned and made safe.

The immediate political consequence of Chernobyl was to strengthen the obligation on states to report comprehensively and immediately any nuclear incident to the IAEA; anti-nuclear movements were encouraged in all the rich countries and increased their pressure on governments; the international community had to accept financial responsibility for the consequences of the incident, setting an important precedent. The idea of an international regime for higher safety standards and for ensuring protection against nuclear accidents gained much ground.

International Regimes for Environmental Protection

Despite all the difficulties of defining the general objective of environmental protection and of designing internationally enforceable regimes, some progress has been made. International organizations (such as the IAEA) have assumed responsibilities for research, exchange of information, regulation, control of the application of rules, and even management of natural resources. The tissue of cooperative institutions and arrangements is at several levels – global, regional, sub-regional, multilateral, and bilateral – depending on the nature of the problems.

Some problems are truly global, such as the protection of whales and the ozone layer, others are local, such as the purity of water, which may be a matter for cooperation between neighbouring states. Some relatively old agreements cover this topic, such as the 1944 International Boundary and Water Commission between Mexico and the United states.[57] When arguments about the trade-off between economic development and environmental protection span international frontiers, they tend to be inconclusive. More and more such disputes have been emerging over pollution, such as that of Lake Michigan and the Saint Lawrence, or of the Rhine polluted by the pharmaceutical and chemical industries of Basel and by the potash mines of Alsace.[58]

The regional level of international organization has assumed a major role in environmental protection, especially in Europe. Although the Treaty of Rome contained no explicit reference to the environment (because of lack of knowledge in the 1950s of environmental hazards), between 1967 and 1991 the EC adopted no fewer than eighty Directives containing measures of environmental protection directly applicable in the member states.[59] Some, such as standards of water purity in the United Kingdom and the protection of small birds in the south-west of France, were highly controversial and provoked strong political reactions. Although the protection of small birds is a marginal case, members of the EC take the view that common environmental rules are essential in the construction of a single market.[60] Pressure to adopt high standards within Europe, such as reducing sulphur dioxide emissions from coal-burning power stations, can result in economic and political difficulties; one example is making British pits non-viable and undermining UK government plans for coal industry privatization. The EC/EU is a special case of intensive regional cooperation although it is a model which may be adopted in other regions. Regional environmental problems, such as pollution of the Mediterranean,[61] sometimes have to be tackled without the help of a pre-existing regional organization which can bring together the interested states.

The system of international arrangements, including global, regional and bilateral agreements, for environmental protection is emerging as a real constraint on the exercise of state sovereignty. Undertakings given in these agreements are very difficult to ignore and contravening them is regarded by the environmentalist lobby as tantamount to a criminal act. Influential international non-governmental organizations and transfrontier political coalitions have been established which apply pressure to governments and international organizations. Perceptions of territorial sovereignty are changing because in environmental policy states no longer appear to have the right to approve some activities within their frontiers.[62]

Broadcasting

The intrusions into state territory made possible by international telecommunications have an enormous, if immeasurable, impact on mentalities and cultural identities. International radio broadcasting has been a powerful instrument for pursuing military, political and economic objectives during most of the twentieth century. The first use of radio for military and political objectives was in 1915 when Germany developed a regular radio news service used by a number of neutral countries: the news bulletins contained coded messages for German agents as well as giving a German version of the progress of the war.[63] Lenin recognized the potential of broadcasting for propaganda purposes. In 1922 a central radiotelegraphy station was operating in Moscow which could be received throughout Russia and over most of western Europe. By 1933 Radio Moscow was broadcasting in ten European languages to promote the Marxist-Leninist cause and the objectives of Soviet foreign policy. From the same year, Hitler greatly expanded German foreign language broadcasting and eventually the British responded, just before the Second World War. During the Second World War, radio was used as an instrument of subversion to weaken the will to resist both of opposing troops and of civilian populations.

As soon as relations between the USSR and the USA deteriorated, the Voice of America began (in 1947) its Russian-language broadcasts; it was flanked by the much more stridently propagandist Radio Free Europe (1948) and Radio Liberty (1953) in which east European *émigré* influence was strong. The BBC also broadcast in Russian and the east European languages, while Radio Moscow responded with broadcasts in all western European languages, as well as jamming western broadcasts which could be received on Soviet territory. The latter response was interpreted as evidence that western broadcasts had a genuine effect. The power of the western media was also felt in other ways. Their dominance of news-gathering and news dissemination, as well as their capacity to produce entertainment which had global appeal, resulted in the projection of a heavily biased western worldview into Third World countries.

Both the Cold War use of broadcasting and the global dominance of the western, mainly American, media were in due course subject to vigorous left-wing criticism and criticism from Third World governments. Noam Chomsky was a late but distinguished critic of broadcast Cold War propaganda.[64] He argued that the United States' presentation of international relations as a Cold War legitimated US interests in Third World countries and aggressive US constraint strategies around the globe. According to Chomsky, the true threat was not from Soviet Communism but from national liberation movements which threatened American investments in Third World countries. This was a splendid over-simplification but it drew attention to the indisputable element of bias in any presentation of a world-view through the medium of broadcasting and to the fact that this medium was bound to be an instrument largely controlled by dominant political and economic powers.

The influence of the western media in the poor countries has been variously described as electronic colonialism, cultural domination and media imperialism.[65] These phrases were invented by university-based left-wing scholars, advancing one form or another of dependency theory (discussed in chapter 2). They represented the poorer countries as pawns in the hands of advanced capitalist countries, often held in thrall by their own belief systems which had been deliberately manipulated by western capitalist interests. Demands were formulated for a new world information order and this was embodied in UNESCO's 1979, *International Commission for the Study of Communication: Final Report*, which suggested a number of radical ways of reducing western media dominance. The allegedly partial and prejudiced nature of this report was one of several factors which led the British and American governments to withdraw from UNESCO as an incompetently managed organization which had become dominated by Third World criticism of the United States and Israel.

The appearance of direct television broadcasting by satellite provided potentially an even more powerful instrument of transfrontier influence than radio, particularly in the case of broadcasting services devoted to news and information (CNN is currently the only global satellite news service). A specific image of global relations can be projected along with selective factual, linguistic, political and social propaganda which, though unlikely to affect decisively the outcome of particular crises, can, through cumulative long-term effects, powerfully influence perceptions of the issues at stake in global competition. The end of the Cold War does not presage the termination of international conflict over such matters as the environment, exploitation of scarce and valuable resources, or economic competition between an increasing number of dynamic states. In future, control of information and of powerful means of communication is likely to be more, rather than less, important.

There have been few attempts to create an international regime for regulating direct television broadcasting. A UN General Assembly resolution of 1982, concerning principles governing utilization by states of artificial satellites, was hostile to direct television broadcasting. Third World governments were concerned about the political implications of unrestricted reception of these satellite broadcasts on their territory. The resolution attracted a large majority but was not supported by the industrialized countries who had access to the necessary technology. There is little Third World countries could do to control direct satellite broadcasting, except by going to the extreme of banning the discs and aerials necessary for reception of the broadcasts (a step which Iran took in April 1994). Other moves towards an international regime have been limited to Europe and, far from being restrictive, have been concerned to guarantee free communication of information, unless it conflicts with views of public morality.[66] The European Community was also concerned to arrive at a common European approach to satellite broadcasting so that it could negotiate as a bloc with the United States and Japan.

Freedom of access to television services was the starting-point of the 1984 EC Green Paper, *Television without Frontiers*. The basic principle of the Green Paper was identical with that of the 1989 Council of Europe Convention on Transfrontier Television. An EC Directive of October 1989 treated broadcasting like any other service within the meaning of the Treaty of Rome, subject to the same freedom of circulation within the Europe of the twelve. It stipulated, with the introduction of new technologies of cable and satellite television, that the Community broadcaster, actual or potential, should have equal access to audiences in member states other than the one in which they were established. This freedom to supply television services encounters practical obstacles, as well as the opposition of state-owned television corporations. The difficulty in developing a Europe-wide television service is the strong audience preference for programmes in the indigenous languages.

Although English is an important and widely understood language, the market for English-language television is dominated by American and British satellite broadcasting systems. In order to combat this linguistic dominance Chancellor Kohl and President Mitterrand initiated a Franco-German channel, Arte, which broadcasts simultaneously in German and French. Although it has attracted critical acclaim, its audience ratings are disappointing. A French-based continuous news service, Euronews, owned mainly by the southern European and Mediterranean public broadcasting systems, has also been launched. Despite these initiatives, the scope for 'television without frontiers', in the sense of Europe-wide television broadcasts, is clearly limited.[67] The French initiative, which resulted in the exception of cultural products (including television programmes and films) from the liberalization of trade in the GATT Uruguay Round finally completed in 1994, and subsequent French attempts to protect the European market from US imports, seem similarly doomed to failure.

International broadcasting marks a powerful breach in frontiers and territorial sovereignty. Radio broadcasting became a widespread phenomenon in the 1930s, with the deliberate aim of political subversion; direct satellite television broadcasting, with the ostensible aim of making profits, became widely available in the 1990s. The latter has already strengthened the position of English as the dominant world language, will help to make the rich countries more attractive as destinations for migrants from the poor countries and will encourage the integration of the global market for consumer goods. But it can also have divisive effects by increasing the awareness of the gap between rich and poor countries, and encouraging the belief that the gap is unbridgeable. The despair provoked risks encouraging military or subversive adventures against the highly industrialized world. It can help an unscrupulous despot to manipulate western opinion (Saddam Hussein was an avid watcher of CNN during the Gulf War). But these are intuitive forecasts and the effects may well be as unexpected as they are unintended.

The radical innovation in telecommunications of the 1990s is the establishment of global computer links, particularly Internet, which gives ready access to noticeboards linking individuals interested in specific topics as well as to vast amounts of information, previously available only within countries. This loss of 'information sovereignty' by states may have more political impact than the development of the printing press. Currently governments are trying to formulate their first responses; some will attempt to find technical means of preventing the dissemination of undesirable information and messages on their territory. Others will seek an international regime which will bring order into what they consider the anarchy of uncontrolled information flows. Neither approach seems promising, and the growing number of individuals linked by common interests who communicate at will through the computer networks across international frontiers will result in fundamental political change.

Conclusion

The activities in uninhabited spaces, particularly those made possible by new technologies, raise questions about the basis of territorial sovereignty. The most direct evidence is the increasing currency of the idea of international regimes, defined as 'collective action by States, based on shared principles, norms, rules and decision-making procedures which constrain the behaviour of individual States'.[68] These are widely considered as essential to resolving the problems of management of uninhabited spaces. If international regimes are necessary for uninhabited spaces, is there any reason why they cannot be instituted for inhabited territory?

States and private interests attempt to extend their 'reach' into empty or uncontrolled spaces whenever they can, using whatever means are to hand. They do so to gain immediate benefit and to claim entitlements but, in addition, to prevent other states and interests from establishing positions which, at some time in the future, may be to their strategic disadvantage. Absolute dominion over uninhabited space is not an option available to states. Arrangements which encourage states to cooperate within recognized fora rather than engage in unrestrained competition are therefore necessary.

The long-term stability of these international regimes is uncertain because their novelty has not allowed the development of accepted rules and expectations concerning their operation; the development of new technologies will open up new and unimagined possibilities for the use of space, and the unpredictable costs and benefits of technical innovation will induce caution by states in accepting binding undertakings. But international regimes are one measure of the extent to which sovereign states are locked into a global system and have more to lose than to gain from retaining or resuming complete liberty of action.

In certain cases, international regimes have been accepted by states as the authoritative legislative body for policies which directly affect their citizens. The European Union (discussed in the Conclusion) is the clearest and most influential example. When such regimes have been firmly established the notion of 'sovereignty', like that of the 'divine right of kings' in the United Kingdom, will be a polite fiction.

Conclusion: The European Union and the Future of Frontiers

Frontiers cannot be separated from the entities which they enclose. In recent history, the international frontier has delimited the sovereign state, a political form which originated in western Europe and spread to all inhabited regions (even though certain states in the less developed world can be described as quasi-states). The clarity of the state frontier is now fading because the exercise of sovereign authority in certain domains is becoming either very difficult or impossible. The increased permeability of international frontiers is both a symptom and a cause of radical change in the characteristics and environment of the state. This change is most evident in Europe, where it has led to extensive speculation about the future of the state.[1]

European integration lacks genuine historical antecedents. It is quite unlike state-building in early modern Europe and the drive towards national self-determination in the nineteenth and twentieth centuries; there is no contemporary equivalent of the federator monarchs who built the European kingdom-states and, as yet, no 'European people' to provide popular support for the European Union. Loyalty to the European Union and belief in its legitimacy must be derived from other sources than those which bind together nations, peoples and local communities. Differences of history, language and culture define the peoples of Europe. As a consequence, European Union can only be based on commitment and loyalty to a European Constitution supported by a powerful coalition of interests. A central element in the building of a loyalty to Europe is extending European citizenship rights which bring tangible benefits for individuals and groups.[2] A genuine sense of solidarity must emerge for the peoples of Europe to accept a common external frontier and the abolition of police controls on frontiers between them. A range of issues to do with location of frontiers, policing of populations and maverick state policies illustrate an uneasy transition between an *ancien régime* and a new order.

The External Frontier of the EU

The location of the external frontier has implications both for the internal development and for the external relations of the European Union. The location will influence the degree of political integration possible, the nature of the constitution of the EU and the operation of its institutions, the extent of policy coordination and harmonization, and both the nature of political alignments and the balance of economic interests within the EU. These themes are familiar in the so-called 'widening or deepening' debate about the future of the Union.

The European Union expanded in 1995 to include Austria and the Scandinavian countries – possibly to be followed early in the twenty-first century by the Visegrád four – Poland, the Czech Republic, Slovakia and Hungary. Such growth risks making its legislative and executive processes more cumbersome, slowing the process of political integration and, perhaps, turning the Union into a loose association of states. In the 1996 inter-governmental conference for developing the European Constitution, pressure will increase for mechanisms to allow some states to progress more quickly towards full monetary and political union which, if it occurs, may establish a new boundary between the core states and the peripheral states of the Union.

The second category of frontier issues for the Union concerns its immediate neighbours. The economic and security interests of the Union are directly engaged in neighbouring countries. All great concentrations of economic or political power tend to have satellite powers around them. Before the collapse of Communist regimes in eastern Europe, the German Democratic Republic and Austria were, for trade purposes, effectively the thirteenth and fourteenth members of the EC. With the collapse of Communism, the Visegrád four have established, as applicants for membership, special relations with the EC/EU. In 1995 the Baltic states signed an association agreement with the EU, with a view to eventual membership. The drawing together of the countries of central Europe produced both positive and negative effects: the frontier regions of Austria and the former West Germany, which had been relatively depressed before 1989, revived with increased trading, commercial and tourist activities. In the Austrian case, there was a large number of new transfrontier joint ventures which were beneficial to both sides.[3] But some industrial activities, such as, in the Waldviertel in

Austria, glass-making and textile manufacture, were displaced to the east because of lower wage costs in the Czech Republic. For the countries bordering the EU to the east, problems of extreme economic inequality with western neighbours have caused anxieties about economic and political subordination to them.[4]

However, inclusion of east-central European countries brings direct EU involvement in frontier tensions of a potentially destabilizing kind, with non-EU neighbours to the east. The EU, for example, has in 1995 for the first time a common frontier with the Russian Federation. The formulation of a common defence and foreign policy for the EU, already difficult because of, amongst other factors, divergences over the relationships between the various European security institutions[5], will become even more difficult the further the external frontier is displaced towards the east. The management of tensions on the external frontier is not merely a matter of adopting the conventional formula of a military alliance ('an attack on one member is an attack on all'); each EU transfrontier relationship requires the formulation of an agreed and detailed strategy.

There are optimistic and pessimistic scenarios for the impact of an expanding external frontier on the European Union. The optimistic scenario is that the relocation of the frontier to the east will expand the area of security and tranquillity which exists in the west of the continent. The European Union's commitment to develop common foreign and defence policies provides an explicit security guarantee to all member states; the Union could be the single most important basis for a future European security order. Minor conflicts on the periphery can be isolated and, in a sense anaesthetized, by the EU; the examples of Gibraltar and Northern Ireland are encouraging, although the issues in these cases concern member states only, and not third countries. The EU creates pressure on the conflicting parties to reach an accommodation because frontier disputes between its member states seem marginal and anachronistic. On the unstable eastern frontiers, small states would be inhibited from pursuing frontier disputes by violent means because they could not win any military confrontation; and maintaining good relations with the EU has benefits, and alienating the EU attracts costs.

The pessimistic scenario is primarily based on two considerations. The first is that the EU is committed to an ever-widening foreign policy and security commitment which may be beyond the EU's decision-making capacities. The lack of an agreed policy in the initial stages and then a lack of firm resolve to intervene in the crisis produced by the disintegration of Yugoslavia supports the pessimistic view. The second is that for the states and peoples, particularly on the eastern frontier, any significant dispute with their neighbours across the external frontier weakens their solidarity with the EU because such conflicts are seen in a different light by the people most directly affected. Such conflicts are likely to be very divisive in the internal politics of the EU because the member states and important interests will diverge sharply on the policies to be adopted. The divisions caused could threaten the cohesion of the Union.

The Greek Case

Greek frontiers provide abundant illustration of the potential threat to EU cohesion posed by local frontier disputes. Greek positions on frontiers are deeply rooted in cultural and ideological attitudes. Prime Minister Andreas Papandreou stated in April 1994 that 'the national patrimony, the Greek language, cultural identity, education and Orthodoxy' should constitute 'the permanent elements of Greek foreign policy'[6]; solidarity with the European Union was not mentioned.

The entirety of Greece's northern frontier, established in its present location in the decade 1913–23, poses problems. Tension exists between Greece and its neighbours: in Epiros with Albania, in the north with Macedonia, in Thrace and in the Aegean with Turkey. In the north-west, the location of the boundary with Albania is regarded as controversial by some Greek irredentists, while the treatment of the Greek minority in Albania and the influx of Albanian economic migrants into Greece are serious issues for the Greek government; in the central section, the emergence of a newly independent state wishing to call itself Macedonia provoked a hostile reaction by Greek opinion and by the Greek government; in the eastern section, in Thrace, there is a significant Turkish minority and tension over further illegal Turkish immigration; and the maritime border with Turkey in the Aegean is the subject of a longstanding dispute over maritime frontiers and sea-bed exploitation.[7] The frontier disputes with Turkey are compounded by the Cyprus problem, where both sides regard themselves as responding to the provocations of the other – the Turks to a pro-union-with-Greece coup in 1974, the Greeks to the Turkish invasion of the same year and the subsequent establishment of the Turkish Republic of Northern Cyprus.

Early in 1994, the 1920s frontier dispute between Albania and Greece was revived. The three main issues were, first, the Hellenic population of southern Albania – the target of continuous propaganda by the orthodox clergy of north-eastern Greece, broadcast by Radio Drynou-pouli. Greek and Albanian estimates differ (400,000 as against 60,000) on the number of Greeks in Albania. The Greeks claimed that this population was subject to harsh repression in the last years of the Hoxha regime and that this persecution has continued. Second, isolated violent incidents occurred, such as the killing of two Albanian soldiers by a Greek 'commando' in April 1994. Third, the beginnings, in 1990–1, of a mass exodus across the Greek frontier placed the Greek authorities in a delicate position because they did not wish to see the disappearance of the Hellenic population of southern Albania. On the other hand, they did not wish to abandon the principle of welcoming the return of Greeks from the Greek diaspora.

The Macedonian question was intensified by the entirely different versions of history offered by propagandists for Greek, Yugoslav and Bulgarian positions. For Greek propagandists since the nineteenth century, the Greek state is the inheritor of classical Greece with a claim to those lands occupied by the Greeks of antiquity. From at least the 1870s, this founding myth of the Greek state was confronted by ethnic divisions in the south-east Balkans and ignored in the struggle between great powers for strategic objectives. From the ethnic standpoint Macedonia was a particularly difficult case – there was no clear Macedonian ethnic identity on which the neighbouring countries could base a strong claim.[8] In the struggle for strategic advantage Austro-Hungary and Germany sought to control the Vardar corridor giving access to Istanbul, and the Russians were determined to thwart them. From both points of view the Macedonian question seemed to lose relevance after the Second World War, although the Bulgarians occasionally revived it, when the USSR sought to create difficulties for Tito.

In September 1991 Yugoslav Macedonia proclaimed its independence. Greece riposted that it could not tolerate an independent country with the historic Greek name of Macedonia or which used other symbols of classical Macedonia, because these implied a claim on part of Greek national territory; Bulgaria, by contrast, announced its willingness to recognize the new Macedonia. This was enough to reignite the conflict, and nationalist feeling in Greece became inflamed. Propaganda was published which attempted to delegitimize claims of a separate Macedonian identity or nation.[9] Strong pressure from the EC was necessary before Greece would accept the name of the Macedonian Republic of Skopje.

In December 1993 Britain, France, Denmark, Germany and Holland recognized the Skopje government and the independent Macedonian state. During the Greek presidency of the European Union in the first six months of 1994, without consulting its European partners, Greece decided to close its frontier with Macedonia. The Greeks demanded that the Skopje government should change its name, its flag (which carried the emblem of the sun of Alexander the Great and Philip of Macedon), and its constitution (which made it a duty to protect Macedonians resident in other countries). Turkey, Bulgaria, Albania, Italy and Macedonia then signed an agreement (18 February 1994) on building a road and rail corridor[10] to prevent the economic strangulation of Macedonia. The Greek government found itself isolated in the European Union and, in April 1994, an action was brought by the EC Commission against Greece before the European Court of Justice for its unilateral trade sanctions against Macedonia. The Greek position was met by almost complete lack of comprehension outside its own borders and interpreted as a manifestation of primitive nationalism which called into question the standing of Greece as a modern state.

The Thrace issue is a consequence of the Greek–Turkish negotiations in 1923 when the two countries agreed to exchange their respective minorities, with the exceptions of the Greeks of Istanbul and the Turks of Thrace, each numbering about 120,000. The Greek population of Istanbul declined to around 3,000 but the Turkish population in Thrace, mainly rural, relatively poor and less mobile, maintained its numbers. The Greek authorities felt threatened by the possibility of Turkish irredentism, encouraged by complaints from Ankara about Greek ill-treatment of the Turkish minority, and by clandestine Turkish immigration. For the Greek government, the acquisition of Thrace in 1923 was the final step in the dismantling of the Ottoman empire, although a militant minority would have liked to seize Constantinople and drive the Turks out of Europe. For the Turks, this loss was deeply felt as an unjust exaction by a victorious coalition. In addition, Bulgaria had an old (no longer voiced) ambition to acquire access to the Aegean through Thrace; the Bulgarians have briefly occupied Thrace three times and their drive to the south was interpreted as in the Russian interest, and perhaps directly inspired by Russia.

These frontier issues are of fundamental concern to Greek governments and to Greek opinion but they are of minor importance for the other governments of the EU, except insofar as they affect the stability of the Union. The interests of the other fourteen member states are: first, that Greece does not allow illegal immigrants across its frontier who could then move freely in the other EC countries; second, to ensure that customs controls are not evaded for fraudulent purposes or for the passage of illegal substances; and third, to maintain stability in the eastern Mediterranean, above all to avoid armed conflict.

The application of Turkey to join the EU could provide a framework for managing Greek–Turkish relations, but EU Turkish membership would produce another set of frontier problems. Turkey's eastern frontier borders on volatile countries such as Iraq, Syria, Georgia and Armenia, and runs through the unstable Kurdish lands. Turkish military attacks on PKK (the Marxist-Leninist Kurdish independence movement) bases in Iraqi territory attracted official EU condemnation in 1995. Building dams in Turkish territory across the headwaters of the Euphrates and the Tigris threatens the interests of Syria and Iraq. Close relations between Turkey and other Turkic peoples of central Asia threaten Russian security interests. If the commitment in the Maastricht Treaty to develop common foreign and defence policies has any substance, the European Union would be involved in this series of difficult and remote frontier questions. Turkish membership of the EU may provide a framework within which progress could be·made on Greek–Turkish bilateral issues, but only at the expense of an even more insecure external EU frontier.

Administration of the External Frontier

Effective management and control of the external frontier were closely linked to the completion of the internal or single market.[11] The Single Market envisaged by the 1985 Single European Act, and developed in detail by the '1992 Programme', required the full implementation of the four freedoms agreed in principle by the member states with the signing of the Treaty of Rome – freedom of movement of persons, goods, services and capital. *Inter alia,* this required the dismantling of the non-tariff barriers to trade embedded in health, safety and industrial standards, professional and trades qualifications, descriptions of goods and administrative procedures. It also required making the external frontier an effective barrier to smuggling and to illegal immigrants, and the dismantling of customs and police controls at the internal frontiers.

Whether the external frontier can be effectively managed and policed depends on how closely national authorities cooperate with one another, which, in turn, requires a high degree of mutual trust in police, administrative and judicial authorities of other member states.[12] The twelve member states made the first collective move towards a harmonized frontier policy at the Rhodes summit in December 1988 when, to fulfil the 1992 programme, national coordinators were appointed to facilitate the implementation of measures necessary, set out in the Palma document. Customs cooperation, except where it touched on criminal law enforcement in the fields of drugs, pornography and arms smuggling, had a much lower political profile and was completed by the target date of 1 January 1993. In addition to an on-line customs intelligence system, exchanges of customs officers were put into effect with a pilot scheme in 1990 and a much more ambitious three-year programme in 1991.

In June 1991, agreement had almost been reached by the European Council on a draft External Frontiers Convention. In the final stages of the negotiation a difference arose between Britain and Spain over the territorial extent of the EC with regard to Gibraltar which, despite two years of attempts to reach a compromise, prevented the Convention being signed. The governments agreed to deem the Convention accepted *de facto* by the member states and to abide by its conditions. Some amendments to the text of the draft Convention were accepted after the ratification of the Maastricht Treaty on Political Union, and the article on the territorial extent of the Union will remain blank until bilateral discussions between Britain and Spain have resolved the issue of Gibraltar.

The basic definition in the Convention was that of the external frontier itself, which was stated to be:

1 a member state's frontier which is not contiguous with a frontier of another member state;
2 airports and seaports, except where they are considered to be internal frontiers for the purposes of instruments enacted under the treaty establishing the European Community.

The draft laid down principles concerning the nature of the controls at external frontiers. Crossing external frontiers was to be controlled by national authorities and carried out in accordance with national law, with due regard to the provisions of the Convention. However, it specified that all persons crossing the external frontier would be subject to visual controls to establish their identity. Specific arrangements for airports were laid down to ensure that flights internal to the EU were kept separate from flights connecting with external states. Reasons for refusing entry included the lack of the necessary documents or a threat to the public policy or national security of member states. A joint list of persons to whom entry is to be refused should be constantly updated by the member states. Rules were laid down for resident non-citizens crossing internal borders, stays of non-citizens other than for a short time and the issue of residence permits. A systematic exchange of information was envisaged, in particular by Article 13.2: 'The creation, organization and operation of a computerised system will be the subject of the Convention on the European Information System.'

The draft Convention leaves virtually all police, administrative and executive control in the hands of the member states, but the member states agree to certain common principles in order to harmonize their practices. The Convention is less ambitious than the Schengen Agreements (1985 and 1990, implemented in March 1995) for measures to compensate for abolition of internal frontiers, to which nine of the twelve members had acceded. The core of the Schengen arrangements are: an information system with on-line access at frontier posts, containing basic information about prohibited immigrants, wanted persons, persons in need of protection, stolen goods; a rapid response system ('Sirène') for mutual assistance when internal frontiers are crossed by wanted persons, suspects and suspect goods; a common visa policy; and a uniform system for asylum-seekers with certain allowances made for the exercise of national discretion.[13]

Britain, Ireland and Denmark[14] did not join the Schengen group and anxieties were expressed among the signatories, particularly in France, about some aspects of the agreement. Amongst other matters, concerns were expressed about the professional competence and integrity of the southern European frontier police, and about the possibility of the spread of Mafia-type criminal organizations into northern Europe. There were heated complaints about lack of parliamentary consultation, either of the European Parliament or the national parliaments. A French parliamentary committee of inquiry denounced 'a technocratic dilution of responsibilities', 'a failure of organization', and 'a lack of democratic accountability'.[15]

The Maastricht Treaty contains all the areas of cooperation envisaged by the Schengen Agreements. If both are implemented at the same time, problems of consistency and coherence between them may arise; there is, therefore, an argument in favour of letting the Schengen Agreements lapse, bringing the twelve EU member states into a common system for policing the external frontier. The counter-argument is that the two member states which remained outside Schengen, Britain and Ireland, are intent on maintaining controls at the internal frontiers and will hinder attempts at establishing a genuine control-free area. Some influential opinion in other member states is reticent about dismantling internal frontier controls; unilateral reimposition of systematic frontier controls on persons is possible if a member state feels that its security is threatened, if there is popular or electoral pressure, or if the controls on the external frontier are deficient.[16]

Doubts about the abolition of internal frontier controls and the efficiency of the administration of the external frontier arose because of new kinds of security threat. Security threats were no longer those of invasion by massive military force but rather the spread of 'disorder' from regions adjacent to the territory of the EU (eastern Europe, North Africa, the Middle East). The first kind of disorder was seen as the spilling over of ethnic, national and religious conflicts, resulting in terrorist action on EU territory or in the influx of large numbers of refugees. The second was the external threat of 'organized crime',[17] mainly involving drugs, but including any criminal traffic from which profits could be made – stolen works of art, export of stolen cars, traffic in women, fraud and extortion. To combat these perceived threats, the European Union is tending, despite the reluctance of some states, to turn into a security community.

When criminal threats from outside the EU became part of the political debate, the weakness of policing arrangements for the external frontier was exposed.[18] Germany's land frontiers are seen to be highly permeable, with the 420 kilometres with Switzerland lightly policed, the 450 kilometres with the Czech Republic relatively secure because of good bilateral cooperation, but with the 430 kilometres shared with Poland, the old Oder–Neisse line, being very difficult to control: 80% of the asylum-seekers arrived across this border in 1992. More than 1 million people entered Germany in 1992 with the apparent intention of staying permanently. In 1992 Spain had significant clandestine immigration from North Africa, and these immigrants frequently reached France before they were apprehended.[19] Italy has a very difficult coastline to police and was administering immigration legislation for the first time in the early 1990s. After the arrival of increasing numbers of people from the former Communist states, Greece, with 1,180 kilometres of land frontiers in difficult terrain, 15,021 kilometres of coastline and more than 2,000 islands, could be represented as a threat for the whole EU.[20]

Whether all the frontiers, in the east and the south, can be policed and controlled to the satisfaction of all EU member states has yet to be demonstrated. But a certain myth of control must gain wide currency to maintain the legitimacy of the EU.

Abolition of Controls at Internal EU Frontiers

The internal frontiers of the EC pose three controversial questions. The first is whether European developments in dismantling frontier controls are different in kind from the erosion of frontiers between all highly developed economies, such as the erosion of frontiers taking place in the regional integration processes of North and South America and of East Asia.

This is a difficult question to answer in the absence of detailed comparative research on transfrontier transactions. Other attempts at regional cooperation have not yet achieved integrated common policies or the introduction of Union law directly applicable in the member states. Optimistic commentaries have, since the late 1970s, been made about developments in South America.[21] A number of initiatives – the Andean group, the Mercosur group (Argentina, Brazil, Uruguay, Paraguay), the Central American free trade area, the G3 associating Mexico, Colombia and Venezuela – have produced slender results. In North America the signing of the North American Free Trade Area Treaty on 10 October 1992 was a major development. The free trade area requires some harmonization of economic policies but does not envisage free movement of persons. In terms of economic dynamism, the most important regional integration process is taking place in eastern Asia (the east Pacific rim) and involves the Association of South-East Asian Nations (Brunei, Indonesia, Malaysia, the Philippines, Singapore and Thailand), the NIE – Newly Industrialized Economies (Hong Kong, South Korea, Singapore and Taiwan), China and Japan. Certain fora have been established – Asian Pacific Economic Cooperation (APEC) and East Asian Economic Caucus (EAEC) but these are in their infancy. The difficult question to answer is whether frontiers are being effaced to a similar extent, although in different ways, in these other regions in terms of trade flows, investment and communications. The European Union has made greater progress in institutional terms but the Pacific rim countries may have a lead in information and communications technologies, and their economic dynamism is leading to ever greater trade and capital flows.

The second question for the European Union is whether an effective political frontier between sovereign jurisdictions can be maintained after its economic functions have been abolished. Harmonization or common policies in environmental protection, trade, competition, state aid, professional qualifications, health and safety standards and other matters are now accepted by the member states. Institutions fulfilling regulatory, judicial and legislative functions have been established; individuals have rights across the whole territory of the Union. Monetary union, with a European central bank, and close cooperation by governments in foreign and defence policy, were formally agreed by the Treaty of European Union. Additional powers have also been given to the European Parliament by that treaty. Cooperation in policing and internal affairs is a key indicator of whether the European Union will develop a state-like constitution. But frontiers still remain obstacles in some domains: different police organization, different criminal justice procedures and different legal systems of the member states are obstacles to crime control in the European Union. The problems of arresting persons in a different European jurisdiction, transferring evidence from one jurisdiction to another, subpoenaing witnesses, different definitions of crime, varying law enforcement policies – all present difficulties and cause expense, delay, misunderstanding and friction. Harmonization of criminal law and criminal law procedures is technically difficult and, at the moment, the political will is lacking to achieve it.

The third controversial question is whether a new European identity is emerging, expressed by a loyalty to the European Union, rivalling that of loyalty to the member states. Loyalty to the Union will, if it is achieved, be centred on the 'constitution of Europe' and the belief that the European Union genuinely promotes general welfare. The regular polling of opinions by Eurobarometer provided evidence that this was happening (although a long economic depression is now having negative effects[22]) and regular participation in direct elections to the European Parliament will help to sustain European solidarity. But questions of identity, loyalty and legitimacy are the most difficult raised by the EU. The way they are provisionally settled will determine the way in which both the internal and external frontiers of the Union are perceived. These perceptions will be an important, and in some cases determining, influence on the frontier policy of governments.

Conclusion

The general purpose of frontiers in the sovereign state was to establish absolute physical control over a finite area and to exercise exclusive legal, administrative and social controls over its inhabitants. But the traditional attributes of 'sovereignty' are clearly being eroded in Europe and frontiers are losing their hard-edged clarity.

But perceptions of territorial limits and territorial constraints are part of social and political processes. A sense of territory is an element (although the characteristics of this element have yet to be established) of what it is to be human.[23] Human consciousness and social organization are profoundly conditioned by territory and frontiers.[24] Boundary-making may be seen as part of the natural history of the human species. Images of frontiers and the conceptions of territorial organization have been part of all major political projects. Territorial ideologies have had widely varying bases – religious dominion, notions of homelands, historical myths, living spaces, natural frontiers, civilizing missions, ethnicity, human biology, claims of natural rights, and the optimal use of space. These are part of the discourse of frontiers, and without them frontiers become unintelligible. Most have motivated people to fight and to die.

The almost universal sense of territorial 'ownership' or belonging implies *inter alia* that the frontier of the territory is a line of exclusion of outsiders or foreigners. Doubts about whether governments and political elites in Europe have been conceiving the frontier in this way are part of the explanation for the increased level of expressions of racism in Europe[25] and of increased alienation of large parts of the electorate from political elites. For practical reasons, it has become increasingly difficult for governments and political elites to consider the frontier as an instrument of exclusion, although they have been compelled by popular pressures to do so in the field of immigration.

The internationalization of industrial, commercial, financial, scientific, professional, sporting and leisure activity means that different boundaries may exist for different purposes. Perceptions of frontiers are changing, from one frontier to several, from line to zone, from physical to cultural, from spatial to functional, from impermeable to permeable.[26] Different professional, social and economic groups within the same society have different conceptions of the space in which their key activities take place. These spaces often transcend, or ignore, the international frontier. Jacques G. Maisonrouge, a senior executive of International Business Machines, has observed: 'For business purposes the boundaries that separate one nation from another are no more real than the equator. They are convenient demarcations of ethnic, linguistic and cultural entities.'[27] The same individual may have different conceptions of space for different purposes.

The mental maps of individuals are, however, malleable and relatively easy to alter, by contrast with the difficulty of changing the political and administrative organization of space. In the post-1945 period, a salient feature of the political map has been the increasing importance of global and regional institutions. Larger groupings of states have sometimes been accompanied by increased autonomy at the sub-state level because state frontiers are no longer viewed as the inviolable cell walls of a sovereign authority. Transfrontier cooperation between municipalities, local authorities, regions and social and economic organizations as on the US–Mexican border can also be observed along all the land frontiers of the EU. The effects of these are complex and will not result in a simple fading of the importance of the international frontier. But an increasing propensity to regard the important frontiers, as anthropologists have,[28] as evidence of cultural discontinuity, may be expected.

Changes in frontiers affect the morale and the self-perception of peoples in the contemporary world. Redefinition of the functions of frontiers in the highly industrialized world can be represented as offering new opportunities to individuals and groups. Opportunities may be for financial reward, new options in educational, cultural and leisure activities or the possibility of forging new political alliances. But changes, whether functional or spatial, in frontiers can be acutely disturbing, altering the balance of power and authority, undermining habits and cultural patterns, threatening identities and creating general feelings of unease and insecurity.

The most difficult and sensitive frontiers are not those of the European Union, but those between the highly industrialized countries and the less developed countries. Frontiers are clearly used to maintain global inequalities. Stronger powers may respect the location of frontiers but may not respect the sovereignties which the frontiers are supposed to delimit. In circumstances where there are gross inequalities of wealth and military capability, attempts to reassert sovereign authority by weaker powers may seem unwarranted and even an act of aggression by the stronger powers. The attempt by the United States to control policies to repress the traffic in narcotic drugs in South America is an illustration. The reactions of the French government to the 1993 electoral victory of the Muslim party in Algeria provides another example. Similar relations between Russia and the former states of the Soviet Union are manifest.

Although cosmopolitan elites may attempt, as far as possible, to ignore international frontiers, large populations will continue to regard them as indispensable instruments of political and social defence. Attempts to harden frontiers, to make them more exclusive, may occur wherever identities and interests appear to be under serious threat. The loss of the ability to control information flows, because of new technologies of communication, has weakened, but not destroyed, the ability of governments to do this. Frontiers as markers of identity and as protectors of interests are unlikely to become redundant in any future which can, at the moment, reasonably be foreseen. Identities will continue to be protected by the exclusion of some human groups and the incorporation of others. Interests will be protected by active frontier policies to exclude undesired goods, services and influences. A world without frontiers in which solidarity with the whole human race dominates all intermediate solidarities remains an utopian dream.

Notes

Introduction

1 For general reviews of contemporary frontiers see Blake 1994b, Foucher 1988. See also Day 1987, Prescott 1987, Tagil 1977.
2 Attempts by social scientists to 'measure' boundary effects on behaviour and values produce obvious results because of the assumptions on which they are based. For example, see MacKay 1968. When statistical analyses of boundary effects are embedded in historical accounts of the development of boundary region, a much enriched account may result. See Rykiel 1985.
3 Although it touches on both literatures, this book is neither a contribution to the debates between neo-realists, liberal institutionalists, functionalists, neo-functionalists and interdependence theorists in international relations nor a book about 'state theory'. For a review of international relations theory see Groom and Light 1994. Recent writings on state theory have regarded the frontier of the state as unproblematic. See Birnbaum 1982, Birnbaum and Badie 1983, De Jasay 1985, Dyson 1980, Evans et al. 1985, Poggi 1978.
4 Some anthropologists hold that boundaries are necessary to any cultural identity. See the 'introduction' to Barth 1969. Evidence about aboriginal societies is fragmentary but even those who live in apparently trackless wastes, such as the Australian aborigines, have highly specific notions of territory.
5 Consideration of frontiers and explicit recognition of the territorial nature of states is very patchy in the western tradition of political philosophy. See Baldwin 1992.
6 Poggi 1978: 92.
7 Anderson 1991.
8 Connor 1969.
9 The relationship between the Nazi regime and an academic discipline

(*Ostforschung* – research on the east) is a chilling example. See Burleigh 1988.

10 Strassoldo 1970.

11 This leads structuralist and post-modernist geographers to regard analysis of space and boundaries as part of a political project. See Davis 1990.

12 Strassoldo 1970 and 1973.

13 For a comment see Blaise 1990.

14 Weigart et al. 1957: 116, 122–4.

15 For a review of the classic literature on the development of a sense of territory in children see Malmberg 1980: 53–64.

16 Goffman (1972) suggests that there is fixed and movable (temporarily occupied such as a restaurant table) personal space.

17 In the 19th c. France was often pictured as a face with Paris as the eye, Brittany as the nose and the Loire estuary as the mouth.

18 Lamb 1968: 8.

19 For a survey of pioneer frontiers see Guichonnet and Raffestin 1974: 65–81.

20 For a comparison between the Iberian and steppe frontiers see Chaunu 1973: i. 33. See also McNeill 1964, Grousset 1965, Wieczynski 1976.

21 Heiberg 1989: 110-11.

22 Peter Sahlins (1989) analyses in this way the process of establishing a social and cultural boundary between France and Spain in the Cerdagne, a small region in the Pyrenees, over a 200-year period.

23 Social boundaries which have no clear spatial reference were considered by Max Weber, who identified 'analytical', 'vertical' and 'organizational' boundaries. See Weber 1947: 139ff.

24 George 1984: 113–25.

25 Oscar Martinez (1994) develops a continuum for relations in the borderlands – alienated borderlands, co-existent borderlands, interdependent borderlands, integrated borderlands.

26 Beaujeu-Garnier and Chabod 1967: 426. Relations between Geneva and its hinterland in France have become much closer since the 1960s. See Grange 1990.

27 This is provoking anxiety in some countries: the 1994 Toubon bill (declared unconstitutional by the Constitutional Council) in France, limiting the use of foreign (essentially English) terms in both state and unofficial publications, is an example.

28 A. P. Cohen 1986: 17.

29 Schmitt 1976, especially pp. 26–37.

30 And some European ones – the Jewish tradition is the most difficult and complex exception.

31 This is a complex body of thought and has taken different forms in Britain, France, Germany and Italy. See Bellamy 1992.

32 For a discussion of some of the issues see Beitz 1994: 123–36.

33 Rawls 1971.

34 Hoffmann 1981.

35 This is not always associated with a conservative position. For example, it is defended by Michael Walzer, a left-liberal. See Walzer 1983.
36 Prescott 1987: 36.
37 See Jennings 1963, de Visscher 1957; and, particularly for French and German legal theory, see Cavin 1971, de Lapradelle 1928.
38 For example, Capotorti 1979: para. 208.
39 Jackson 1990.
40 The terms European Communities, European Community and European Union refer to the same group of institutions (with important legal exceptions) which have changed their name as a result of new international agreements. The first refers to the European Economic Community, European Coal and Steel Community, Euratom from 1957 to 1985; the second to the unification of these communities by the 1985 Single European Act; the third to the reformed institutions following the Treaty of European Union (often known as the Maastricht Treaty) which came into force in 1993.

1 The International Frontier in Historical and Theoretical Perspective

1 For an analysis of theoretical connections between statehood and territoriality see Baldwin 1992.
2 Reading history backwards and 'abridging' traditions are heinous errors for some historians and philosophers of history. For a classic statement of this position see Oakeshott 1991. However, the terms used in political discourse, as well as concepts developed in international law and diplomacy, are based on a highly selective reading of history.
3 See Jolowicz 1952, especially pp. 66–8, 280.
4 In *Puck of Pook's Hill*, 1906.
5 Hanson and Maxwell 1983.
6 Luttwak 1976. Luttwak's argument is effectively demolished in Isaac 1990; see also the review of Isaac by Whittaker, *Times Literary Supplement*, 22 March 1991.
7 See Whittaker 1989.
8 Sitwell 1984.
9 Gagé 1964.
10 Braudel 1984: 66.
11 Rokkan and Urwin 1982.
12 Le Bras 1967: 47–57, McNeill 1939.
13 Southern 1970, Baldwin 1929.
14 Baldwin 1986: 248–58.
15 Charlemagne recognized Byzantium and concluded the Treaty of Aachen in 814 with the eastern Roman empire in an effort to reunite Christendom.
16 Dion 1947: 71–85 describes the work of the 120 boundary commissioners in delimiting the three kingdoms.
17 Some hold the view that the foreign policy of the Russian tsars remained

the pursuit of 'pan-orthodoxy' rather than pan-Slavism. For an example of this view see Thual 1994.

18 The Chinese notion of the 'Middle Kingdom' was the most long-lasting and almost certainly the most complete of all the universalisms. The emperor held his mandate from heaven to rule the centre of civilization (the Middle Kingdom) and the political structure was an element of a total Confucian cosmology in which the social, moral, physical and spiritual domains formed an integrated whole. It was the emperor's duty to lead the less civilized peoples who in turn owed obeisance and tribute to him. A brief survey is given in the introduction to Hsu 1960.

19 Rafferty 1928: vol 6. 156–7.

20 Jean Gottmann (1975) argues that political–territorial communities, analogous to the modern state, emerged somewhat earlier in the fourteenth century.

21 This was for various reasons including the unreliability of requisitioned labour, lack of financial resources, undeveloped administrative structures, political fragmentation and physical threats from within (as important as external threats). See Contamine 1980, especially p. 366.

22 Braudel 1985: 99.

23 Giddens 1981: 11.

24 Quoted in the preface to Burguière and Revel 1989: 17.

25 Braudel 1986.

26 For wide-ranging contributions to the study of the political uses of cartography see Buisseret 1992.

27 Broc 1983.

28 Foucher 1988: 63–96.

29 Eck 1969: 28.

30 Bonenfant 1953: 79.

31 Bloch 1961: ii. 382. But it was difficult to delineate precisely as late as the 17th c. See Girard d'Albissin 1970.

32 Guenée 1986: 17; see also Guenée 1981.

33 Boutier, Dewerpe and Nordman 1984.

34 Fawtier 1961.

35 Nordman and Revel 1989.

36 Godechot 1983: 81.

37 See ch. 5 below for the establishment of the *départements*.

38 Travaux du comité d'études 1918.

39 For an account (perhaps over-drawn) of this process, see Weber 1979; see also Zeldin 1977: ii. 3–28.

40 Weber 1984. See also Smith, 1969.

41 Gullick 1955.

42 For example, the Franco-Spanish boundary, considered the first modern frontier, was agreed at the Treaty of the Pyrenees in 1659 but it was not fully demarcated until the mid-19th c. in the treaties of Bayonne in 1866 and 1868. In this case, disputes did not result in military action but identifying the exact location of the watershed of the Pyrenean mountain chain and

agreeing the extent to which ancient rights of pasturage should influence the exact line of demarcation posed difficult and controversial questions for the frontier commission. See Gómez-Ibanez 1975: ch. 5, Sahlins 1989.

43 The impact of revolutionary states on the international system, and on the classic balance of power, is a controversial matter. Their leaders have undoubtedly been convinced that they were following some iron historical law which required a radical revision of the territorial status quo but their actions can be interpreted as following the main lines of the policies of the *ancien régime*. See Armstrong 1993.

44 The seminal article is Mackinder 1904. According to Mackinder, global geopolitical struggle inevitably took place between those who sought control of the Eurasian heartland and the maritime powers who dominated the rimland of the seas and oceans. If a single power controlled the heartland, according to Mackinder, it would dominate the world: this thinking continued to influence American geopolitical thinking in the post-1945 period. See Dalby 1990; see also Foucher 1988.

45 The best accounts of Marxist thought on the nation-state and nationalism are Connor 1984 and Haupt, Lowy and Weill 1974.

46 Lenin 1964: xxii. 263.

47 Dependency theory was revived by writers such as Murray (1975) and was given a less orthodox Marxist expression in work on Latin America, for example Cardoso and Faletto 1971, Evans 1979.

48 The treatment of nationalism here is necessarily brief and schematic. For a recent brilliant review of theories of nationalism, see Hall 1993.

49 See ch. 2 below.

50 Febvre 1922: 388, and *passim*. See also Ancel 1938 for another elegant rebuttal of the theses of the German geopolitical school.

51 See Parker 1994. Despite Geoffrey Parker's substantial contribution (particularly Parker 1988), the recent literature on geopolitics is thin and unconvincing. The extent to which the revival of geopolitics is marked by nationalist assumptions is documented in Raffestin, Loprano and Pasteur 1995: 279–308.

52 The Nazis supplemented geopolitical arguments with arguments about the actual ethnic composition, or the ethnic characteristics in the past, of the populations of parts of Poland and Lithuania; see Burleigh 1988, especially pp. 155–86. Italian Fascist propagandists followed the Nazi lead; see Lopreno 1991. The association with Nazism and Fascism completely discredited the German geopolitical school, although there have been recent attempts at a partial rehabilitation by French authors. See Korinman 1990, Haushofer 1986; Professor Jacobsen's own massive scholarly work can also be regarded as a rehabilitation – see Jacobsen 1979.

53 Ardrey 1967 and 1972, Dawkins 1976. However, Dawkins, like the more distinguished exponents of sociobiology such as the Nobel Prize-winner Konrad Lorenz (see Lorenz 1966 and the exposition of his ideas in Evans 1975 and Wilson 1975), did not consider territoriality, as such, to be determined by the human genome but as a by-product of biologically

determined human aggression, or the expression of human beings as 'survival machines' or 'hidden biological prime movers', a view for which there is scant evidence.

54 *Revue de l'Institut de Sociologie* 1984, especially pp. 360–2.

55 The very term 'sociobiology' is regarded by many as a provocation and associated with biological reductionism – see the critique of Kaye (1986). Some of the most perceptive critics of sociobiology admit, however, that there is a biological basis to human behaviour. Lerner 1992.

56 Bodin 1962. Bodin's account of sovereignty was complex, but he insisted that sovereignty was indivisible.

57 Skinner 1978.

58 Novak 1970: 3.

59 Boulding 1962.

60 Amongst his many works see in particular Wallerstein 1976.

61 Kindelberger 1969: 4, Keohane and Nye 1977: 353.

62 This general view of causation has influenced political geographers who have tried to distance themselves from political ideology in order to seek (in vain) a more objective and scientific appraisal of spatial relationships. Geographers, when they have escaped the geopolitical fallacy of believing spatial relationships are fundamental causal factors, have argued that there is, in Yves Goblet's phrase, a 'universality of interdependencies' and that physical, economic and human interdependencies across political frontiers are to be found almost everywhere: Goblet 1956: 148–62.

63 Monnet was concerned to avoid offending national sentiments, which were easily aroused in the years following 1945.

64 For a discussion of the Serbian case see ch. 2, for the Israeli case see ch. 3, and for the Greek case see the conclusion.

65 See ch. 3.

66 Braudel 1985: 218.

2 Self-Determination, Secession and Autonomy: European Cases of Boundary-Drawing

1 For the literature on self-determination see Knight and Davies 1987.

2 Who the 'people' are remains a problem in contractarian theory. See David Held's essays in Held 1991 and 1993.

3 Mill 1861: 547.

4 Lansing 1921, particularly pp. 97–101.

5 Tudjman 1981: 29.

6 Tunkin 1974: 1.

7 The relationship between Marxist-Leninist theory and the practice of Soviet nationality policy is difficult to analyse without reference to other policies. See Duncan 1988: 180–200.

8 Jennings 1956: 56.

9 Emerson 1960: 298–9. For a short review of the arguments against self-determination see Buccheit 1978: 20–31.

10 The usual response to this anxiety is that the claim of most small groups is ludicrous and only the more important human groups, with a shared history, have the right to self-determination. For a recent development of this view see Margalit and Raz 1990.

11 The French revolutionaries, however, introduced the practice of the plebiscite to legitimize a change of sovereignty (in the case of Belgian provinces annexed by France). The small number of examples of plebiscites to sanction changes in sovereignty between the French Revolution and the First World War were not models of free expression of the wishes of the populations concerned because strong pressure was brought to bear on the electorate. See Rousseau 1964: 28–47.

12 Immanuel Kant offers the best philosophical justification of national independence, although he admitted that there is an element of subjective judgement in deciding which nations should have independence. See Williams 1983, particularly pp. 250–1.

13 John Hall (1993) argues that it is easier to define 'nationalism' than the 'nation', but admits that no comprehensive theory of nationalism is possible.

14 Renan 1992: 5.

15 De Gaulle 1954: 1–2.

16 Plamenatz 1960.

17 Anderson 1991: 7.

18 Capotorti 1979.

19 Wight 1977: ch. 6.

20 See Azcárate 1945, Cobban 1945 (rev. edn 1969), Cruttwell 1937, Farley 1986, Mattern 1921.

21 The bitter memories of the 1920 Polish occupation of Vilna survived in the 1990s. During negotiations in February 1994 in Warsaw, Lithuania demanded that the Polish–Lithuanian Treaty settling the frontier between the two countries should contain a condemnation of the occupation; this was successfully resisted by the Polish government.

22 Wambaugh 1933, Johansson 1988: 155.

23 Wambaugh's discussion of this remains, despite the lack of post-Second World War examples, the most authoritative. See Wambaugh 1933: i. 442–7.

24 The community of states has sought to make frontiers the most durable of institutions. Even if a sovereign state disappears: 'The principle of the successor state taking over *ipso jure* all of its predecessor's boundaries and boundary regimes has for a long time been recognised as one of the basic principles of the law of state succession' (Tyranowski 1985: 465). This was confirmed by the 1978 Vienna Convention on Succession of States in respect of Treaties (Article 11) and the treaties with respect to boundaries were distinguished from all other treaties which were held to be of a less binding character. What this means may be variously interpreted but the intention is clear.

25 The experience of an Alsatian, born in 1862 and dying in 1951, illustrates

the lack of consultation for transfers of territory. Sovereignty over Alsace changed four times between France and Germany without his opinion once being directly asked. Husser 1989.

26 Other examples are: the Spanish regions of Catalonia and the Basque Provinces, Corsica and Scotland which voted in favour of devolution in 1979 but with a majority insufficient to reach the qualified majority threshold laid down in the enabling legislation.

27 Heslinga 1979.

28 For a detailed history of the issues up to the package agreement of 1969 see Alcock 1970.

29 One optimistic scenario was that the spread of bilingualism would lead to a new equilibrium between the ethnic groups without necessarily undermining their specific identity. See Gubert 1982.

30 The three major contributions in English to the study of the Jura question are Campbell 1982, Jenkins 1986, McRae 1983.

31 Jenkins 1986: 90–107.

32 See for example Béguilin and Charpilloz 1982, Béguilin and Schaffter 1974, Charpilloz 1976, Fell 1976, Schaffter 1968.

33 See for example Aubry 1983, Flückiger 1977.

34 Ideas of a larger area were discarded because the Protestants risked being put in a minority, and suggestions of a smaller area, in which Protestants would be the overwhelming majority, were rejected on the grounds that the smallness of the province established might make it non-viable.

35 Whyte 1983.

36 Whyte 1991.

37 Bruce 1994.

38 Hintjens, Loughlin and Olivesi 1994.

39 The lack of evidence about the origins of the Basques and their language is reviewed in a historical *tour de force* in Collins 1990.

40 Boulangé and Cavenaile 1991.

41 Kolarz 1946.

42 Tighe 1990: 40–1.

43 Some Hungarian statements are interpreted as veiled irredentism. A persistent problem is that any mention of 'autonomy' in eastern Europe is often interpreted as a first move towards secession. See Schöpflin 1993.

44 Roux 1993. The origin of the Serbian nation in Kosovo has led the Serb Orthodox Bishop of Prizren to say: 'Even if Serbs disappeared completely from Kosovo, the Serbian State would keep Kosovo within its territory because it is the soul of Serbia; when the soul is detached from the body it becomes nothing more than a corpse which decomposes.' *Le Monde,* 22 October 1992.

45 'Romania's Minorities', *The Times,* 19, 20 November 1991.

46 For a survey of the problems of self-determination see Müllerson 1994.

47 But Moldova and Azerbaijan (temporarily) failed to ratify the Alma Ata Declaration of December 1991 setting up the CIS.

48 For example, on 11 September 1991, the Catalonian national day (the

Diada), thousands of demonstrators carried banners through the streets of Barcelona proclaiming 'Independence is possible' in the presence of representatives from Lithuania and Slovenia. *Financial Times,* 16 September 1991.

49 Losser 1990.

50 The small number of Germans still living in the former German lands also helped to dampen irredentist sentiment.

51 Fritsch-Bournazel 1991: 31.

52 The exodus continued even after the official proclamation of German unity in the autumn of 1990, with an estimated 100,000 leaving in the three months following that proclamation. The birth rate in the new Länder dropped by 50% and in 1993 the Institute of Population Sciences in Wiesbaden was predicting a continuous decline through out-migration of the population until the end of the century. *Le Monde,* 9 October 1993.

53 For the background see Banac 1984.

54 *Financial Times,* 16 September 1988.

55 The frontier between the eastern and western Roman empires was in almost exactly the same place as the frontier between Serbia and Croatia.

56 Particularly Tchossitch 1991.

57 Quoted in Tudjman 1981: 22.

58 For an account and explanation see Woodward 1995.

59 The nature and effects of the deterioration of the economy are reviewed in Hewitt and Winston 1991. Controversy about whether ethnic and national unrest was one of the causes or one of the results of economic unrest is likely to continue.

60 For a guide to Soviet federalism see the introduction to Lapidus, Zaslavsky and Goldman 1992.

61 *Frankfurter Allgemeine Zeitung,* 13 December 1989.

62 Before these legal texts were adopted all fifteen Union republics had declared their 'sovereignty' and all except two, the Russian Federation and Kazakhstan, had declared their 'independence'. The difference between the two concepts was not entirely clear.

63 For a statement of this position see the interview of V. Landsbergis, the first President of the new Lithuanian Republic, in *Autrement* 1991: 226–7.

64 See especially Lemarq 1992 and Sokologorsky 1992.

65 *Le Monde,* 28 August 1991.

66 A curious territorial anomaly was created by the establishment of the Baltic states – the Russian enclave of Kaliningrad. This was the result of the division of the old German province of East Prussia between Poland and the USSR at the end of the Second World War. The Polish official position is that it should remain Russian. The Lithuanians aspire to part of it, but are opposed by Russia. Unofficial suggestions included converting it into a national home for Gypsies and returning at least the city of Kaliningrad (formerly Königsberg) to Germany. *Le Monde,* 8–9 March 1992; Lepesant 1993.

67 *Financial Times,* 20 July 1993.

68 For a survey of all the nations and ethnic groups of the former Soviet Union see Caratini 1990.
69 However, the parliamentary elections of February 1994 in Moldova produced a majority in favour of preserving independence and hostile to union with Romania.
70 *Le Monde,* 25–6, 27 August 1991.
71 Russian populations oustide the Russian Federation may be used to advance Russia's strategic and political interests. This is particularly the case for the self-proclaimed Dniestr Republic, which envisages an eventual union with the Russian Federation even though separated by 1,000 kilometres of Ukrainian territory. Moscow authorities appear to give this tacit support. See Socor 1994.
72 See Radvanyi 1992: 71.
73 *Le Monde,* 13 July 1993.
74 The Russian ministers of foreign affairs and defence stated in 1994 that Russia does not need international authorization for 'peace-keeping' operations within the CIS area. This was a move towards reconstituting the ex-USSR as a security community. The monetary union with Belarus of April 1994 and the Russian pressure on the Ukraine to form a 'common economic space' were the first steps towards the reconstitution of a wider economic union.
75 Although now dated, the basic source on the religious strands of former Soviet Central Asia is the works of Bennigsen. See Bennigsen and Lemercier-Quelquejay 1981, Bennigsen and Wimbush 1986.
76 *Independent,* 5 April 1991.
77 Roy 1991.
78 Wehrlé 1993.
79 *Le Monde,* 18 July 1992.
80 The Volkswagen plant in Bratislava does not seem to have a promising future: *Financial Times,* 6 August 1993.
81 The Poles and the Irish were both Catholic as well as oppressed peoples. This combination attracted the sympathies of both the right and the left in other European countries.

3 Themes in African and Asian Frontier Disputes

1 Reza Djalili 1990.
2 Piscatori 1986: 40–75.
3 Of these Vietnam has been reunited, Yemen briefly so (1990–4) and Korea remains partitioned, with potentially serious regional security implications.
4 Lamb 1968: 228–9.
5 Stereotyping of the continents pre-dated the 19th c. The Renaissance *mappae mundi* and the descriptive geographical works of the later 16th and early 17th c. had lavish pictorial images of the continents which usually represented Europe as more advanced in science and armaments than the

other continents. But it was not until much later that the two stereotypes mentioned entered the popular imagination.

6 Asiwaju 1990: 26.
7 Jackson 1990: 68–9.
8 Gallais 1982: 114; see also Sautter 1982.
9 K. M. Barbour, by superimposing a political map for tropical Africa on a tribal map, estimated that at least '187 tribal territories' were bisected by political boundaries. He emphasized the unreliability of this estimate because of the conceptual confusion surrounding terms such as 'tribes' and 'tribal territories'. Barbour 1961: 312–13.
10 Udo 1982: 211–12.
11 Barbour 1961.
12 Asiwaju 1985.
13 Udo 1982: 210, Drysdale and Blake 1985: 81–2.
14 Kapil 1966.
15 Brownlie 1979 remains the indispensable work of reference.
16 The literature on the development of frontiers in the Maghreb is particularly rich. See *inter alia*, Laroui 1977, Nordman 1975, Trout 1969.
17 Anderson 1987.
18 Hanlon 1986, Lemon 1991.
19 The approach in this chapter owes much to Smith 1983.
20 Jackson 1990: 42.
21 Brownlie 1971: 360–1.
22 The Organization of African Unity is one of several important examples of regional organizations playing an important role in maintaining the territorial status quo. See Lyon 1970.
23 Benmassaoud Trédano 1989: 60–4, Bourjorl-Flecher 1981.
24 Boateng 1978: 17–18.
25 McEwan 1971: 51–4, 108–9.
26 Benmassaoud Trédano 1989: 164–82.
27 *Libération*, 28–9 July 1990.
28 Until the time of Nasser, an Egyptian aspiration was 'the unity of the Nile', in other words, the annexation of Sudan.
29 *Independent*, 14 August 1992.
30 Touval 1972: 196–202, 281 and *passim*, Young 1966: 167–208. The separatist movement of Casamance, active since 1982 in Senegal, is a case where the geography of the province (isolated between Guinea-Bissau and the Gambia with only its eastern extremity attached to the rest of Senegal) is the primary factor.
31 Lemarchand 1962. See also Neuberger 1986.
32 Hodges 1983, C. M. Brown 1991.
33 Benmassaoud Trédano 1989: 136–41.
34 *Le Monde*, 14–15 August, 1 September 1989.
35 *Le Monde*, 3 August 1991.
36 *Le Monde*, 13 March 1992: 'L'Impossible référendum'.
37 Drysdale 1964.

38 Samatar 1985; for an interesting Marxist account see J. Markakis 1987; for an extended discussion of the Somali sense of nationhood see Touval 1963.
39 Chalier 1966.
40 Ottoway 1982, Radcliff 1986.
41 Japan became an imperial power in its own right and subjected China to similar indignities.
42 Gong 1984: 173.
43 Joyeux 1991: i. 93.
44 For the maps and the Indian reaction to them see Indian Ministry of Information and Broadcasting, 1962.
45 See Woodman, 1969.
46 The first All-China Soviet Congress of November 1931 stated: 'All Mongolians, Tibetans, Miao, Koreans and others living on the territory of China shall enjoy the full right to self-determination i.e. they may either join the Union of Chinese Soviets or secede from it and join their own state as they prefer.' Brandt, Schwartz and Fairbank, 1952: 223. The Chinese Communists revised their view after taking power in 1949.
47 Joyeux 1989.
48 Lu Chih 1986, especially pp. 3–4; see also Lamb 1964, 1966 and Maxwell 1970.
49 *Le Monde*, 23 May 1991.
50 See below, ch. 5.
51 See below, ch. 6. The islands of Quemoy and Matsu, occupied by Taiwan but lying very close to the Chinese mainland, were subject to bombardment by the forces of the People's Republic of China in 1959, but there have been no recent incidents.
52 The southern half of Sakhalin had been acquired by Japan at the Treaty of Portsmouth after the Russo-Japanese War of 1904–5.
53 Zhirinovsky's geopolitical ideas concerning eastern Europe are reminiscent of the 1914 political map and expressed in terms of the pre-1945 political discourse of intensely competitive nationalism.
54 Choudhary 1972: 11.
55 Choudhary 1972.
56 For a detailed account see Choudhury 1974.
57 These included the 1965 Declaration on the Inadmissibility of Intervention in the Domestic Affairs and the Protection of their Independence and Sovereignty and the 1970 Declaration of the Principles of International Law concerning Friendly Relations and Cooperation among States in Accordance with the Charter of the United Nations. On the other hand the 1966 Strict Observance of the Prohibition of the Threat or the Use of Force in International Relations and the Rights of Peoples to Self-Determination emphasized the right of colonial peoples to seek and receive all support in their struggles for self-determination.
58 Choudhury, 1973: 62–89.
59 Lévy 1973.
60 This is consistent with India's position on the Nagas, a hill people on the

north-eastern frontier who have fought a long guerrilla war. The Indian government has refused to accept the Naga claim to self-determination on the grounds that they are already part of the Indian state. See Maxwell 1973.

61 Finnie 1990: 150.
62 For the problem of counting the Kurds see Heraclides 1991: 131.
63 Recent books on the Kurds include Bulloch and Morris, 1992, Kreyenbroek and Sperei 1992, Laizer 1991. Most of the best literature on the Kurds is now dated, although there has been exhaustive press coverage in the aftermath of the Gulf War and the repression of the Kurdish revolt by Saddam Hussein. See particularly Bois 1966, Chaliand 1980, Edmonds 1957, Jawad 1981.
64 *Le Monde*, 26 June 1993.
65 *The Economist*, 'On Misery Mountain'; 'Operation Desertion: America and the Kurds,' 13 April 1991, pp. 68, 43.
66 Israel, Jordan, Syria and Lebanon have a mutual interest in cooperating to utilize the Jordan but, as a result of the pressures of increasing population and continuing political tension, this cooperation has not taken place. See Lowi 1993.
67 For the practical implementation of this in the occupied territories see Harris 1980.
68 See Kipnis 1987a, 1987b and 1991.
69 Armstrong 1993.
70 Parsons 1995.

4 Boundaries within States: Size, Democracy and Service Provision

1 See ch. 2.
2 Slovakia had a brief period of 'autonomy' as a Nazi puppet state during the Second World War.
3 The mistake of Michael Hechter (1975) is to assume a consistent relationship in the regional division of labour – one of systematic exploitation of the peripheral regions by the centre. It is, however, undeniable that exploiting relationships exist and that individuals with strong cultural markers from the peripheral regions (language, dialect, social behaviour, skills) are excluded from access to metropolitan centres of power.
4 Keating 1988.
5 For a discussion of recent trends see Batley and Stoker 1991.
6 Tarrow 1978: 1.
7 Ouzouf-Marignier 1986.
8 For this argument see Nordman and Revel 1989, especially pp. 132–42.
9 A good example is the classic text Buchanan and Tulloch 1962. See also Dryzek 1990.
10 Bennett 1980: 298–300.
11 Particularly the distinguished studies of Peter Katzenstein: 1984 and 1985.

12 Russett (1968) argues that the largest 'states' are neither proportionately larger nor smaller than 2,000 years ago. See also Sharpe 1989.

13 A distinguished exception is Dahl and Tufte 1973. The presence of many variables, in addition to size, makes the task of isolating the effect of size almost impossible. Geraint Parry and his collaborators, in their thorough study of political participation in the United Kingdom, although aware of the problem, do not tackle the question of the effect of size of local communities. See Parry, Moyser and Day 1992.

14 Also, like Madison, one of the founding fathers of the American republic, he regarded the division between local and national affairs was unproblematic. With the extension of government services this division has become very difficult to draw.

15 Dahl and Tufte 1973: 51–6.

16 Blair, in Batley and Stoker 1991: 53. The lower tier of English local government is very much larger than the European norm.

17 Dahl and Tufte 1973: 14.

18 For a review of the relevant literature see Bulpitt 1983: chs 1 and 2, Rhodes 1981, Rhodes and Wright 1989: Introduction.

19 See for example Priore and Sabel 1984, especially pp. 251–80.

20 Mény 1986: 1.

21 Goblet 1956: 100.

22 The Joxe schema may be confirmed or overtaken by the Pasqua proposals of May 1994 for seven inter-regional groupings for infrastructure planning. *Le Monde,* 18 May 1994.

23 The manner of the incorporation of the territory into the state helps to explain variations in the strength of regional identities. The distinction drawn by Stein Rokkan and Derek Urwin between 'union states' and 'unitary states' is useful. Union states were established by a process of accretion of entities which retained some autonomy, whereas unitary states are established through conquest around a single dominant centre. Rokkan and Urwin 1982: 11.

24 However, in 1989 the Catalan and in 1990 the Basque parliaments voted a declaration of principle reaffirming their right to self-determination.

25 Gourevitch 1978: 52–3.

26 For discussions of the work of the Commission see Brand 1974, Pearce 1980, Redcliffe-Maud and Wood 1974.

27 British changes diverge from the European pattern in other respects. Local government was weakened by the establishment of semi-independent authorities for local development and the delivery of services, as well as the insistence on traditional local government services being put out to tender. See the excellent review in King 1993.

28 Leonardi 1992, especially p. 5.

29 Despite the scepticism of eminent authorities such as Raymond Aron, in the 1970s, and Roy Jenkins, in the 1990s, about European citizenship, Elizabeth Meehan (1993) makes a powerful case for the importance of these rights.

30 Fitzmaurice 1993. Three Euregios (only two of which function) have been established across the sensitive German–Polish frontier.
31 Council of Europe. Documents. CME/Loc (76) 27.
32 Arnold 1977, Arnold-Plassière 1979; for a general study see Guichonnet and Raffestin 1974: 166–218, von Malchus 1973 and 1975 and, for more recent developments, see Freeman and Pulikowski 1992.
33 For the establishment and early history of this association see R. Baumert, 1969; for later developments see Roth 1981.
34 Anderson 1982.
35 *Le Monde,* 24 August 1991.
36 The direct loss of employtment in 1992–3 was serious. In Hendaye, the autoport used by road transport for clearing customs was deserted, with the loss of 240 jobs; in customs the number of officers was decreased from fifty-five to seven. The unemployment rate doubled to 18% and in Irun it reached 30%.
37 *Le Monde,* 5–6 September 1993.
38 Jardel 1982.
39 *Le Monde,* 10–11 October 1993.
40 *Le Monde,* 12–13 May 1991. However, a treaty signed in Bayonne between France and Spain on 10 March 1995 was a new start, giving local authorities the right to form transfrontier consortia to provide services and promote joint ventures.
41 Ricq 1981 and 1990.
42 Vernier 1993.
43 This was a reversal of the 'polluter pays' principle (first given influential backing by the 'transfrontier pollution group' of the OECD; see OECD 1979) which has been urged on governments by the OECD and the EU. In this case the polluted paid the polluter to reduce his noxious activities.
44 The Luxembourg government had opposed the Cattenom station from 1979 when it abandoned the building of its own station at Remerchen on safety grounds. The Luxembourg prime minister, Jacques Santer, bitterly criticized the French position on Cattenom saying that siting of power stations was a matter of national sovereignty *and* neighbouring states. A transfrontier popular agitation was mounted against this and other nuclear power stations on the upper Rhine. *Le Monde,* 14 October 1986.
45 Anderson, 1982 and 1983.
46 De Rougemont 1968 and 1970.
47 For an overview see Martinez 1986.
48 Asiwaju 1986, 1990: 11, 35–45.
49 Greño Velasco 1977: 23–4.
50 This region is now intensively studied. Contributions of especial interest are in Herzog 1992, particularly Morales and Tamayo-Sanchez (pp. 49–68), Sklair, (pp. 69–88), de la Garza and Vargas (pp. 89–112); for recent developments see Ganster and Valenciano 1992.

5 Frontiers and Migration

1 An important debate is contained in Brown and Shue 1981; the debate has been renewed in Barry and Goodin 1992.
2 Walzer 1992: 31. Another defence of this position is Carens 1989: 31–49.
3 Chaney 1981.
4 Pogge, 1994: 89–122.
5 Lichtenberg 1981: 79–100.
6 In 1968 the celebrated student agitator in Paris.
7 Cohn-Bendit and Schmidt 1992.
8 Cohn-Bendit 1993: 22–31.
9 In Britain internal border controls have been imposed between Northern Ireland and the rest of the UK. Northern Ireland residents could be refused the right to travel to the mainland.
10 Zolberg 1989: 406. See also the various contributions to Kritz, Keely and Tomasi 1981.
11 Particularly United Nations 1990, United Nations Development Program 1991, United Nations Food and Population Agency 1991; the annual reports of the Système d'Observation Permanente sur les Migrations for OECD are an invaluable source for member countries; see also Wils 1991: 281–99.
12 Dowty 1987: 186.
13 Talbott 1971: 525.
14 *Current Digest of the Soviet Press* 1983.
15 CDU/CSU Group in the German Bundestag 1977: 27.
16 Pufendorf 1934: bk 8, ch. 11, s. 4.
17 Hirschman 1970, especially pp. 3–20, 120–1.
18 See Johnston 1972.
19 Plender 1988.
20 Basic sources include McEverdy and Jones 1978, Broek and Webb 1978, McNeill, 1978; for the contemporary period see Castles and Miller 1993, Chaliand 1994.
21 See Gildea 1987, especially pp. 3–27, 141–70.
22 Lengereau 1990: 55.
23 Japan was an exception among the rich countries in that it has never welcomed immigrants. Some foreigners were stranded after Japan's failed imperial adventure in the first half of the 20th c. In 1990 there were estimated to be about 1 million Koreans (from the 2 million in 1945) and 150,000 Chinese in Japan. Relatively small groups of clandestine immigrants, mainly comprising people whose physical appearance is similar to that of the Japanese, entered the country on tourist visas and stayed on to work illegally. In 1989 legislation allowed limited, and short-term, immigration for purposes of professional and technical training, but it also included heavy fines on employers for each illegal immigrant employed. Japan, for geographical, social, cultural and ethnic reasons, could control immigration more effectively than other highly developed countries.

24 For the phases of immigration in western Europe since 1945 see Salt 1981: 133–57.
25 Cited in Arendt 1958: 283.
26 Fielding 1993: 10.
27 Dummett and Niessen 1993, Hargreaves 1992: 74–86. In material terms, the right to permanent residence matters more than citizenship. See Brubaker 1989: 145–62.
28 Marie 1987; for a balanced collection of studies see King 1993. There remain problems of comparing migrant flows even within the EU because countries, to mention only the most obvious problems, adopt different definitions of immigrants, treat asylum-seekers in different ways and collect statistics differently. See Eurostat 1993: n. 12.
29 See Eurobarometer poll of 1988 for perceptions of different categories of immigrants.
30 The Eurobarometer poll of spring 1993 surprisingly reported Italy as the least welcoming country with 64% of respondents saying that there were too many immigrants.
31 Kleff 1991: 83–97.
32 Some can, however, buy their entry. Hong Kong Chinese who wish to come to Britain prior to the 1997 takeover by the People's Republic of China can do so if they bring £150,000 investment capital. Miles 1991: 284.
33 The practice differed from revolutionary theory. The 1791 French Constitution granted citizenship unequivocally to individuals born of French fathers or resident in France. Children born of immigrants only became automatically French by virtue of a law of 1889. See Brubaker 1992.
34 Illegal immigration subsequently became such an important issue that rules governing temporary immigration were modified by legislation in 1980, 1982 and 1993.
35 Moulier Boutang, Garson and Silberman 1986; Documentation Française 1986.
36 *Le Monde,* 23 March 1991. Barreau proposed that the way forward was to have quotas of immigrants for particular professions. This had virtually no support.
37 Montanari and Cortese 1993: 212–33.
38 Divine 1957, Kritz 1983, Papademetriou and Miller 1983.
39 An example is the vigorous argument by Julian Simon that, in order to maintain economic leadership, the United States should welcome as many immigrants as possible because immigrants bring expertise, money and an indomitable will to succeed. He argued in favour of 1 million immigrant visas per year with revisions upwards until problems started to appear. This kind of argument is not made in European countries. See Simon 1989.
40 Palmieri 1981: p. xvii.
41 See Weintraub 1990, especially pp. 178–92.
42 In the 1940s and 1950s, Afro-Americans moved in a great wave of internal migration from south to north, to ghettos in the great northern cities. See Lehmann 1991: 3–107. This movement has been characterized as a disaster

by, amongst others, Brian Barry, who uses it as an argument against regarding free movement, even within a country, as necessarily beneficial. Barry and Goodin 1992: 284.

43 For a digest of information on the 1986 and 1990 Acts see Landes, Caldwell and Siegel 1991.

44 At the western end of the frontier, Governor Wilson of California success-fully campaigned in favour of withdrawing, because of cost, all social services, including emergency health care, from illegal immigrants. In 1994, on parallel lines, Governor Chiles of Florida, demanded $1,500 million from the federal government for the cost of education, health and social services which the state had to provide for 345,000 illegal immigrants whom the immigration authorities had failed to stop at the frontier.

45 Indeed, in 1993 the Clinton administration proposed new measures to strengthen the border patrol as well as to tighten up regulations on asylum-seekers.

46 *Projet* 1992, *Pouvoirs* 1992.

47 For a collection of analyses of this change see Glazer 1985.

48 An exception was the movement of US citizens into Canada, especially when they moved into occupations central to the maintenance of Canada's cultural identity.

49 Tentative moves had been made towards adopting a common immigration policy before. See Wrochno-Stanke 1982.

50 Wihtol de Wenden 1992: 101–11.

51 *Financial Times*, 26–7 January 1991: For an analysis of the possible impact of the liberalization of the Russian emigration law see de Tinguy 1992, *Hommes et migrations* 1992.

52 *Financial Times*, 28 December 1990. Despite this stance, and the Clinton administration's refusal in 1994–5 to allow any more Haitian and Cuban refugees into the US, the overall record of admission of refugees by successive American administrations has been more liberal than in any other country except Germany.

53 See particularly Joly and Poulton 1992, King 1994.

54 Before 1989 the East German authorities encouraged the passage of asylum-seekers through Berlin in order to embarrass the West German government.

55 Kemper 1993, Heinelt 1993.

56 *Le Monde*, 23 July 1990.

57 United Nations High Commissioner for Refugees 1979, Goodwin-Gill 1983.

58 *Le Monde*, 7 December 1990.

59 Lawless and Seccombe 1986.

60 Birks and Sinclair 1980.

61 According to the Egyptian government, 2 million of its citizens were in Iraq on the eve of the Gulf War. *Le Monde*, 31 August 1989.

62 It is not possible to obtain accurate year-by-year figures of the origins of immigrants. See Khader 1991: 186–7.

63 Longuenesse 1986.

64 Fargues 1985.
65 Seccombe 1988: 155.
66 Walzer 1992: 164–71.
67 *The Times*, 20 February 1985.
68 *The Independent*, 14 July 1989.
69 *Le Monde*, 20 August 1985.
70 *The Independent*, 3 January 1990.
71 Gordenker 1987: 14–15, Lévy 1973, Oliver 1978.
72 *Le Monde*, 25 May 1993.
73 Figures of the UN High Commissioner for Refugees quoted in *Le Monde*, 15 August 1991.
74 Jackson 1990: 150.
75 Kuper 1981.
76 O'Neill 1994: 85.

6   Uninhabited Zones and International Cooperation

1 Honoré 1961.
2 Waldron 1988: 28.
3 Malaurie 1989 and 1992.
4 There have been a number of estimates of doubtful reliability. See Splettstoesser and Dreschhoff 1990.
5 See discussions in Lovering and Prescott 1979 and more recently Triggs 1987; there are also three useful contributions in Schofield 1994.
6 Peterson 1988.
7 Auburn 1982: 1.
8 *Antarctic Treaty System Handbook,* 1989: p. viii, Joyner and Chopra 1988.
9 Morris 1990.
10 Smith 1990: 6.
11 *Financial Times,* 16 October 1989.
12 Peterson 1988: 2.
13 For the text of the treaty and all other relevant legal instruments relating to the Antarctic see Bush 1982–8.
14 In 1993 a private member's bill was introduced in the United Kingdom House of Commons (Antarctic bill – bill no. 14, 1993) with the purpose of regulating British activity in the continent. The debate showed the considerable interest in the issues of environmental protection among MPs, despite Britain's geographical distance from Antarctica.
15 Electoral pressures in 1988 (the potential importance of the ecology vote) helped to change the French socialist government's position. The Australian government was also converted to a more stringent environmental regime when a closely fought general election was imminent. *Le Monde,* 10 October 1989.
16 This was only a partial defection because the two countries did not seek to

undermine the ATS at the thirty-year review conference of the system held in 1991.

17 Greenpeace also suspected that the motivation for the airstrip was, in the longer term, economic exploitation. It has subsequently suffered serious storm damage.

18 See Peterson 1988: 175–93.

19 Sir Arthur Watts provides a characteristically robust defence of the solidity of the legal basis of the Antarctic treaties. Watts 1992: 294–8.

20 Charney 1991.

21 Gilmore 1994: 1–45, Alexander 1986.

22 Johnston 1988.

23 Nanda 1986.

24 Denman 1984.

25 The legal issues are complex in maritime boundary-drawing and are subject to fine legal analysis. See especially Weil 1989.

26 For example, Craven, Schneider and Stimson 1989; more generally see Blake 1987, Earney 1990 and Kwiatkowska 1989.

27 The best account remains Wilson 1979–80. For more recent developments see Clogg 1991: 12–23, Brown 1991: 9–16.

28 Greece has no legal entitlement to be considered an archipelagic state, something which would have supported this claim.

29 See below p. 164.

30 Brown 1991: 15.

31 McDonald 1988–9.

32 *Le Monde,* 25 May 1989.

33 *Libération,* 8 August 1991.

34 See Lowi 1993: 54–78.

35 Prescott 1987: 53, Martin et al. 1985.

36 It was also subject to radically different interpretations. See Parenti 1986: 156–60.

37 Weber 1983: 191–4.

38 The right of overflight of international straits lying within territorial waters, even for military flights, is, however, included in the 1982 Law of the Sea Convention and, according to some authorities, was already part of customary international law.

39 For the texts of these see Zwann 1988; for a review of all the treaties and agreements on outer space or having implications for space travel and exploration see Reynolds and Merges 1989, especially chs 3–8.

40 There was no treaty ban on anti-satellite technology and it was relatively easy to develop. See Nye and Schear 1987, especially pp. 1–2.

41 Some, however, argue that the effect of Articles I and IV of the treaty is to ban all military activity.

42 Krepon et al. 1990. France, in partnership with Italy and Spain, developed in the 1990s a new generation of observation satellites (Helios 1 and 2) and a radar satellite (Osiris), but these have not yet been marketed.

43 Reijnen and de Graff 1989.

44 By the 1976 Bogotá Declaration eight equatorial states (Brazil, Colombia, Congo, Ecuador, Indonesia, Kenya, Uganda and Zaire) claimed sovereign rights over that part of the geostationary orbit above their territory – the rest, they admitted, was 'the common heritage of mankind'. They based their claim on two propositions – first that the 1967 Treaty did not define outer space; second, that they were not provided with the relevant technical information when the 1967 Treaty was negotiated. A basic weakness of this claim was the difficulty, in practice, of asserting sovereign rights at the altitude of the geostationary orbit (35,800 kilometres). Also, the 1969 and 1979 Conventions on outer space ban the appropriation of outer space, the moon and other celestial bodies. The Bogotá Declaration has been ignored by all states with satellite launching capabilities.

45 Cocca 1986: 17–24, Matte 1987.

46 For a review of these see Martin 1992.

47 However, Ambassador Benedick argues strongly the case for some states proceeding more quickly than others in raising environmental standards in order to raise the standards of 'global stewardship'. Benedick 1991: 206.

48 The standard work for these Conventions and for subsequent international agreements is Lyster 1985. International law on environmental protection is not restricted to treaties specifically devoted to the issue but may also be an incidental part of treaties such as the 1960 Treaty concerning the frontier between the Netherlands and the Federal Republic of Germany.

49 See Thacher 1992: 183–211. This collection is a basic source on the philosophical, legal, political and institutional issues of international environmental protection.

50 Ships and aircraft have been regarded as major international polluters and, as a consequence, the IMO has adopted rules (exceptionally difficult to enforce) against cleaning out of bilges, and the ICAO has made rules against noise and gas emissions.

51 In 1970 the OECD established a committee for the environment which has produced a series of studies, declarations of principle and recommendations, particularly OECD 1974, 1976, 1978.

52 The EC has played the most important role in terms of enforceable directives which apply to its member states. Its first major project was the First Action Programme on the Environment (1974–6).

53 Notably the 1968 European Convention for Water, 1972 European Convention for Soils, 1970 Declaration on the Environment.

54 Bath 1992: 113. Environmental damage has not only been the result of activities conducted in Mexico. One notable example of US pollution was the increased salinity in the Colorado River system, resulting from the Welton–Mohawk irrigation project in the United States (now resolved).

55 The illegal dumping of dangerous waste remains a serious problem. For the United States–Mexico frontier see Bath 1992: 116–17.

56 By the 1985 Vienna Convention for the Protection of the Ozone Layer, the 1987 Montreal Protocol and the 1990 London Revisions of the Montreal Protocol.

57 This agreement unusually gives diplomatic immunity and freedom of movement to officials of both nationalities to inspect water shortage and pollution
   problems: Weintraub 1990: 168. In February 1992, after much criticism of
   the, often US-generated, pollution of the Mexican frontier region, the two
   countries adopted an Action Plan for the Environment of the Mexican–United States Frontier Region. This plan, although lacking adequate
   financial support, is a model of flexible cooperation.
58 The 1975 Bonn Agreement was never implemented by the French, because
   of a revolt by French mayors and environmentalist groups against dumping
   the waste from the potash mines in disused mine-shafts, which they alleged
   would damage the water table.
59 Romi 1993: 227–35.
60 The interconnection of environmental and economic matters was seen
   clearly by the protagonists of zero growth in the early 1970s (Dennis
   Meadows and his associates at MIT), the Club of Rome and the Greenpeace
   movement. It was explicit in international agreements such as the 1987
   Montreal Protocol on the phasing out of the use of CFC gases, and in
   influential reports such as the 1987 Brundtland Report. However, it is only
   in the context of the EC that a direct link is made between environmental
   and economic regulation.
61 See Haas 1990.
62 When faced with harsh economic necessities, governments' concern for the
   environment weakens and new international agreements are hard to reach.
   The outcome of the 1992 Rio de Janeiro World Environment Conference
   which brought together 150 heads of state and government was confirmation
   of this. Their presence, during a period of world economic recession,
   indicated the importance they attributed to the subject (or their sensitivity
   to political/electoral pressures), but the outcome was a vague declaration of
   principles and no firm undertakings.
63 Wasburn 1992: ch. 1.
64 Chomsky 1982.
65 See, for example, McPhail 1981.
66 Where stations are broadcasting pornography for profit by selling decoders,
   it is possible to ban the marketing of these devices. The station Red Hot
   Dutch had its revenues withheld in this way by a British government
   decision in 1993.
67 Négrine and Papthanassopoulos 1990: 35ff.
68 List and Rittberger 1992: 86.

Conclusion: The European Union and the Future of Frontiers

1 For an important example of this speculation see *Political Studies* 1994.
2 The impact is, and is likely to remain, uneven across various categories of
  the population of the Union. Treaty-based rights, Directives and European
  Court of Justice decisions implementing them have, for example, had a

differential impact on the position of women. See Buckley and Anderson 1988, Meehan 1993: 101–20.

3 'Les Régions frontalières sortent de leur torpeur', *Le Monde*, 4 November 1993.

4 The Visegrád four have made considerable efforts to adapt to the market economy of the European Union in the hope that early membership of the EU will give them access to key decision-making fora. See ECSA-Europe 1993. Their citizens have greater faith in the beneficial effects of the European Union than do citizens of the member states. See the Eurobarometer poll of December 1990.

5 Wörner et al. 1993; the whole process of multilateral cooperation in security matters has been subject to readjustment since 1989 – see Brenner 1995.

6 *Le Monde*, 19 April 1994.

7 See ch. 6.

8 The ethnic composition of the population of Macedonia in the late 19th and early 20th c. was the subject of widely different assessments by Bulgarians, Greeks, Serbs, Germans and Turks. See Shaw 1977: ii. 208, Castellan 1991: 355.

9 See Institute of International Political and Strategic Studies n.d.

10 About 500 kilometres of road and rail had either to be built or upgraded. This posed serious financial and logistical problems.

11 Considerable territorial complexity on the fringes of the European Union raises problems of administration and control which have not yet been resolved. This complexity is composed of several elements: sovereign micro-states which are enclaves in EU territory (Andorra, Monaco, San Marino, the Vatican); enclaves of Germany in Switzerland and Switzerland in Italy; 'free zones' which are not considered part of national territory for customs purposes (Gex and Haute-Savoie in France, Gorizia and Livigno in Italy); territories which, though linked to member states, are not considered part of the EU (Channel Islands, Faeroe Islands, Greenland); dependencies and overseas territories which may or may not be part of the EU or its customs territory. No one individual case is important but collectively they pose considerable difficulties.

12 These matters are extensively discussed in Anderson and den Boer 1994 and Anderson et al. 1995.

13 Considerable legislative and constitutional adaptation had been undertaken to bring national law into conformity with the Convention. France amended its Constitution, Germany its Basic Law, and most of the partners had to revise their asylum laws in ways which in France, the Netherlands and Germany caused considerable domestic controversy.

14 The Danish position changed after German pressure and the 1995 accession to the EU of other Scandinavian states.

15 République Française – Sénat – Deuxième Session Extraordinaire – 1993–4 – no. 262. *Annexe au procès verbal; de séance du 25 janvier 1994. Rapport d'information fait au nom de la mission commune d'information chargée*

d'examiner la mise en place et le fonctionnement de la Convention d'Application de l'Accord du 14 juin 1985.

16 Passport controls were temporarily reintroduced in 1995 at Schipol airport in the Netherlands because the system of smart cards for passengers from within the Schengen area to cross the frontier was shown to be open to abuse from those coming from outside.

17 For an analysis of organized crime, the problems of definition of the phenomenon, and the extent to which it is regarded as an external threat see Anderson 1993.

18 Busch 1993, Diederichs 1993, Pastore 1993.

19 République Française *loc. cit.* pointed out that the majority – 64% in 1992 – of illegal immigrants were stopped at the internal frontiers of the EC.

20 République Française – Sénat – Session Ordinaire – 1992–3 – no. 384. *Annexe au procès verbal de la séance du 23 juin 1993.*

21 For example, Prats 1978: 22. 'Since the. beginning of the 1960s, Latin America has been engaged in a process apparently leading to the disintegration of the political frontier ... from the desire to develop regional economies and mobilise under-utilised resources.'

22 For example, the Eurobarometer surveys reported a decline in France (from 60% in 1987 to 40% in 1993) of numbers who thought that membership of the EU brought benefits to France.

23 For an illustration of this assumption, see Goffman 1972, especially pp. 52.

24 See Trier 1966.

25 The argument of Balibar and Wallerstein (1989) is that, as state boundaries are losing some of their exclusionary function, other mechanisms for exclusion are strengthening: 'We believe that, in traditional or remodelled forms ... racism is not decreasing but is growing in the contemporary world.'

26 See Lacasse 1974.

27 Barnett and Muller 1974: 14.

28 'What is called "culture" is a fragment of humanity which, from the point of view of the research at hand and of the scale on which the latter is carried out, presents significant discontinuities in relation to the rest of humanity.' Lévi-Strauss 1963.

Bibliography

Alcock, A. E. 1970: *The History of the South Tyrol Question*. London: Michael Joseph.

Alexander, L. M. 1986: The Delimitation of Maritime Boundaries. *Political Geography Quarterly*, 5 (1), 19–25.

Alliès, P. 1980: *L'Invention du territoire*. Paris: Presses Universitaires de Grenoble.

Ancel, J. 1938: *La Politique des frontières*. Paris: Gallimard.

Anderson, B. 1991: *Imagined Communities: Reflexions on the Origin and Spread of Nationalism*. Rev. edn, New York: Verso.

Anderson, E. 1987: Water Resources and Boundaries in the Middle East. In G. H. Blake, and R. N. Schofield (eds), *Boundaries and State Territory in the Middle East and North Africa*, Wisbech: Menas Press, 85–98.

Anderson, M. 1982: Scenarios for Conflict in Frontier Regions. In R. Strassoldo and G. Delli Zotti (eds), *Cooperation and Conflict in Border Areas*, Milan: Franco Angeli, 145–78.

—— 1983: The Political Problems of Frontier Regions. In M. Anderson (ed.), *Frontier Regions in Western Europe*. London: Frank Cass.

—— 1993: *Control of Organised Crime in the European Community*. Edinburgh: Project Group on European Police Co-operation, Working Paper no. 9.

—— and den Boer, M. (eds) 1994: *Policing across National Boundaries*. London: Pinter.

—— *et al.* 1995: *Policing the European Union*. Oxford: Oxford University Press.

Antarctic Treaty System Handbook 1989. 6th edn, Cambridge: Polar.

Ardrey, R. 1967: *The Territorial Imperative: A Personal Enquiry into the Animal Origins of Property and Nations*. London: Collins.

—— 1972: *The Social Contract. A Personal Enquiry into the Evolutionary Origins of Order and Disorder*. London: Collins.

Arendt, H. 1958: *The Origins of Totalitarianism*. 2nd edn, New York: Verso.

Armstrong, D. 1993: *Revolution and World Order: The Revolutionary State in International Society.* Oxford: Clarendon Press.

Armstrong, J. A. 1982: *Nations before Nationalism.* Chapel Hill: University of North Carolina Press.

Arnold, M. 1977: *La Coordination des schémas d'aménagement du territoire des régions frontalières: le cas de l'Alsace, de la Rhénanie-Palatinat, du Pays de Bade et de la Suisse du Nord-Est.* Strasbourg: Council of Europe.

Arnold-Plassière, M. 1979: La Coopération transfrontalière régionale en matière d'aménagement du territoire: Étude du cas de la vallée du Rhin. Strasbourg: Ph.D. thesis.

Asiwaju, A.I. (ed.) 1985: *Partitioned Africans: Ethnic Relations Across Africa's International Boundaries, 1884–1984.* London: Hurst, and University of Lagos Press.

—— 1986: Problem solving along African Borders: Case Study of the Nigeria–Benin Border since 1889. In O. J. Martinez (ed.), *Across Boundaries: Transborder Interaction in Comparative Perspective,* El Paso: Western Texas Press 159–90.

—— 1990: *Artificial Boundaries.* New York: Civiletis International.

Aubry, G. 1983: *Sous la coupole pas sous la coupe.* Tavannes: Agecopresse.

Auburn, F. M. 1982: *Antarctic Law and Politics.* London: Hurst.

Autrement, 1991 no. 50: special number, *Pays Baltes.*

Averick, S. and Rosen, S. 1985: *The Importance of the 'West Bank' and Gaza to Israel's Security.* Washington and Tel Aviv: American–Israeli Public Affairs Committee.

Azcárate, P. 1945: *The League of Nations and National Minorities: An Experiment.* Washington: Carnegie Foundation.

Bacon, E. F. 1954: Types of Pastoral Nomadism in Central and South West Asia. *South Western Journal of Anthropology,* 10, 44–65.

Bainville, J. 1915 (rev. edn, 1933): *Histoire de deux peuples.* Paris: Nouvelle Librairie Nationale (Fayard).

Baldwin, J. W. 1986: *The Government of Philip Augustus: Foundations of French Royal Power.* Berkeley: University of California Press.

Baldwin, S. 1929: *Organisation of Medieval Christianity.* New York: Holt.

Baldwin, T. 1992: Territoriality. In H. Gross and R. Harrison (eds), *Jurisprudence: Cambridge Essays,* Oxford: Oxford University Press, 207–30.

Balibar, E. and Wallerstein, I. 1989: *Race, nation, classe: les identités ambiguës.* Paris: La Découverte.

Banac, I. 1984: *The National Question in Jugoslavia.* Ithaca: Cornell University Press.

Barbour, K. M. 1961: A Geographical Analysis of Boundaries in Inter-Tropical Africa. In K. M. Barbour and R. M. Prothero (eds), *Essays in African Populations,* London: Routledge & Kegan Paul, 303–23.

Barker, E. 1956: *The Approach to Self-Government.* Cambridge: Cambridge University Press.

—— Clark, G. N. and Vaucher, P. 1955: *The European Inheritance.* Oxford: Clarendon, Press, 3 vols.

Barnett, R. J. and Muller, R. E. 1974: *Global Reach: The Power of the Multinational Corporation*. New York: Simon & Schuster.

Barry, B. and Goodin, R. E. (eds) 1992: *Free Movement: Ethical Issues in the Transnational Migration of People and Money*. Brighton: Harvester Wheatsheaf.

Barth, F. (ed) 1969: *Ethnic Groups and Boundaries*. London: Allen & Unwin.

Bath, C. R. 1992: The Emerging Environmental Crisis along the United States–Mexico Border. In L. A. Herzog (ed), *Changing Boundaries in the Americas: New Perspectives on the US–Mexican, Central American and South American Borders*, San Diego: University of California Center for US–Mexican Studies, 113–32.

Batley, R. and Stoker, G. (eds) 1991: *Local Government in Europe*. London: Macmillan.

Baumert, R. 1969: *La 'Regio'*. Paris: Dalloz.

Beaujeu-Garnier, J. and Chabot, G. 1967: *Urban Geography*. London: Longman.

Béguelin, R. and Charpilloz, A. 1982: *Les Racines de l'unité jurassienne*. Delémont: Rassemblement Jurassien.

— and Schaffter, R. 1974: *L'Autodétermination du peuple jurassien. Ses conséquences*. Delémont: Rassemblement Jurassien.

Beitz, C. R. 1979: *Political Theory and International Relations*. Princeton: Princeton University Press.

— 1994: Cosmopolitan Liberalism and the States System. In C. Brown (ed.), *Political Re-structuring in Europe*, London: Routledge, 123–36.

Bellamy, R. 1992: *Liberalism and Modern Society*. Cambridge: Polity.

Benedick, R. E. 1991: *Ozone Diplomacy: New Directions in Safeguarding the Planet*. Cambridge, Mass.: Harvard University Press.

Benmassaoud Trédano, A. 1989: *Intangibilité des frontières coloniales et espace étatique en Afrique*. Paris: Librairie Générale de droit et de Jurisprudence.

Bennett, R. J. 1980: *The Geography of Public Finance*. London: Methuen.

Bennigsen, A. A. and Wimbush, S. E. 1986: *Muslims of the Soviet Union: A Guide*. Bloomington: University of Indiana Press.

— and Lemercier-Quelquejay, C. 1981: *Les Musulmans oubliés. Les Peuples musulmans de l'Union soviétique*. Paris: La Découverte.

— and Wimbush, S. E. 1979: *Muslim National Communism in the Soviet Union*. Chicago: University of Chicago Press.

Billington, R. A. 1966: *America's Frontier History*. New York: Holt, Rinehart & Winston.

Birks, J. S. and Sinclair, C. A. 1980: *International Migration and Development in the Arab Region*. Geneva: International Labour Office.

Birnbaum, P. 1982: *La Logique de l'État*. Paris: Fayard.

— and Badie, P. 1983 *Sociologie de l'État*. New edn, Paris: Grasset.

Biucchi, B. and Gauderd, G. (eds) 1981: *Régions Frontalières*. Paris: Georgi Saint Saphorin.

Blair, P. 1991: Trends in Local Autonomy and Democracy: Reflections from a

European Perspective. In R. Batley and G. Stoker (eds), *Local Government in Europe: Trends and Developments*, London: Macmillan, 41–57.

Blaise, C. 1990: *The Border as Fiction*. Orono: Borderlands Monograph Series, 4.

Blake, G. H. (ed.) 1987: *Maritime Boundaries and Ocean Resources*. London: Croom Helm.

— (ed.) 1994a: *Maritime Boundaries*. London: Routledge.

— (ed.) 1994b: *World Boundaries Series*. London: Routledge 5 vols (each volume cited under volume editor).

— and Schofield, R. N. (eds) 1987: *Boundaries and States Territory in the Middle East and North Africa*. Wisbech: Menas Press.

Bloch, M. 1961: *Feudal Society*. Chicago: University of Chicago Press, 2 vols.

Boateng, E. A. 1978: *A Political Geography of Africa*. Cambridge: Cambridge University Press.

Bodin, J. 1962: *The Six Books of the Commonweale*, ed. C. D. Macrae. Facsimile edn, Cambridge, Mass.: Harvard University Press.

Body-Gendrot, S., d'Hellencourt, B. and Rancoule, M. 1989: Entrée interdite: La Législation sur l'immigration en France, au Royaume-Uni et aux États-Unis. *Revue Française de Science Politique*, 39, 50–74.

Bois, T. 1966: *The Kurds*. Beirut: Khayats.

Bonenfant, P. 1953: A Propos des limites médiévales. In *Eventail de l'histoire vivante; offert par l'amitié d'historiens, linguistes, géographes, économistes, sociologues, ethnologues à Lucien Febvre*, Paris: Colin, 2 vols.

Boulangé, B. and Cavenaile, R. 1991: *La Belgique des Origines à l'état fédéral*. 2nd edn. Brussels: Erasme.

Boulding, K. E. 1962: *Conflict and Defense: A General Theory*. New York: Harper.

Bourjol-Flecher, D. 1981: Heurs et Malheurs de l'Uti Possidetis: L'Intangibilité des frontières africaines. *Revue Juridique et Politique: Indépendance et Coopération*, 3, 811–35.

Boustani, R. 1990: *Atlas du monde arabe*. Paris: Bordas.

Boutier, J., Dewerpe, A. and Nordmann, D. 1984: *Un tour de France royal: Le Voyage de Charles IX (1564–1566)*. Paris: Aubier Montaigne.

Brand, J. 1974: *Local Government Reform in England 1888–1974*. London: Croom Helm.

Brandt, C., Schwartz, B. and Fairbank, J. 1952: *A Documentary History of Chinese Communism*. London: Allen & Unwin.

Braudel, F. 1973: *Capitalism and Material Life, 1400–1800*. Trans. M. Kochan, London: Weidenfeld and Nicolson.

— 1980: *L'Identité de la France*. Paris: Arthaud Flammarion.

— 1985: *Civilisation and Capitalism*, iii: *The Perspective of the World*. London: Collins.

Brenner, M. (ed.) 1995: *Multilateralism and Western Strategy*. London: Macmillan.

Broc, N. 1983: Quelle est la plus ancienne 'carte moderne' de la France? *Annales de Géographie*, 92, 513–30.

Broek, J. O. M. and Webb, J. W. 1978: *A Geography of Mankind*. 3rd edn, New York: McGraw Hill.

Brown, C. (ed.) 1994: *Political Re-structuring in Europe*. London: Routledge.

Brown, C. M. 1991: Diplomacy and the Western Sahara Conflict. *Diplomatic Record*, 2, 233–53.

Brown, J. 1991: *Delicately Poised Allies: Greece and Turkey*. London: Brassey.

Brown, P. G. and Shue, H. (eds) 1981: *Boundaries: National Autonomy and its Limits*. Totowa: Rowman & Littlefield.

Brownlie, I. 1971: *Basic Documents on African Affairs*. Oxford: Oxford University Press.

—— 1979: *African Boundaries: a Legal and Diplomatic Encyclopedia*. London: Hurst.

Brubaker, W. R. (ed.) 1989: *Immigration and the Politics of Citizenship in Europe and North America*. New York: University Press of America.

Brubaker, W. R. 1992: *Citizenship and Nationhood in France and Germany*. Cambridge, Mass.: Harvard University Press.

Bruce, S. 1994: *What do the Ulster Protestants Want?* Oxford: Oxford University Press.

Buccheit, L. C. 1978: *Secession: The Legitimacy of Self-Determination*. New Haven: Yale University Press.

Buchanan, J. M. and Tulloch, G. 1962: *The Calculus of Consent: Logical Foundations of Constitutional Democracy*. Ann Arbor: University of Michigan Press.

Buchholz, H. 1994: The Inner-German Border. Consequences of its Establishment and Abolition. In C. Grundy-Watt, (ed.), *Eurasia*, London: Routledge, 55–62.

Buckley, M. and Anderson, M. (eds) 1988: *Women, Equality and Europe*. London: Macmillan.

Buisseret, D. (ed.) 1992: *Monarchs, Ministers and Maps: The Emergence of Cartography as a Tool of Government in Early Modern Europe*. Chicago: Chicago University Press.

Bull, H. and Watson, A. (eds) 1984: *The Expansion of International Society*. Oxford: Oxford University Press.

Bulloch, J. and Morris, H. 1992: *No Friends but the Mountain*. London: Viking.

Bulpitt, J. G. 1983: *Territory and Power in the United Kingdom*. Manchester: Manchester University Press.

Burgière, A. and Revel, J. (eds) 1989: *Histoire de France*. Paris: Seuil, 2 of 4 vols.

Burleigh, M. 1988: *Germany turns Eastwards: A Study of* Ostforschung *in the Third Reich*. Cambridge: Cambridge University Press.

Busch, H. 1993: Spanien, die Grenze nach Süden. *Bürgerrechte & Polizei*, 45 (2) 58–63.

Bush, W. M. (ed.) 1982–8: *Antarctica and International Law; a Collection of Inter-State and National Documents*. Dobbs Ferry, NY: Oceana Publications, 4 vols.

Byran Collester, J. and Burnham, H. 1975: Eurocontrol: A Reappraisal of Functional Integration. *Journal of Common Market Studies,* 13 (4) 345–67.

Campbell, D. B. 1982: Nationalism, Religion and the Social Bases of Conflict in the Swiss Jura. In S. Rokkan and D. W. Urwin (eds), *The Politics of Territorial Identity*, London: Sage, 279–307.

Capotorti, F. 1979: *Study on the Rights of Persons Belonging to Ethnic, Religious and Linguistic Minorities.* New York: UN Doc. E/CN. 4/Sub. 2/384/Rev. 1.

Caratini, R. 1990: *Dictionnaire des nationalités et des minorités en URSS.* Paris: Larousse.

Cardoso, F. H. and Faletto, E. 1971: *Dependency and Development in Latin America.* Berkeley: University of California Press.

Carens, J. H. 1989: Membership and Morality: The Admission to Citizenship in Liberal Democracies. In W. R. Brubaker (ed.), *Immigration and the Politics of Citizenship in Europe and North America*, New York: University Press of America, 31–49.

Castellan, G. 1991: *Histoire des Balkans, XIVᵉ–XXᵉ siècle.* Paris: Fayard.

Castles, S. and Miller, M. 1993: *The Age of Migration: International Migration Movements in the Modern World.* London: Macmillan.

Cavin, J. F. 1971: *Territorialité, nationalité, et droits politiques.* Lausanne: Imprimerie Held.

CDU/CSU Group in the German Bundestag 1977: *White Paper on the Human Rights Situation in Germany and of the Germans in Eastern Europe.*

Chaliand, G. (ed.) 1980: *People Without a Country: The Kurds and Kurdistan.* London: Zed Press.

—— et al., 1994: *Atlas des migrations.* Paris: Seuil.

Chalier, T. 1966: A propos des conflits de frontière entre la Somalie, l'Ethiopie et le Kenya. *Revue Française de Science Politique*, 2, 310–19.

Chaney, E. M. 1981: Migrant Workers and National Boundaries: The Basis for Rights and Protections. In P. G. Brown and H. Shue (eds), *Boundaries: National Autonomy and its Limits*, Totowa: Rowman & Littlefield, 37–78.

Charney, J. I. 1991: *The New Nationalism and the Use of Common Spaces: Issues of Marine Protection and the Exploitation of Antarctica.* Totowa: Allanheld, Osmun.

Charpilloz, A. 1976: *Le Jura irlandisé.* Vevy: Galland.

Chaunu, P. 1973: *L'Espagne de Charles Quint.* Paris: Société d'Édition de l'Enseignement Supérieur, 2 vols.

Chazan, N. (ed.) 1991: *Irredentism in International Politics.* London: Adamantine Press.

Chomsky, N. 1982: *Towards a New Cold War.* New York: Pantheon.

Choudhary, S. 1972: *A Study in International Legal Norms and Permissive Conscience.* New Delhi: Asian Publishing House.

Choudhury, C. W. 1972: Bangladesh: Why it Happened. *International Affairs*, 48 (2) 242–9.

—— 1973: The Emergence of Bangladesh and the South East Asia Triangle. *Year Book of World Affairs*, 62, 62–89.

—— 1974: *The Last Days of a United Pakistan.* Bloomington: Indiana University Press.

Clogg, R. 1991: Greek-Turkish Relations in the post 1974 Period. In D. Constas (ed.), *The Greek–Turkish Conflict in the 1990s: Domestic and External Influences,* London: Macmillan, 12–23.

Cobban, A. 1945: *The Nation State and National Self-Determination.* Oxford: Oxford University Press (rev. edn London: Collins, 1969).

Cocca, A. 1986: The Common Heritage of Mankind: Doctrine and Principle of Space Law. *Proceedings of the Twenty-Ninth Colloquium on the Law of Outer Space,* Washington: International Institute of Space Law, 17–24.

Cohen, A. P. (ed) 1986: *Symbolising Boundaries.* Manchester: Manchester University Press.

Cohen, S. B. 1986: *The Geopolitics of Israel's Border Question.* Boulder: Westview Press.

Cohn-Bendit, D. 1993: Europe and its Borders: the Case for a Common Immigration Policy. In S. Ogata et al., *Towards a Common Immigration Policy,* Brussels: Philip Morris Institute for Public Policy Research, 23–31.

—— and Schmidt, T. 1992: *Heimat Babylon: Das Wagnis der multikulturellen Gesellschaft.* Hamburg: Hoffmann und Campe.

Colby, C. C. (ed.) 1938: *Geographical Aspects of International Relations.* Chicago: University of Chicago Press.

Cole, J. W. and Wolfe, E. R. 1974: *The Hidden Frontier.* New York: Academic Press.

Collins, R. 1990: *The Basques.* 2nd edn, Oxford: Basil Blackwell.

Connor, W. 1969: Myths of Hemispheric, Continental, Regional and State Unity. *Political Science Quarterly,* 84 (4) 555–82.

—— 1984: *The National Question in Marxist-Leninist Theory and Practice.* Princeton: Princeton University Press.

Contamine, P. 1980: *La Guerre au moyen âge.* Paris: Presses Universitaires de France.

Cooper, J. S. 1985: Reconstructing History from Ancient Inscriptions. *Sources (and Monographs) from the Ancient Near East,* 11 (1).

Craven, J. P., Schneider, J. and Stimson, C. (eds) 1989: *The Implications of Extended Maritime Jurisdiction in the Pacific.* University of Hawaii: Law of the Sea Institute.

Cruttwell, C. R. M. F. 1937: *A History of Peaceful Change in the Modern World.* Oxford: Oxford University Press.

Current Digest of the Soviet Press 1983: The Law on the USSR State Border, 34 (51), 15–20.

Curzon of Kedleston, Lord 1907: *Frontiers.* Oxford: Oxford University Press.

Dahl, R. A. and Tufte, E. R. 1973: *Size and Democracy.* Stanford: Stanford University Press.

Dalby, S. 1990: American Security Discourse: The Persistence of Geopolitics. *Political Geography Quarterly,* 9, 171–88.

Davis, M. et al. 1990: *Fire in the Hearth: The Radical Politics of Place in America.* New York: Verso.

Dawkins, R. 1976: *The Selfish Gene*. New York: Oxford University Press.

Day, A. J. (ed.) 1987: *Border and Territorial Disputes*. 2nd edn, London: Keesings Reference Publications.

De Jasay, A. 1985: *The State*. Oxford: Blackwell.

de la Garza, R. O. and Vargas, C. 1992: The Mexican-Origin Population of the United States as a Political Force in the Borderlands: From Paisanos to Ponchos to Potential Political Allies. In L. A. Herzog (ed.), *Changing Boundaries in the Americas*, San Diego: University of California Press, 89–112.

de Gaulle, C. 1954: *Mémoires de Guerre*. Paris: Plon, 3 vols.

de Lapradelle, P. G. 1928: *La Frontière: Étude de Droit International*. Paris: Éditions Internationales.

Demandt, A. (ed.) 1990: *Deutschlands Grenzen in der Geshichte*. Munich: Beck.

De Marchi, B. and Boileau, A. M. (eds) 1982: *Boundaries and Minorities in Western Europe*. Milan: Angeli.

Denman, D. R. 1984: Markets under the Seas. London: IEA, Hobart Paper no. 17.

de Rougemont, D. (ed.) 1968, 1970: *L'Europe des Régions*. Geneva: Institut des Études Européennes.

de Tinguy, A. 1992: Émigration de l'ex URSS: La Grande Inconnue. *Esprit*, 183, 114–27.

de Visscher, C. 1957: *Theory and Reality in Public International Law*. Trans. P. E. Corbett, Princeton: Princeton University Press.

Diederichs, O. 1993: Die Sicherung der deutschen Ostgrenze. *Bürgerrechte & Polizei*, 45 (2), 24–9.

Dion, R. 1947: *Les Frontières de la France*. Paris: Hachette.

Divine, R. A. 1957: *American Immigration Policy, 1924–1952*. New Haven: Yale University Press.

Djalili, M. J. 1990: Territoire et frontières dans l'idéologie islamiste contemporaine. *Relations Internationales*, 62, 387–407.

Documentation Française 1986: *La Lutte contre les trafics de main d'oeuvre*. Paris: Imprimerie Nationale.

Doggan, M. 1993: Le Nationalisme en Europe: Déclin à l'Ouest, résurgence à l'Est. In E. Philippart, (ed.) *Nationalisme et frontières dans la nouvelle Europe*, Brussels: Éditions Complexe.

Dowty, A. 1987: *Closed Borders: The Contemporary Assault on the Freedom of Movement*. New Haven: Yale University Press.

Drysdale, A. and Blake, G. H. 1985: *The Middle East and North Africa: A Political Geography*. Oxford: Oxford University Press.

Drysdale, J. 1964: *The Somali Dispute*. London: Pall Mall.

Dryzek, J. S. 1990: *Discursive Democracy: Politics, Policy, and Political Science*. Cambridge: Cambridge University Press.

Dummett, A. and Neissen, J. 1993. *Immigration and Citizenship in the European Union*. Brussels: CCME Briefing Paper no. 14.

Duncan, P. 1988: Ideology and the National Question: Marxism-Leninism and Nationality Policy of the Communist Party of the Soviet Union. In S. White, and A. Pravda (eds), *Ideology and Soviet Politics*, London: Macmillan, 180–200.

Dunleavy, P. et al. (eds) 1993: *Developments in British Politics 4*. London: Macmillan.

Dyson, K. 1980: *The State Tradition in Western Europe*. Oxford: Oxford University Press.

Earney, F. 1990: *Marine Mineral Resources*. London: Routledge.

Ecevit, Z. H. 1981: International Labour Migration in the Middle East and North Africa: Trends, Effects, Policies. In M. M. Kritz, C. B. Keely and S. M. Tomasi (eds), *Global Trends in Migration Theory and Research on International Population Movements*, New York: Center for Migration Studies, 259–75.

Eck, A. 1969: *Le Moyen Age Russe*. 2nd edn, Paris: Mouton.

ECSA-Europe 1993: *The Legal, Economic and Administrative Adaptations of Central European Countries to the European Community*. Baden Baden: Nomos.

Edmonds, C. J. 1957: *Kurds, Turks and Arabs*. Oxford: Oxford University Press.

Emerson, R. 1960: *From Empire to Nation: The Rise of Self-Assertion of Asian and African Peoples*. Cambridge, Mass.: Harvard University Press.

—— 1972: Self-Determination. *American Journal of International Law*, 65 (3), 459–74.

Enscalada, V. 1979: *Air Law*. Alphen aan den Rijn: Sijthoff and Noordhoff.

Eurostat 1993: *Statistiques rapides: Populations et conditions sociales*. Brussels: European Communities.

Evans, P. 1979: *Dependent Development: The Alliance of Multinational, State, and Local Capital in Brazil*. Princeton: Princeton University Press.

—— and others (eds), 1985: *Bringing the State Back In*. Cambridge: Cambridge University Press.

Evans, R. I. (ed) 1975: *Konrad Lorenz: The Man and his Ideas*. New York: Harcourt Brace Jovanovic.

Fargues, P. 1985: Du Nil au Golfe. Problèmes de l'émigration égyptienne. *Population*, vol. 1.

Farley, L. T. 1986: *Plebiscites and Sovereignty: The Crisis of Political Illegitimacy*. Boulder: Westview.

Fawtier, R. 1961: Comment le roi de France, au début du XIVe siècle, pouvait-il se représenter son royaume?' In *Mélanges offerts à P. E. Martin*. Geneva: Comité des Amis P. E. Martin, 65–77.

Featherstone, M. (ed.) 1990: *Global Culture: Nationalism, Globalization and Modernity*. London: Sage.

Febvre, L. 1922: *La Terre et l'évolution humaine*. Paris: La Renaissance du Livre (repr. Paris: Albin Michel, 1970).

—— 1973: *Frontière:* The Word and the Concept. In P. Burke (ed.), *A New Kind of History from the Writings of Febvre*, London: Routledge & Kegan Paul, 208–18.

Fell, R. 1976: *Un Canton du Jura: Pourquoi?* Delémont: Rassemblement Jurassien.

Fielding, A. 1993: Mass Migration and Economic Restructuring. In R. King (ed.), *Mass Migration in Europe: The Legacy and the Future.* London: Belhaven Press 7–18.

Finnie, D. H. 1990: *Shifting Lines in the Sand: Kuwait's Elusive Frontier with Iraq.* London: Tauris.

Fitzmaurice, J. 1993: Regional Cooperation in Central Europe. *West European Politics,* 16 (3), 380–400.

Flückiger, F. 1977: *Unité jurassienne? Notion de 'peuple' et celle d''état.* Berne: Association des Amis du Jura bernois.

Foucher, M. 1986: *L'Invention des frontières.* Paris: Fondation pour les Études de la Défense Nationale.

—— 1988: *Fronts et frontières: Un tour du monde géopolitique.* Paris: Fayard.

—— 1990: *Les Frontières de la nouvelle Europe. Politique étrangère,* 3, 575–87.

Freeman, O. and Pulikowski, P. 1992: *Les Collectivités territoriales et la coopération transfrontalière.* Warsaw.

Fritsch-Bournazel, R. 1991: *L'Allemagne unie dans une nouvelle Europe.* Brussels: Éditions Complexe.

Frontiers: Planning for Consumer Change in Europe 1991. Henley: Centre for Forecasting and Research International.

Gagé, J. 1964: *Les Classes sociales dans l'Empire Romain.* Paris: Payot.

Gallais, J. 1982: Poles d'État et frontières en Afrique contemporaine: *Cahiers d'Outre Mer,* 38, 114–21.

Ganster, P. and Valenciano, E. O. 1992: *The Mexican–US Border Region and the Free Trade Agreement.* San Diego State University: Institute for Regional Study of the Californias.

Gasser, A. 1978: *Berne et le Jura: 1815–1977.* Berne: Imprimerie Fédérative.

Gellner, E. 1983: *Nations and Nationalism.* Oxford: Oxford University Press.

George, P. 1984: *Géopolitique des minorités.* Paris: Presses Universitaires de France.

Giddens, A. 1981: *A Contemporary Critique of Historical Materialism,* i: *Power, Property and the State.* London: Macmillan.

Gildea, R. 1987: *Barricades and Borders. Europe, 1800–1914.* Oxford: Oxford University Press.

Gilmore, W. C. 1994: Sea and Ocean Bed. *Stair Encyclopedia of Scots Law,* xxi. 1–45, London: Butterworths.

Girard d'Albissin, N. 1970: *Genèse de la frontière Franco-Belge: Les Variations des limites septentrionales de la France de 1659 à 1789.* Paris: Picard.

Girot, P. O. 1994: The Inter-Oceanic Canal and Boundaries in Central America. In id. (ed.), *The Americas,* London: Routledge, 58–71.

Glazer, N. (ed.), 1985: *Clamour at the Gates: The New American Immigration.* San Francisco: ICS Press.

Goblet, Y. M. 1956: *Political Geography and the World Map.* London: Praeger.

Godechot, J. 1983: *La Grande Nation. L'Expansion révolutionnaire de la France.* 2nd edn, Paris: Aubier Montaigne.

Goertz, G. and Diehl, P. F. 1992: *Territorial Changes and International Conflict.* London: Routledge.

Goffman, E. 1972: *Relations in Public.* Harmondsworth: Penguin.

Gómez-Ibanez, D. A. 1975: *The Western Pyrenees.* Oxford: Oxford University Press.

Gong, G. W. 1984: China's Entry into International Society. In H Bull and A. Watson (eds), *The Expansion of International Society.* Oxford: Oxford University Press, 171–84.

Goodwin-Gill, G. S. 1983: *The Refugee in International Law.* Oxford: Clarendon Press.

Gordenker, L. 1987: *Refugees in International Politics.* London: Croom Helm.

Gottman, J. 1973: *The Significance of Territory.* Charlottesville: University of Virginia.

Gould, P. and White, R. 1986: *Mental Maps.* 2nd edn, London: Allen & Unwin.

Gourevitch, P. 1978: Reforming the Napoleonic State: The Creation of Regional Governments in France and Italy. In S. Tarrow, P. J. Katzenstein and L. Graziano (eds), *Territorial Politics in Industrial Nations,* New York: Praeger, 28–63.

Grange, D. J. 1990: La Question frontalière franco-genevoise depuis 1945. *Relations Internationales,* 63, 313–28.

Green, S. W. and Perlman, S. M. (eds) 1985: *The Archeology of Frontiers and Boundaries.* Orlando: Academic Press.

Greño Velasco, J. E. 1977: Problema institutionel de la integración frontizera. *Integración Latinoamericana,* 17 Buenos Aires: Inter-American Development Bank/Instituto para la Integración de América Latina.

Gresh, A. (ed.) 1993: *À l'Est, les nationalismes contre la démocratie?* Brussels: Éditions Complexe.

Groom, A. J. R. and Light, M. (eds) 1994: *Contemporary International Relations: A Guide to Theory.* London: Pinter.

Grousset, R. 1965: *L'Empire des Steppes.* Paris: Payot (repr. 1989).

Gubert, R. 1982: The Problems of Inter-Ethnic Relations in Alto Adige with Reference to the New Demand for Bilingualism by Italians. In B. De Marchi, and A. M. Boileau (eds), *Boundaries and Minorities in Western Europe,* 211–28.

Guenée, B. 1981: La Géographie administrative de la France à la fin du Moyen Age. *Politique et histoire du Moyen Age.* Paris: Publications de la Sorbonne, 41–71.

—— 1986: Des Limites féodales aux frontières politiques. In P. Nora (ed.), *Les Lieux de mémoire,* i, *La Nation,* Paris: Seuil 11–34.

Guichonnet, P. and Raffestin, C. 1974: *Géographie des frontières.* Paris: Presses Universitaires de France.

Gullick, E. 1955: *Europe's Classic Balance of Power.* Ithaca: Cornell University Press.

Haas, P. M. 1990: *Saving the Mediterranean: The Politics of International Environmental Cooperation.* New York: Columbia University Press.

Habermas, J. 1992: Citizenship and National Identity: Some Reflections on the Future of Europe. *Praxis International,* 12 (1), 1–19.

Hall, J. A. 1993: Nationalism: Classified and Explained. *Daedalus,* 122 (3), 1–28.

Hanlon, J. 1986: *Beggar Your Neighbours: Apartheid Power in Southern Africa.* Bloomington: Indiana University Press.

Hanson, W. and Maxwell, G. 1983: *The Antonine Wall: Rome's North West Frontier.* Edinburgh: Edinburgh University Press.

Harding, S. and Phillips, D. 1986: *Contrasting Values in Western Europe.* London: Macmillan.

Hargreaves, A. 1992: Migration Controls, Open Frontiers and European Union. *Journal of Area Studies,* 1, 74–86.

Harris, W. W. 1980: *Taking Root: The Israeli Settlement in the West Bank, the Golan and Gaza–Sinai, 1967–80.* New York: Wiley.

Haupt, G., Lowy, M. and Weill, C. 1974: *Les Marxistes et la question nationale, 1848–1914.* Paris: Maspero.

Haushofer K. 1986: *De la Géopolitique.* Paris: Fayard.

Hechter, M. 1975: *Internal Colonialism: The Celtic Fringe in British National Development.* London: Routledge & Kegan Paul.

Heiberg, M. 1989: *The Making of the Basque Nation.* Cambridge: Cambridge University Press.

Heinelt, H. 1993: Immigration and the Welfare State. *German Politics,* 2 (1), 78–96.

Held, D. (ed.), 1991: *Political Theory Today.* Oxford: Blackwell.

—— (ed.) 1993: *Prospects for Democracy: North, South, East, West.* Cambridge: Polity.

Hennessy, A. 1978: *The Frontier in Latin American History.* Albuquerque: University of New Mexico Press.

Heraclides, A. 1991: *The Self-determination of Minorities in International Politics.* London: Frank Cass.

Herz, J. H. 1961: The Rise and Demise of the Territorial State. In J. D. Rosenau (ed.), *International Politics and Foreign Policy,* New York: Free Press of Glencoe, 80–6.

Herzog, L. A. (ed.) 1992: *Changing Boundaries in the Americas: New Perspectives on the US–Mexican, Central American and South American Borders.* San Diego: University of California Press.

Heslinga, M. W. 1979: *The Irish Border as a Cultural Divide.* Assen: Van Gorcum.

Hewitt, A. and Winston, V. H. (eds) 1991: *Milestones in Glasnost and Perestroika: The Economy.* Washington: Brookings Institution.

Hintjens, H., Loughlin, J. and Olivesi, C. 1994: The Status of Maritime and Insular France. *Regional Politics and Policy,* 4 (3), 110–31.

Hirschman, A. O. 1970: *Exit, Voice and Loyalty.* Cambridge, Mass.: Harvard University Press.

Hobsbawm, E. and Ranger, J. (eds) 1983: *The Invention of Tradition.* Oxford: Oxford University Press.

Hodges, J. T. 1983: *Western Sahara: The Roots of a Desert War.* London: Lawrence Hill.

Hoffman, H. (ed.) 1987: *Arab–Israeli Relations in Israel.* Bristol: Wyndham Hall.

Hoffmann, S. 1981: *Duties beyond Borders*. Syracuse: Syracuse University Press.

Hofstadter, R. and Lipset, S. M. (eds) 1968: *Turner and the Sociology of the Frontier*. New York: Basic Books.

Hommes et migrations 1992: June special number: *Migrations Est-Ouest*.

Honoré, A. M. 1961: Ownership. In A. G. Guest (ed.), *Oxford Essays in Jurisprudence*, Oxford: Oxford University Press, 107–47.

Hsu, I. C. Y. 1960: *China's Entrance into the Family of Nations*. Cambridge, Mass.: Harvard University Press.

Huout, J.-L. 1989: *Les Sumériens*. Paris: Errance.

Hurrell, A. and Kingsbury, B. (eds) 1992: *The International Politics of the Environment*. Oxford: Clarendon Press.

Husser, P. 1989: *Un Instituteur alsacien: Entre France et Allemagne. Journal de Philippe Husser 1914–1951*. Paris: Hachette.

Ignatieff, M. 1993: *Blood and Belonging: Journeys into the New Nationalism*. London: BBC Books Chatto & Windus.

Indian Ministry of Information and Broadcasting 1962: *Chinese Aggression in Maps*. New Delhi.

Inglehart, R. 1990: *Cultural Shift in Advanced Industrial Societies*. Princeton: Princeton University Press.

Institute of International Political and Strategic Studies. n.d.: *The Macedonian Affair: A Historical Review of the Attempts to Create a Counterfeit Nation*. Athens.

La Integración frontizera en la sub-región andina. La Paz: Instituto International de integración 1985.

Ireland, G. 1938: *Boundaries, Possessions and Conflicts in South America*. Cambridge, Mass.: Harvard University Press.

—— 1941: *Boundaries, Possessions and Conflicts in Central and North America and the Caribbean*. Cambridge, Mass.: Harvard University Press.

Isaac, B. 1990: *The Limits of Empire: The Roman Army in the East*. Oxford: Clarendon Press.

Jackson, R. H. 1990: *Quasi-States: Sovereignty, International Relations and the Third World*. Cambridge: Cambridge University Press.

Jacobsen, H.-A. 1979: *Karl Haushofer: Leben und Werk*. Boppard am Rhein: Harald Boldt, 2 vols.

Jardel, J.-P. 1982: Alpazur: a New Transfrontier Region. In R. Strassoldo and G. Delli Zotti (eds), *Cooperation and Conflict in Border Areas*. Milan: Angeli, 87–100.

Jawad, S. 1981: *Iraq and the Kurdish Question 1958–1970*. Ithaca: Cornell University Press.

Jenkins, J. R. G. 1986: *Jura Separatism in Switzerland*. Oxford: Oxford University Press.

Jennings, I. 1956: *The Approach to Self-Government*. Cambridge: Cambridge University Press.

Jennings, R. 1963: *The Acquisition of Territory in International Law*. Manchester: Manchester University Press.

Johansson, R. 1988: *Small States in Boundary Conflicts: Belgium and the Belgian–German Border, 1914–1919.* Lund: Lund University Press.

Johnson, J. T. 1975: *Ideology, Reason and the Limitations of War: Religious and Secular Concepts, 1200–1740.* Princeton: Princeton University Press.

Johnston, D. M. 1988: *The Theory and History of Ocean Boundary Making.* Kingston: McGill–Queens University Press.

Johnston, H. J. M. 1972: *British Emigration Policy: 1815–1830: 'Shovelling out Paupers'.* Oxford: Clarendon Press.

Jolowicz, H. F. 1952: *Historical Introduction to the Study of Roman Law.* Cambridge: Cambridge University Press.

Joly, D. and Poulton, R. 1992: *Refugees: Asylum in Europe?* London: Minority Rights Group Report.

Joyeux, F. 1989: *Les Frontières du Vietnam: Histoire des frontières de la péninsule indochinoise.* Paris: Harmattan.

—— 1990: Vietnam en quête de nouvelles frontières. *Relations Internationales,* 64, 387–407.

—— 1991: *Géopolitique de l'extrême orient.* Brussels: Éditions Complexe, 2 vols.

Kapil, S. 1966: On the Conflict Potential of Inherited Boundaries in Africa. *World Politics,* 18 (4), 656–73.

Katzenstein, P. J. 1984: *Corporatism and Change: Austria, Switerland, and the Politics of Industry.* Ithaca: Cornell University Press.

—— 1985: *Small States in World Markets: Industrial Policy in Europe.* Ithaca: Cornell University Press.

Kaye, H. L. 1986: *The Social Meaning of Modern Biology: From Social Darwinism to Sociobiology.* New Haven: Yale University Press.

Keating, M. 1988: *State and Regional Nationalism: Territorial Politics and the European State.* Brighton: Harvester.

Kegley, C. (ed.) 1993: *The New International Realities: The Neoliberal Challenge to Realist Theories of World Politics.* New York: St Martin's Press.

Kemper, F.-J. 1993: New Trends in Mass Migration in Germany. In R. King (ed.), *Mass Migration in Europe,* London: Belhaven Press, 256–74.

Keohane, R. and Nye, R. 1977: *Power and Interdependence: World Politics in Transition.* Boston: Little, Brown.

Khader, B. 1991: Les Migrations vers le Golfe. *Relations Internationales,* 66, 183–98.

Kindleberger, C. 1969: *American Business Abroad.* New Haven: Yale University Press.

King, M. 1994: Policing Refugees and Asylum Seekers in the 'Greater Europe'. In M. Anderson and M. den Boer (eds), *Policing across National Boundaries.* London: Pinter, 69–84.

King, R. (ed.) 1993: *Mass Migration in Europe: The Legacy and the Future.* London: Belhaven Press.

Kipnis, B. A. 1987a: Geopolitical Ideologies and Regional Strategies in Israel. *Tijdschrift voor Economische en Sociale Geografie,* 78, 125–38.

—— 1987b: Regional Development and Strategy Considerations in Multicommunity Land of Israel. In J. H. Hofman (ed.), *Arab-Jewish Relations in Israel,* London: Wyndham Hall, 21–44.

—— 1991: Geographical Perspectives on Peace Alternatives for the Land of Israel, In N. Kliot and S. Waterman (eds), *The Political Geography of Conflict and Peace*, London: Belhaven Press, 217–28.

Kleff, H. G. 1991: Les Turcs à Berlin avant et aprés la chute du Mur. *Revue Européenne des Migrations Internationales*, 7 (2), 83–97.

Klusmeyer, D. B. 1993: Aliens, Immigrants, and Citizens: The Politics of Inclusion in the Federal Republic of Germany. *Daedalus*, 122 (3), 81–114.

Knight, D. B. and Davies, M. 1987: *Self-Determination: An Interdisciplinary Annotated Bibliography*. London: Garland.

Kolarz, W. 1946: *Myths and Realities of Eastern Europe*. London: Lindsay Drummond.

Korinman, R. 1990: *Quand l'Allemagne pensait le monde: Grandeur et décadence d'une géopolitique*. Paris: Fayard.

Kratochwil, F. V., Rohrlich, P. and Mahajain, H. 1985: *Peace and Disputed Sovereignty: Reflections on Conflict over Territory*. New York: University Press of America.

Krepon, M. et al. 1990: *Commercial Observation Satellites and International Security*. New York: Macmillan and the Carnegie Foundation for International Peace.

Kreyenbroek, P. G. and Sperei, S. 1992: *The Kurds*. London: Routledge.

Kritz, M. M. (ed.) 1983: *US Immigration and Refugee Policy: Global and Domestic Issues*. Lexington: Heath.

—— Keely, C. B. and Tomasi, S. M. (eds) 1981: *Global Trends in Migratory Theory and Research in International Population Movements*. New York: Center for Migration Studies.

Kruszewski, Z. A. 1972: *The Oder–Neisse Boundary and Poland's Modernization: The Socio-Economic and Political Impact*. New York: Praeger.

Kuper, E. 1981: *Genocide: Its Political Use in the 20th Century*. New Haven: Yale University Press.

Kwiatkowska, B. 1989: *The 200 Mile Exclusive Economic Zone in the New Law of the Sea*. Dordrecht: Nijhoff.

Lacasse, J. P. 1974: Les Nouvelles Perspectives de l'étude des frontières politiques. *Cahiers de Géographie de Québec*, 18, 4.

Laffan, R. G. D. 1918: *The Serbs: The Guardians of the Gate*. Repr. London: Dorset Press, 1989.

Laizer, S. 1991: *Into Kurdistan*. London: Zed Press.

Lamb, A. 1964: *The China-Indian Border: The Origin of the Disputed Territories*. Oxford: Oxford University Press.

—— 1966: *The MacMahon Line*. London: Routledge & Kegan Paul, 2 vols.

—— 1968: *Asian Frontiers: Studies in a Continuing Problem*. London: Pall Mall Press.

Landes, A., Caldwell, B. E. and Siegel, M. A. 1991: *Immigration and Illegal Immigrants*. Wylie Texas: Information Plus.

Lansing, R. 1921: *The Peace Negotiations: A Personal Narrative*. Boston: Houghton Mifflin.

Lapidus, G. W., Zaslavsky, V. and Goldman, P. (eds) 1992: *From Union to*

Commonwealth: Nationalism and Separatism in the Soviet Republics. Cambridge: Cambridge University Press.

Laroui, A. 1977: *Les Origines sociales et culturelles du nationalisme marocain, 1830–1912.* Paris: Maspero.

Lattimore, O. D. 1940: *Inner Asian Frontiers of China.* Oxford: Oxford University Press, repr. 1988.

Lavisse, E. 1924: *Vue générale de l'histoire politique de l'Europe.* 16th edn, Paris: Colin.

Lawless, R. I. and Seccombe, I. J. 1986: Travailleurs migrants et débuts de l'industrie pétrolière. *Maghreb-Machrek*, no. 112.

Le Bras, G. 1967: The Sociology of the Church in the Early Middle Ages. In S. L. Thrupp (ed.), *Early Medieval Society*, New York: Appleton-Century-Crofts, 47–57.

Lehmann, N. 1991: *The Promised Land.* New York: Knopf.

Lemarchand, R. 1962: The Limits of Self-Determination: The Case of the Katanga Secession. *American Political Science Review*, 56 (2), 404–16.

Lemarq, G. 1992: L'Indépendance des états baltes et la question des nationalités. *Hérodote*, 64 (January–March), 136–47.

Lemon, A. 1991: Apartheid as Foreign Policy: Dimensions of International Conflict in Southern Africa. In N. Kurit and S. Waterman (eds), *The Political Geography of Conflict and Peace*, London: Belhaven Press.

Lengereau, F. 1990: *Les Frontières allemandes, 1919–1989: frontières d'Allemagne et en Allemagne. Aspects Territoriaux de la Question allemande.* Bern: Peter Lang.

Lenin, V. I. 1964: Imperialism, the Highest Form of Capitalism. In *Collected Works.* London: Lawrence and Wishart, xxii. 185–304.

Leonardi, R. 1992: The Role of Sub-National Institutions in European Integration. *Regional Politics and Policy*, 1 and 2 (2), 1–13.

Lepesant, G. 1993: Mutations de l'espace économique et politique de la région frontalière germano-polonaise et de Kaliningrad. *Cahiers de l'observatoire de Berlin*, Berlin: Centre National de Recherches Scientifiques, 25.

Lerner, R. M. 1992: *Final Solutions: Biology, Prejudice and Genocide.* Pittsburgh: Pennsylvania University Press.

Lévi-Strauss, C. 1963: *Structural Anthropology.* New York: Basic Books.

Lévy, B.-H. 1973: *Bangladesh, nationalisme dans la révolution*, Paris: Maspero.

Lichtenberg, J. 1981: National Boundaries and Moral Boundaries: A Cosmopolitan View. In P. G. Brown and H. Shue (eds), *Boundaries*, Totowa: Rowman & Littlefield, 79–100.

Light, M. and Groom, A. J. R. (eds) 1985: *International Relations: A Handbook of Current Theory.* Boulder: Lynne Reiner.

Lindberg, L. and Scheingold, S. (eds) 1971: *Regional Integration: Theory and Research.* Cambridge, Mass.: Harvard University Press.

List, M. and Rittberger, V. 1992: Regime Theory and International Environmental Management. In A. Hurrell and B. Kingsbury (eds), *The International Politics of the Environment*, Oxford: Clarendon Press, 85–109.

Longuenesse, E. 1986: Migrations et société dans les pays du Golfe. *Maghreb-Machrek,* no 112.

Lopreno, D. 1991: La Géopolitique du fascisme italien: La Revue mensuelle *Géopolitica. Hérodote,* 63 (October–December) 116–29.

Lorenz, K. 1966: *On Aggression.* New York: Harcourt Brace & World.

Losser, A. 1990: La Frontière interallemande: Exemple type de frontière 'passoire' dans le domaine économique. *Relations Internationales,* 64, 371–86.

Lovering, J. F. and Prescott, J. R. V. 1979: *Last of Lands: Antarctica.* Melbourne: Melbourne University Press.

Lowi, M. R. 1993: *Water and Power: The Politics of a Scarce Resource in the Jordan River Basin.* Cambridge: Cambridge University Press.

Lu Chih, H. 1986: *The Sino-Indian Border Dispute.* Boulder: Greenwood.

Luard, E. (ed.) 1970: *The International Regulation of Frontier Disputes.* London: Thames & Hudson.

Luttwak, E. N. 1976: *The Grand Strategy of the Roman Empire.* Baltimore: Johns Hopkins University Press.

Lutz, W. (ed.) 1991: *Future Demographic Trends in Europe and North America.* London: Academic Press.

Lyon, P. 1970: Regional Organizations and Frontier Disputes. In E. Luard (ed.), *The International Regulation of Frontier Disputes,* London: Thames & Hudson, 109–40.

Lyster, S. 1985: *International Wildlife Law.* Cambridge: Grotius.

McDonald, R. 1988–9: *The Problem of Cyprus.* London: International Institute of Strategic Studies.

McEverdy, C. and Jones, R. 1978: *Atlas of World Population.* Harmondsworth: Penguin.

McEwan, A. C. 1971: *International Boundaries in East Africa.* Oxford: Oxford University Press.

MacKay, J. R. 1969: The Interactance Hypothesis and Boundaries in Canada. In B. J. L. Berry and D. F. Marble (eds), *Spatial Analysis: A Reader in Statistical Geography,* Englewood Cliffs, NJ: Prentice-Hall, 122–9.

Mackinder, H. J. 1904: The Geographical Pivot of History. *The Geographical Journal,* 23, 421–37.

McLean Petras, E. 1981: The Global Labour Market in the Modern World Economy. In M. M. Kritz, C. B. Keely and S. M. Tomasi (eds), *Global Trends in Migratory Theory,* New York: Center for Migration Studies, 44–63.

McLuhan, M. 1962: *The Gutenberg Galaxy.* Toronto: University of Toronto Press.

—— 1967: *The Medium is the Message.* New York: Random House.

—— and Powers, B. R. 1989: *The Global Village: Transformations in World Life and Media in the 21st Century.* New York: Oxford University Press.

McNeill, J. T. 1939: The Feudalization of the Church. In J. T. McNeill, H. Spinka and W. H. Willoughby (eds), *Environmental Factors in Christian History,* Chicago: University of Chicago Press, 187–205.

McNeill, W. H. 964: *Europe's Steppe Frontier, 1500–1800.* Chicago: Chicago University Press.

—— 1978: Human Migration: A Historical Overview. In W. H. McNeill and R. Adams (eds), *Human Migration: Patterns and Policies*, Bloomington: Indiana University Press.

McPhail, T. L. 1981: *Electronic Colonialism: The Future of International Broadcasting.* London: Sage.

McRae, K. D. 1983: *Conflict and Compromise in Multilingual Societies: Switzerland.* Waterloo: Wilfrid Laurier University Press.

Malaurie, J. 1989: *Les Derniers Rois de Thulé: Avec les Esquimaux polaires face à leur destin.* 5th edn, Paris: Plon.

—— 1992: L'Arctique soviétique, face aux miroirs brisés de l'occident. *Hérodote*, 64 (January–March), 194–219.

Malmberg, T. 1980: *Human Territoriality: Survey of Behavioural Territories in Man with Preliminary Analysis and Discussion of Meaning.* Paris: Mouton.

Mann, M. 1993: Nation States in Europe and other Continents: Diversifying, Developing, not Dying. *Daedalus*, 122 (3), 115–40.

Margalit, A. and Raz, J. 1990: National Self-determination. *Journal of Philosophy*, 57, 439–61.

Marie, C.-V. 1987: *Les Migrations en Europe occidentale.* Paris: Council of Europe.

Markakis, J. 1987: *National and Class Conflict in the Horn of Africa.* Cambridge: Cambridge University Press.

Martel, A. 1965: *Les Confins saharo-tripolitaine de la Tunisie, 1881–1911.* Paris: Presses Universitaires de France, 2 vols.

Martin, P. J. et al. 1985: *Shawcross and Beaumont: Air Law*, vol. i. London: Butterworth.

Martin, P.-M. 1992: *Droit des activités spaciales.* Paris: Masson.

Martinez, O. J. (ed.) 1986: *Across Boundaries: Transborder Interaction in Comparative Perspective.* El Paso: Western Texas Press.

—— 1994: The Dynamics of Border Interaction: New Approaches to Border Analysis. In C. H. Schofield (ed.), *Global Boundaries*, London: Routledge, 1–15.

Matte, N. M. 1987: The Common Heritage of Mankind Principle in Outer Space. *Annals of Air and Space Law*, 12, 313–36.

Mattern, J. 1921: *The Employment of the Plebiscite in the Determination of Sovereignty.* Baltimore: Johns Hopkins University Press.

Maxwell, N. 1970: *India's China War.* London: Cape.

—— 1973: India and the Nagas. London: Minority Rights Group, report no. 17.

Mazrui, A. A. 1991: *Cultural Forces in World Politics.* London: Curry.

Meehan, E. 1993: *Citizenship in the European Community.* London: Sage.

Mény, Y. 1986: The Political Dynamics of Regionalism: Italy, France, Spain. In R. Morgan (ed.), *Regionalism in European Politics*, London: Policy Studies Institute, 1–28.

Miles, R. 1991: Who Belongs? The Meaning of the British Nationality and Immigration Law. *Journal of Law and Society*, 18 (2), 279–86.

Mill, J. S. 1861: *Considerations on Representative Government.* In J. M.

Robertson (ed.) *The Collected Works of J. S. Mill*, vol. xix. London: Routledge & Kegan Paul, 1977.

Minority Rights Group 1985: *The Kurds*. London: MRG, report no. 23.

Molle, W. 1990: *Economics of European Integration*. Aldershot: Dartmouth.

Montanari, A. and Cortese, A. 1993: South to North Migration in a Mediterranean Perspective. In R. King (ed.), *Mass Migration in Europe*, London: Belhaven Press, 212–33.

Morales, R. and Tamayo-Sánchez, J. 1992: Urbanization and Development of the United States–Mexico Border. In L. A. Herzog (ed.), *Changing Boundaries in the Americas*, San Diego: University of California Press, 49–68.

Morris, M. (ed.) 1990: *Great Power Relationships in Argentina, Chile and Antarctica*. New York: St Martin's Press.

Moulier-Boutang, Y., Garson, J. V. and Silberman, R. 1986: *Économie politique des migrations clandestines de main d'oeuvre*. Paris: Publi-sud.

Müllerson, R. 1994: *International Law, Rights and Politics: Developments in Eastern Europe and the CIS*. London: Routledge.

Murray, R. 1975: The Internationalization of Capital and the Nation State. In H. Radice (ed.), *International Firms and Modern Imperialism*. Harmondsworth: Penguin, 107–34.

Naff, T. 1984: The Ottoman Empire and the European States-System. In H. Bull and A. Watson (eds), *The Expansion of International Society*, Oxford: Oxford University Press, 153–66.

Nanda, V. P. 1986: The Exclusive Economic Zone. *Political Geography Quarterly*, 5 (1), 9–13.

Nay, A. 1991: *Introduction aux statuts de l'étranger*. Brussels: Story Scienta.

Nayer, A. and Nys, M. 1992: *Les Migrations vers l'Europe occidentale: Politique migratoire et politique d'Intégration en Belgique*. Brussels: Fondation Roi Baudouin.

Négrine, R. and Papthanassopoulos, S. 1990: *The Internationalisation of Television*. London: Pinter.

Neuberger, B. 1986: *National Self-Determination in Post-Colonial Africa*. Boulder: Lynne Reiner.

Noiriel, P. 1988: *Le Creuset français: Histoire de l'immigration (XIXᵉ–XXᵉ siècles)*. Paris: Seuil.

Nora, P. (ed.) 1986–1992: *Les Lieux de mémoire*. Paris: Gallimard, 5 vols.

Nordman, D. 1975: *La Notion de frontière en Afrique du Nord: Mythes et réalités vers 1830 vers 1912*. Paris: Thesis Montpellier III.

—— and Revel, J. 1989: La Formation de l'espace français. In A. Burguière and J. Revel (eds), *Histoire de France*, Paris: Seuil, i. 33–169.

Novak, B. C. 1970: *Trieste 1941–1954: The Ethnic, Political, and Ideological Struggle*. Chicago: Chicago University Press.

Nye, J. S. and Shear, J. A. (eds) 1987: *Seeking Stability in Space: Anti-Satellite Weapons and the Evolving Space Regime*. New York: University Press of America.

Oakeshott, M. 1991: The Activity of Being an Historian. In id., *Rationalism in Politics and Other Essays*, new edn, Indianapolis: Liberty Press, 137–67.

OECD 1974: *Problems of Transfrontier Pollution.* Paris
—— 1976: *Legal Aspects of Transfrontier Pollution.* Paris.
—— 1979: *OECD and the Environment.* Paris.
Ogata, S. et al. 1993: *Towards a European Immigration Policy.* Brussels: Philip Morris Institute.
Oliver, T. W. 1978: *The United Nations in Bangladesh.* Princeton: Princeton Univeristy Press.
O'Neill, O. 1994: Justice and Boundaries. In C. Brown (ed.), *Political Restructuring in Europe*, London: Routledge, 69–88.
Ottoway, M. 1982: *Soviet and American Influence in the Horn of Africa.* New York: Praeger.
Ouzouf-Marignier, M. V. 1986: Politique et géographie lors de la création des départements français. *Hérodote*, 40 (January–March) 140–60.
Palmieri, V. H. 1981: Foreword. In M. M. Kritz (ed.), *Immigration and Refugee Policy*, Lexington: Heath, xi–xxi.
Papademetriou, D. G. and Miller, M. J. 1983: *The Unavoidable Issue: US Immigration Policy in the 1980s.* Philadelphia: Institute for the Study of Human Issues.
Parenti, M. 1986: *Inventing Reality: The Politics of the Mass Media.* New York: St Martin's Press.
Parker, G. 1988: *The Geopolitics of Domination: Territorial Sovereignty in Europe and the Mediterranean from the Ottoman Empire to the Soviet Union.* London: Routledge.
—— 1994: Political Geography and Geopolitics. In A. J. R. Groom and M. Light (eds), *Contemporary International Relations*, London: Pinter, 170–81.
Parry, G., Moyser, G. and Day, N. 1992: *Political Participation and Democracy in Britain.* Cambridge: Cambridge University Press.
Parsons, A. 1995: *From Cold War to Hot Peace: UN Interventions, 1947–1994.* London: Michael Joseph.
Pastore, M. 1993: Italien als Einwanderungsland. *Bürgerrechte & Polizei*, 45 (3), 62–6.
Pearce, C. 1980: *The Machinery of Change in Local Government 1888–1974.* London: Allen & Unwin.
Pentland, C. 1973: *International Theory and European Integration.* London: Faber.
Peterson, M. J. 1988: *Managing the Frozen South: The Creation and Evolution of the Atlantic Treaty System.* Berkeley: University of California Press.
Petit de Prego, M. A. 1982: L'Indépendance et la solution fédérale: Le Projet fédéral de José Artigas. *Problèmes de frontières dans le tiers monde.* Paris: Harmattan, 153–65.
Philippart, E. (ed.) 1993: *Nations et frontières dans la nouvelle Europe.* Brussels: Éditions Complexe.
Piscatori, J. P. 1986: *Islam in a World of Nation States.* Cambridge: Cambridge University Press.
Plamenatz, J. 1960: *On Alien Rule and Self-Government.* Oxford: Oxford University Press.

Plender, R. 1988: *International Migration Law.* Dordrecht: Nijhoff.

Pogge, T. W. 1994: Cosmopolitanism and Sovereignty. In C. Brown (ed.), *Political Re-structuring in Europe,* London: Routledge, 89–122.

Poggi, G. 1978: *The Development of the Modern State.* London: Hutchinson.

Political Studies 1994: 42, special number: *Contemporary Crisis of the Nation State?*

Pouvoirs 1992: 62, special number: *Islam dans la cité.*

Prats, R. 1978: *La Théorie de la frontière confrontée à l'intégration économique latino-américaine. Le Concept de la frontière institutionnelle d'intégration.* Paris: Institut des Hautes Études de l'Amérique Latine III.

Prescott, J. R. V. 1987: *Political Frontiers and Boundaries.* London: Allen & Unwin.

Prescott Webb, W. 1962: *The Great Frontier.* Boston: Houghton Mifflin.

Priore, M. J. and Sabel, C. F. 1984: *The Second Industrial Divide.* New York: Basic Books.

Problèmes de frontières dans le tiers monde. Journées d'études du 20 et 21 mars 1981. Laboratoire 'Connaissances du Tiers Monde'. Published with the assistance of the Conseil Scientifique de l'Université de Paris VII.

Problèmes de frontières dans le tiers monde. Paris: Harmattan 1982.

Projet 1992: 23 (autumn), special number: *Musulmans en terre d'Europe.*

Pufendorf, S. 1934: *De Jure Naturae et Gentium.* Trans. C. W. Oldfather, Cambridge, Mass.: Harvard University Press.

Radcliff, W. 1986: *Follow the Leader in the Horn: The Soviet–Cuban Presence in East Africa.* Washington: Cuban American National Foundation.

Radvanyi, J. 1992: Et si la Russie, à son tour éclatait? *Hérodote,* 64 (January-March), 63–73.

Rafferty, R. W. (ed.) 1928: *The Works of the Right Honourable Edmund Burke,* vol. vi. Oxford: Oxford University Press.

Raffestin, C., Loprano, D. and Pasteur, Y. 1995: *Géopolitique et histoire.* Lausanne: Payot.

Ratzel, F. 1897: *Politische Geographie.* Munich: Oldenberg.

Rawls, J. 1971: *A Theory of Justice.* Oxford: Oxford University Press.

Redcliffe-Maud, Lord and Wood, B. 1974: *English Local Government Reformed.* Oxford: Oxford University Press.

Reijnen, G. C. M. and de Graff, W. 1989: *The Pollution of Outer Space, in Particular of the Geostationary Orbit: Scientific, Policy and Legal Aspects.* Dordrecht: Nijhoff.

Renan, E. 1992: *Qu'est-ce qu'une nation?* (1881). Paris: Presses Pocket.

République Française – Sénat – Session Ordinaire – 1992–3 – no. 384. *Annexe au procès verbal de la séance du 23 juin 1993.*

République Française – Sénat – Deuxième Session Extraordinaire de 1993–4, no. 262. *Annexe au procès verbal de la séance du 25 janvier 1994. Rapport d'information fait au nom de la mission commune d'information chargée d'examiner la mise en place et le fonctionnement de la Convention d'Application de l'Accord du 14 juin 1985.*

Revue de l'Institut de Sociologie 1984: 3/4, special number: *Territorialité.* Université Libre de Bruxelles.

Reynolds, G. H. and Merges, R. P. 1989: *Outer Space: Problems of Law and Policy.* London: Westview Press.

Reza Djalili, M. 1990: Territoire et frontière dans l'idéologie islamiste contemporaine. *Relations Internationales,* 63, 305–12.

Rhodes, R. A. W. 1981: *Control and Power in Central–Local Government Relations.* Farnborough: Gower.

—— and Wright, V. (eds) 1989: *Tensions in the Territorial Politics of Western Europe.* London: Frank Cass.

Ricq, C. 1981: *Les Travailleurs frontaliers en Europe.* Paris: Anthropos.

—— 1990: *La Main d'œuvre frontalière en Suisse.* Geneva: Institut des Études Européennes.

Robertson, R. 1990: Mapping the Global Condition: Globalization as the Central Concept. In M. Featherstone (ed.), *Global Culture,* London: Sage, 15–30.

Rokkan, S. and Urwin, D. W. (eds) 1982: *The Politics of Territorial Identity.* London: Sage.

Romi, R. 1993: *L'Europe et la protection juridique de l'environnement.* Paris: Victoires.

Rosenau, J. N. 1980: *The Study of Global Interdependence.* London: Pinter.

Roth, V. 1981: Analyse und Evaluation bestehender Kooperationsmodelle im Raume Basel. In B. Biucchi and G. Gauderd (eds), *Régions frontalières,* Paris: Georgi Saint Saphorin.

Rousseau, C. 1964: *Cours de droit international public.* Paris: Cours Polycopie.

Roux, J.-P. 1970: *Traditions des nomades de la Turquie méridionale.* Paris: Maisonneuve.

Roux, M. 1993: *Les Albanais en Yugoslavie.* Paris: Maison des Sciences de l'Homme.

Roy, O. 1991: Asie centrale: Le Calme avant la tempête. *Le Monde,* 29 August.

Russett, B. M. 1968: Is there a Long-Run Trend towards Concentration in the International System. *Comparative Political Studies,* 1 (1) 103–22.

Rykiel, Z. 1985: Regional Integration and Boundary Effect in the Katowice Region. In J. B. Goddard and Z. Taylor (eds), *Proceedings of the 7th British–Polish Geographical Seminar, May 23–30 1983,* Warsaw: Polish Scientific Publishers.

Sack, R. D. 1986: *Human Territoriality: Its Theory and History.* Cambridge: Cambridge University Press.

Sahlins, P. 1989: *Boundaries: The Making of France and Spain in the Pyrenees.* Berkeley: University of California Press.

Salt, J. 1981: International Labour Migration in Western Europe: A Geographical Review. In M. M. Kritz, C. B. Keely, and S. M. Tomasi, (eds), *Global Trends in Migratory Theory,* New York: Center for Migration Studies, 133–57.

Samatar, S. S. 1985: The Somali Dilemma: Nation in Search of a State. In A. I. Asiwaju (ed.), *Partitioned Africans,* London: Hurst, and University of Lagos Press, 155–93.

Sautter, G. 1982: Quelques réflexions sur les frontières africaines. In *Problèmes de frontières dans le tiers monde*, Paris: Harmattan, 41–50.

Schaffter, R. 1968: *Les Impératifs de la liberté*. Delémont: Rassemblement Jurassien.

Schmitt, C. 1976: *The Concept of the Political*. Trans. George Schwab, New Brunswick, NJ: Rutgers University Press.

Schofield, C. H. (ed.) 1994: *Global Boundaries*. London: Routledge.

—— and Schofield, R. N. (eds) 1994: *The Middle East and North Africa*. London: Routledge.

Schöpflin, G. 1993: *Hungary and its Neighbours*. Paris: Chaillot Papers no. 7.

Seccombe, I. J. 1988: International Migration, Arabisation and Localisation in the Gulf Labour Market, In B. R. Pridham (ed.), *The Arab Gulf and the Arab World*, London: Croom Helm, 153–88.

Sharpe, L. J. 1989: Fragmentation and Territoriality in the European State System: *International Political Science Review*, 10 (3), 223–38.

Shaw, M. N. 1986: *Title to Territory in Africa*. Oxford: Oxford University Press.

Shaw, S. J. 1977: *History of the Ottoman Empire*. Cambridge: Cambridge University Press, 2 vols.

Sheffer, G. (ed.) 1986: *Modern Diasporas in International Politics*. London: Croom Helm.

Simon, J. L. 1989: *The Economic Consequences of Immigration*. Oxford: Blackwell; Washington: Cato Institute.

Simonet, J. 1992: *Pratiques du management en Europe*. Paris: Éditions d'Organisation.

Sitwell, N. H. H. 1984: *Outside the Empire: The World the Romans Knew*. London: Paladin.

Skinner, Q. 1978: *The Foundation of Modern Political Thought*. Cambridge: Cambridge University Press, 2 vols.

Sklair, L. 1992: The Maquila Industry and the Creation of a Transnational Capitalist Class in the United States–Mexico Border Region. In L. A. Herzog (ed.), *Changing Boundaries in the Americas*, San Diego: University of California Press. 69–88.

Slatta, R. W. 1992: Historical Frontier Imagery in the Americas. In L. A. Herzog (ed.), *Changing Boundaries in the Americas*, San Diego: University of California Press, 25–48.

Smith, A. 1990: *Antarctica:* An Analysis of the Political and Territorial Issues arising from the Antarctic Treaty System. Edinburgh: diss., Department of Politics, University of Edinburgh.

Smith, A. D. 1983: *State and Nation in the Third World: The Western State and African Nationalism*. New York: St Martin's Press.

Smith, N. B. 1969: The Idea of the French Hexagon. *French Historical Studies*, 6 (2), 139–55.

Socor, V. 1994: Moldava. *RFE/RL Research Reports*, 3 (16) (22 April), 17–22.

Sokologorsky, I. 1992: Les Russes en Estonie. *Hérodote*, 64 (January–March), 148–62.

Southern, R. W. 1970: *Western Society and the Church in the Middle Ages.* Harmondsworth: Penguin.

Splettstoesser, J. F. and Dreschoff, G. M. (eds) 1990: *Mineral Resources Potential of Antarctica.* Washington, DC: American Geophysical Union.

Steinberg, J. 1976: *Why Switzerland?* Cambridge: Cambridge University Press.

Stoetzel, J. 1983: *Les Valeurs du temps présent.* Paris: Presses Universitaires de France.

Strassoldo, R. 1970: *From Barrier to Junction: Towards a Sociological Theory of Borders.* Gorizia: ISIG.

—— (ed.) 1973: *Confini e Regioni.* Trieste: Lint.

—— and Delli Żotti, G. (eds) 1982: *Cooperation and Conflict in Border Areas.* Milan: Angeli.

—— and Gubert, R. 1973: The Boundary: An Overview of its current theoretical status. In R. Strassoldo (ed.), *Confini e Regioni*, Trieste: Lint, 29–57.

Système d'Observation Permanente sur Les Migrations (SOPEMI), Annual Reports, OECD.

Tägil, S. 1977. *Studying Boundary Conflicts.* Stockholm: Scandinavian University Books.

Talbott, S. (ed.), 1971: *Khrushchev Remembers.* London: Little, Brown.

Tarrow, S. 1978: Introduction. In S. Tarrow, S. P. Katzenstein and L. Graziano (eds), *Territorial Politics in Industrial Nations*, New York: Praeger, 1–27.

Tchossitch, D. 1991: *Le Temps de la mort.* Trans. D. Babic, Paris: L'Age d'Homme, 2 vols.

Thacher, P. S. 1992: The Role of the United Nations. In A. Hurrell and B. Kingsbury (eds), *The International Politics of the Environment*, Oxford: Clarendon Press, 183–211.

Thual, F. 1994: *Géopolitique de l'Orthodoxie.* Paris: Dunod.

Tighe, C. 1990: *Gdansk: National Identity in the Polish–German Borderlands.* London: Pluto Press.

Touval, S. 1963: *Somali Nationalism.* Cambridge, Mass.: Harvard University Press.

—— 1972: *The Boundary Politics of Independent Africa.* Cambridge, Mass.: Harvard University Press.

Travaux du Comité d'Études 1918: *L'Alsace-Lorraine et la frontiére du Nord-Est.* Paris: Imprimerie Nationale.

Trier, J. 1966: Zaun und Mannring. In *Beiträge zur Geschichte der Deutschen Sprache und Literatur*, 66, 232–64.

Triggs, G. D. (ed.) 1987: *The Antarctic Treaty Regime: Law, Environment and Resources.* Cambridge: Cambridge University Press.

Trompenaars, F. 1994: *L'Entreprise multiculturelle.* Paris: Maxima-Laurent du Mesnil.

Trout, F. E. 1969: *Morocco's Saharan Frontiers.* Geneva: Droz.

Tsoukalis, L. 1993: *The New European Economy: The Politics and Economics of Integration.* Oxford: Oxford University Press.

Tudjman, F. 1981: *Nationalism in Contemporary Europe.* East European Monographs, New York: Columbia University Press.

Tunkin, G. I. 1974: *Theory of International Law.* Trans. W. E. Butler, Cambridge, Mass.: Harvard University Press.

Turner, F. J. 1953: *The Frontier in American History.* London: Holt (1st pub. 1894: Madison: State Historical Society of Wisconsin).

Tyranowski, J. K. 1985: Boundaries and Boundary Treaties in the Law of State Succession. In *Thesaurus Acroasium* Thessaloniki, xiv *National and International Boundaries*, 459–540.

Udo, R. K. 1982: *The Human Geography of Tropical Africa.* London: Heinemann.

United Nations 1990: *World Population Prospects 1990.* New York: Population Studies 120.

United Nations Development Program 1991: *Human Development Report.* New York: Oxford University Press.

United Nations Educational, Scientific and Cultural Organization 1979: *International Commission for the Study of Communication Problems: Final Report.* Paris.

United Nations Food and Population Agency. 1991: *Population Issues.* New York.

United Nations High Commissioner for Refugees 1979: *Collection of International Instruments concerning Refugees.* Geneva.

Veliz, C. 1967: *Latin America and the Caribbean. A Handbook.* London: Blond.

Vernier, A. 1993: *Rapport sur l'aménagement du territoire dans les régions frontalières.* Paris: Confédération des Travailleurs Chrétiens–Institut de Recherches Economiques et Sociales.

von Malchus, V. 1973: Méthodes et pratiques de la coopération internationale des régions frontalières européennes. In R. Strassoldo (ed.), *Confini e Regioni,* Trieste: Lint, 179–98.

—— 1975: *Partnerschaft an europäischen Grenzen.* 2nd edn, Bonn: Europa Union.

Waldron, J. 1988: *The Right to Private Property.* Oxford: Clarendon Press.

Wallerstein, I. 1976: *The Modern World-System: Capitalist Agriculture and the Origins of the European World-Economy in the Sixteenth Century.* New York: Academic Press.

—— 1990: Culture as the Ideological Battleground of the Modern World System. In M. Featherstone (ed.), *Global Culture,* London: Sage, 31–55.

Walzer, M. 1981: The Distribution of Membership. In P. G. Brown and H. Shue (eds), *Boundaries,* Totawa: Rowman & Littlefield, 16.

—— 1983: *Spheres of Justice.* Oxford: Blackwell.

—— 1992: The New Tribalism: Notes on a Difficult Problem. *Dissent,* 39 (2) 164–71.

Wambaugh, S. 1933: *Plebiscites since the World War.* Washington: Carnegie Foundation, 2 vols.

Wasburn, P. C. 1992: *Broadcasting Propaganda: International Radio Broadcasting and the Construction of Political Reality.* London: Praeger.

Watts, A. 1992: *International Law and the Antarctic Treaty System.* Cambridge: Grotius.

Weber, E. 1979: *Peasants into Frenchmen: The Modernization of Rural France, 1970–1914*. London: Chatto & Windus.

—— 1984: L'Hexagone. In P. Nora (ed.), *Les Lieux de Mémoire*, ii: *La Nation* 97–8.

Weber, L. 1983: European Organization for the Safety of Air Navigation (Eurocontrol). In *Encyclopedia of Public International Law*, vi. 191–4, Amsterdam: North Holland.

Weber, M. 1947: *The Theory of Social and Political Organisation*. Oxford: Oxford University Press.

Wehrlé, F. 1993: Les Chemins de la désintégration de la Tchécoslovaquie. In A. Gresh (ed.), *À l'Est*, Brussels: Éditions Complexe, 89–100.

Weigart, H. W. et al. 1957: *Principles of Political Geography*. New York: Appleton-Century-Crofts.

Weil, P. 1989: *The Law of Maritime Delimitation: Reflections*. Cambridge: Grotius.

Weintraub, S. 1990: *A Marriage of Convenience: Relations between Mexico and the United States*. New York: Oxford University Press.

Whittaker, C. R. 1989: *Les Frontières de l'Empire Romain*. Annales littéraires de l'Université de Besançon, vol. lxxxv.

Whyte, J. H. 1983: The Permeability of the UK–Irish Border: A Preliminary Reconnaissance. *Administration*, 31 (3), 300–15.

—— 1991: *Interpreting Northern Ireland*. Oxford: Clarendon Press.

Wieczynski, L. 1976: *The Russian Frontier: The Impact of the Borderlands upon the Course of Early Russsian History*. Richmond: University of Virginia Press.

Wight, M. 1977: *Systems of States*. Leicester: Leicester University Press.

Wihtol de Wenden, C. 1992: Le Choc de l'Est, un tournant historique pour les migrations? *Esprit*, 183 (July), 101–11.

Williams, H. L. 1983: *Kant's Political Philosophy*. Oxford: Blackwell.

Wils, A. B. 1991: Survey of Immigration Trends and Assumptions about Future Migration. In W. Lutz (ed.), *Future Demographic Trends in Europe and North America*, London: Academic Press, 281–99.

Wilson, A. 1979–80: *The Aegean Dispute*. Adelphi Papers no. 195, London: International Institute of Strategic Studies.

Wilson, E. O. 1975: *Sociobiology: The New Synthesis*. Cambridge, Mass.: Harvard University Press.

Wilson, R. W. 1992: *Compliance Ideologies: Rethinking Political Culture*. Cambridge: Cambridge University Press.

Windass, S. 1970: The League and Territorial Disputes. In E. Luard (ed.), *The International Regulation of Frontier Disputes*, London: Thames & Hudson, 31–85.

Wisard, F. 1988: *Le Jura en question: Analyse des discours sur 'l'unité du Jura'*. Lausanne: Institut de Science Politique.

Wolf, E. 1982: *Europe and the Peoples without History*. Berkeley: University of California Press.

Wood, B. 1976: *The Process of Local Government Reform 1966–74*. London: Allen & Unwin.

Wood, H. J. 1950: The Far East. In W. G. East and O. H. K. Spate (eds), *The Changing Map of Asia: A Political Geography*, London: Methuen, 249–303.

Woodman, D. 1969: *Himalayan Frontiers: A Political Review of the Russian, Chinese, Indian and British Rivalries.* London: Barrie & Rockliff.

Woodward, S. L. 1995: *Balkan Tragedy: Chaos and Dissolution after the Cold War.* Washington: Brookings Institution.

Wörner, M. et al. 1993: *What is European Security after the Cold War?* London: Philip Morris Institute.

Wrochno-Stanke, K. 1982: Immigrant Workers in Western Europe and European Integration. In B. De Marchi and A. M. Boileau (eds), *Boundaries and Minorities in Western Europe*, Milan: Angeli, 271–84.

Young, C. 1966: The Politics of Separatism: Katanga 1960–1963. In G. M. Carter (ed.), *Politics in Africa: Seven Cases.* New York: Harcourt Brace.

Zacher, M. W. and Mathew, R. A. 1993: Liberal International Theory: Common Threads, Divergent Strands. In C. Kegley (ed.), *New International Realities*, New York: St Martin's Press.

Zeldin, T. 1974, 1977: *France, 1870–1945.* 2 vols. Oxford: Oxford University Press.

Zolberg, A. R. 1981: International Migrations in Political Perspective. In M. M. Kritz, C. B. Keely and S. M. Tomasi (eds), *Global Trends in Migratory Theory*, 3–27.

—— 1989: The Next Waves: Migration Theory for a Changing World. *International Migration Review*, 23 (3), 403–30.

Zwann, T. L. (ed.) 1988: *Space Law: Views of the Future.* London: Kluwer.

Index